Skills For Maximising Your Graduate Experience

Thinking About Your Research

Communicating Your Research

Your Future And The Workplace

Ted VanderNoot, Ph.D.

Victoria VanderNoot, Ph.D.

Cognitrix Ltd.
London, U.K.
www.cognitrix.com

Disclaimer:

The authors and publisher have taken all reasonable care in preparing this book. Mistakes brought to their attention (info@cognitrix.com) will be considered immediately and corrected at the earliest opportunity.

The information, procedures and opinions contained in this book may not be suitable for every individual or every situation.

The information, procedures and opinions stated in this book:

- are not guaranteed nor warranted to produce any particular results; and
- are not a substitute for suitable professional advice.

The publisher and the authors disclaim any liability arising from the use of the information, procedures and opinions contained in this book.

British Library Cataloguing in Publication data available.

ISBN 978-0-9562487-4-9

Published in the UK in 2012 by Cognitrix Ltd.

Second printing 2020.

Contents

Preface

Why Did We Write This Book?

The idea to write this book came out of more than a few lively discussions over the years about our experiences getting our PhDs. A recurring theme of those chats was how little information about how to actually *do* research was imparted during the process of gaining our PhDs. Much of what we've learned, we learned "the hard way" in the years since we finished our PhDs. Time and again we said to each other "... if only we had known that ...". Worse yet, many of our colleagues also seem to have had similar experiences.

Most students have little trouble acquiring the technical aspects of performing their subject/discipline but the soft-skills (thinking and communication) that support their technical skills are often sadly neglected. In fact, a lot of schools and programs offer little in the way of formal courses related to these skills. Yet they are crucial for a successful career. How can you learn to think like a researcher and plan a research project that is designed to answer a question rather than simply collect data? How can you communicate your ideas to others and convince them of your conclusions or recommendations?

We feel that research degrees *should* be like an apprenticeship. Unfortunately, Supervisors and Principal Investigators are increasingly busy and have less time for personal coaching and teaching. Postgraduate students in large groups will receive an even smaller share of their supervisor's time. How much they can learn from other students and postdoctoral fellows to replace input from their supervisor(s) is variable. This book aims to fill that gap.

We decided to write this book to include all the things we would have liked to have learned about *how to do research* while we were still doing our PhDs! It's the book we wished we'd read when we were starting out.

Who Is This Book For?

This book is for postgraduate *research* students (MPhil, MSc or PhD) from any field or discipline such as aeronautical engineering, biology, business management, chemistry, civil engineering, computer science, electronics, environmental science, genetics, geography, history, mathematics, nursing, oceanography, psychology, physics, sociology ...

This book presumes that you have already decided to do a research degree and you now want to make the best of it.

What Is Our Approach?

We have aimed to make this book practical. For that reason, we have not littered it with references and notes. If you are interested in going into more depth in a topic, then you can find more material online or in your Library. Or you can have your graduate school book some of Ted's workshops which were the basis for this book.

The chapters in this book target the weak areas we have observed from working with postgraduate students and the problems and questions that have come up during the various workshops which Ted has run. We have assumed that postgraduate students will be able to learn the technical aspects of their discipline, and from our experience, this is a safe assumption.

We haven't included a separate chapter on defending your thesis because there is too much variation in how vivas are organised in different disciplines and countries to give any useful and specific advice. Your supervisor(s) will be in a better position to give you appropriate advice. Nevertheless, the chapters on reasoning, presenting and writing will help in writing your thesis and preparing for your defence.

We also haven't discussed "managing your supervisor". (... a dangerous myth in our opinion. Feel free to read someone else's fantasies on this matter.)

What Will This Book Help You To Do?

This book will help you to:

- Define your research question.
- Plan your research so that it answers your research question.
- Think about your results.
- Structure a logical case.
- Present your case (spoken or written) in a clear and concise way.
- Think about what comes after your research degree.
- Prepare an effective covering letter and CV/Résumé and then perform well in the interview.

Acknowledgements

Thanks to Jo James and Dr. Julie Reeves (both at the *University of Southampton*) and Mimi Phung for their helpful comments on an earlier draft.

Thanks to Christine VanderNoot (*Cognitrix Ltd.*) for her insightful and *relentless* editorial efforts. Her favourite questions were: "What are you trying to say?" and "How can you say this plainly and simply?" She kept reminding us that for some of the students reading this book, English would be their second or third language.

- 1 -
A Degree Requires The Right Attitude And Approach

When we wrote the first draft of this book and asked colleagues to read it and give us feedback, a universal comment was "What about a chapter on dealing with your supervisor?". We think this says something about the quality of research supervision when most people consider that coping with your supervisor(s) deserves a chapter!

Realistically though, getting the most out of your graduate school experience involves more than just your research supervisor(s).

You ...

First And Foremost, Take Responsibility For Your Learning.

It is up to *you* to ensure that you get what you need from the graduate school experience. Be proactive and take the initiative whenever possible. Cultivate an attitude of being a paying customer. Regardless of whether you receive a stipend as a research or teaching assistant, you are almost certainly paying tuition as well and that tuition entitles you to expect a certain level of service from your postgraduate institution (or graduate school in North America). Treat your postgraduate time like an apprenticeship – you are obtaining valuable on-the-job training. Remember, you are learning how to do research more generally, not only the specifics and details of a particular field.

Choose Your Research Supervisor Carefully.

This is a complex process and we are not going to claim to have a crystal ball for making *that* decision. But it is important to remember, you are shopping for them as much as they are shopping for postgraduates. Your supervisor(s) will have a tremendous impact on the direction of your early career. Make this decision carefully and try to make the best choice for ***you,*** not what someone else says is the best choice.

Obviously you will need to decide on research area in which you would like to work. This will most often be in the same field as your undergraduate degree but you should not feel trapped by this. It is just as valid to move into adjacent fields if your interests and general aptitudes warrant it. Depending on the discipline, it may also be possible to make a more radical jump on moving to postgraduate work. However, be prepared to do a fair bit of remedial work and study to get yourself to where others started out in that discipline.

Once you have decided which research area to focus upon, you will need to look into the reputation of researchers in the chosen field who are willing to take on postgraduates. You will need to decide whether you want to work with someone who is just starting out or someone who is well established. A younger faculty member will likely have enthusiasm and new ideas but may still struggle, themselves, with some of the concepts covered in this book. An established researcher will have had many years to learn and perfect their skills, but may have lost their enthusiasm and/or may be resistant to new ideas or ways of doing things.

You need to evaluate the size of the research group. A large group often means someone fairly prestigious – someone well-funded and successful can afford to maintain large groups. There is a certain caché or status that comes from working in such groups, but be prepared, there are associated costs too. If the group is large, how much time do you think the supervisor will have for you? This will necessarily mean less one-to-one interaction with you but could mean that you have the opportunity to work with and learn from others in the group. A smaller group will mean more direct access to the supervisor and the opportunity for one-to-one learning. When looking for a supervisor, talk to the people in the group (if possible) and try to find out the dynamics of the group and the management style of the supervisor. Will these work for you?

In addition, you will have to factor in basics like geographic location (are you able to relocate?) and whether you will be able to do your degree full-time or do it part-time while earning money to support yourself. You will need to find both a program and a supervisor who is amenable to your needs.

Actively Seek And Develop Additional Skills To Support Your Career.

It is dangerous to assume that you will absorb and develop these skills as you go along. We don't learn to drive or play tennis by simply watching TV or reading books, we learn by practising a lot and challenging ourselves. The same reasoning would apply to making presentations, writing papers, planning a research project, *etc.*

Manage Your Time And Tasks.

Time and task management could be a book in itself and we will only touch the surface of it here. Depending on the program, there may be subject-specific course work, your research, some amount of teaching assistance and supplemental skills-development.

The course work is clearly related to learning the theory and fundamentals of your chosen speciality at the beginning of your postgraduate research degree. It will probably involve lectures, assignments and tests/exams.

The research itself is obviously important to both you and your supervisor(s). It forms the basis of your thesis and any other publications that come out of your postgraduate experience. As well as the research you do on your own, this will involve regular meetings with your supervisor(s) and networking with the larger research community.

Teaching assistance, helping more junior students, is also extremely valuable because it helps to develop teaching skills which will be of use if you pursue an academic career and lead a group of your own. It also can help you to learn and sharpen your communication skills. Learning to explain things to a novice so that they understand requires you to not only know your subject well but to be able to present it clearly and concisely.

The development of supplemental skills will help your research and contribute to your future employability. These supporting skills might include presentation skills, writing skills, IT skills, creative thinking, problem solving and so on. Realistically assess your strengths and weaknesses and then look for courses/workshops that will develop your weak areas.

During your postgraduate degree, you will have numerous demands upon your time (course-work, research, teaching assistance, supplemental skills-development, personal commitments, ...). You must recognise that you have a fixed amount of time available. You will need to actively and deliberately choose how you distribute your time among the various activities.

Completing your postgraduate degree requires consistency and discipline. Regular work beats crash efforts. Think of it more like a marathon rather than a series of sprints. You get a degree for original and valuable research. Lots of trivial results or simply being busy is not enough to get a degree.

Work or results that won't appear in your thesis or contribute to your career should be strenuously avoided. Ask yourself, and if necessary ask your supervisor(s), the following questions:

- How is doing this relevant/useful to answering my research question?
- How does this contribute towards my thesis?
- How does this contribute to my career?

In your postgraduate experience and throughout your career in fact, you will encounter a variety of tasks which are:

- unimportant and not urgent;
- unimportant but urgent;
- important but not urgent; and
- important and urgent.

The first and the last items in this list are easy decisions about whether or not they get done. The two in the middle cause the most difficulty. Unimportant but urgent tasks do ***not*** become worth doing simply because someone thinks they are urgent. Urgency simply means the deadline is close and not that it is necessarily important. And of course, the important but not urgent tasks ***do not lose*** their importance just because there is no specific deadline for getting them done. Important tasks like writing papers can fall into this category! No one can deny how important they are to your future career, but unless there is a specific deadline for perhaps a special journal issue, it is easy to let the writing of the paper slide to tomorrow or next week or next month. If you are not careful, you'll find yourself scooped and someone else will publish your idea first. And when you come to look for your next position, you won't have as many publications to your credit as other candidates.

One approach to making time for the important but not urgent tasks is to *salami slice* them into such small pieces that it becomes easy to fit each little piece into your day. Each day you do one small bit that may take as little as 5 or 10 minutes. Overtime, the little bits add up, often surprisingly quickly! For example, if you wanted to write a paper for publication, then you might spend 5 to 10 minutes each day doing one of the following:

- Get the *Guidelines for Authors* from the journal website.
- Collect your notes and research materials into one pile.
- Review your data and analyses.
- Work on structuring a logical case to support your conclusion(s).
- Prepare one diagram or one table.
- Write one paragraph.

This book was written using the *salami slice* approach over a period of eighteen months. It may have taken that long but it got done!

Network! Network! Network!

While doing research can be largely independent endeavour, it is not without its social element. It is essential to be able to communicate the results of your research to a wider audience. You need to be known for doing good work. This is essential not only because it contributes to the knowledge of your particular field but also for more individually relevant reasons: future collaborations, possible job offers and future funding.

Get your supervisor to introduce you to everyone! You never know when someone you meet might offer you a job. You never know when you will meet a new colleague and form a new collaboration.

Try to participate in a collaboration of some kind during your postgraduate experience. Even if it is simply someone in your own university or department but outside your own research area or group. This broadens your horizons, can be beneficial to both parties, and looks good on a résumé. A lot of very interesting work goes on in overlapping regions of different fields.

Meet people from other departments! Discussing your research with people from outside your speciality is extremely useful. Never, never underestimate the power of stupid questions from people who don't know! And when people outside your field can understand what you are doing and why it is important, then you know you are explaining it well. Finally, there have been numerous times we've seen someone with a research problem discover that someone in another field has already solved that kind of problem, which means you don't need to reinvent the wheel.

Social media are becoming more important and you should definitely explore what they have to offer. However spending several hours a day on *Facebook, Twitter* or even *LinkedIn* is a poor substitute for actually doing your research. So far, there aren't any degrees awarded for time spent on *Facebook, Twitter* or *LinkedIn!*

Manage Your Online Professional Image/Reputation.

In addition to networking, it is essential that you manage your online presence because it will be too late to fix it when it is time to look for a job. Never post (or if necessary remove) anything that does not contribute to a professional impression. Consider your internet presence as if it was going to be a matter of permanent and public record.

- There are sites that archive older versions of websites and let you see how they looked 5 or 10 years ago!
- Material can be copied from one website by another website, often without the first website's knowledge or permission.

Anything you post on the web can come back to haunt you many years later. Look at your internet presence (web-pages and/or social networking) with the eyes of potential employers. What conclusions would strangers draw, based upon what you have presented?

The more serious the position you are applying for, the more thoroughly the employer will explore your past. For example:

- security-sensitive positions (government, police, security services);
- reputation-sensitive positions (legal firms, banks);
- ethically-sensitive positions (schools, charities).

If your web presence indicates signs of:

- poor judgement;
- illegal behaviour (under-age drinking, drug-use);
- indiscreet or unprofessional behaviour;

then you probably won't be invited for an interview.

I know of one young lady whose *Facebook* page consisted of 300+ photos of her at parties. If you were an employer, then what would be your impression of this applicant?

... And Your Supervisor(s)

They Are Human Beings, Not Gods.

Probably one of the biggest roadblocks to learning effectively in the early stages stems from dysfunctional relationships with supervisors. Many beginning students have an unhealthy fear of their supervisors. Firstly, supervisors are human beings, not gods. They have knowledge and skills, but they aren't perfect. They can make mistakes or jump to the wrong conclusion like anyone else. Secondly, they learned their trade 10, 20 or 30 years ago and the research environment has changed since they began. Unfortunately, some of them haven't kept up. You will need to learn from their strengths, and we hope, cope with or manage their weaknesses. Bear in mind that it is also possible to learn from their weaknesses; if nothing else you can see what doesn’t work! You can learn from others how to do the things that your supervisor does not do well.

Moreover, they were typically hired for their research ability, not their teaching or supervisory skills. Many institutions have little or poor training in teaching and/or supervision and some schools don't even require new academic staff to take any teaching courses. They are essentially being expected to perform tasks for which they have little specific training or experience. Sure, they went through graduate school too ... observing how to teach from folks who also were not taught how to teach ... it is a never-ending cycle. We once heard it said that if you had two good teachers during your graduate school experience then you should count yourself lucky!

The supervisor-student relationship is like any other, trust needs to be developed. They need to know that you will do your best and ask questions when needed. You need to know that they will actually teach you how to do research and not just let you flounder. You are a student working towards an examinable degree! You are not an employee who must do whatever the boss says. And remember, it is a partnership – they need graduate students and graduate students need supervisors.

Interacting With Your Supervisor(s)

Try to have regular and frequent meeting times with your supervisor(s). This will ultimately depend upon their workload but nothing takes the place of actual face-to-face time. Remember that their time is valuable, so be as concise and organised as you can be and plan ahead to avoid wasting your time and theirs. Believe us, this will be appreciated. Cultivate an efficient approach to meeting with your supervisor(s). For example, prepare notes to make sure all the topics get covered and you proceed quickly. It is a good idea to start off with a brief status check:

- What have you done since the last meeting?
- What worked as expected?
- What hasn't worked?
  - What steps did you take to remedy matters?
  - Is it working now?
  - What is your contingency plan?
- What do you have planned next and why those items?
- Are there any areas where you need assistance?

This format efficiently gets you on the same page and provides an opportunity to check your reasoning and understanding. Make sure that you give them a true status check – they need to know both the good and the bad. It benefits neither you nor your supervisor to only talk about the good. If you are having a problem with some area, they may have the answer or an idea of what to check next. Learning how to work independently is extremely important but spinning your wheels is counter-productive. It may be that you aren't doing anything wrong. It may be that the anticipated result is just not happening the way it was expected. Many beautiful theories have been sacrificed on the altar of empirical evidence.

Also, if your supervisor doesn't suggest it, ask to meet from time to time away from his or her office – in the laboratory or wherever else you do most of your actual research. Some of the best supervisors we have known routinely spend time in the lab, observing their team while they are doing research. This doesn't have to be an ordeal, just a change of venue and an informal discussion of the day-to-day activities. This gives the opportunity to keep the supervisor aware of how long the research is taking (something that tends to be forgotten once the researcher steps away from hands-on research to run a research group) and it allows a check on how the data is being collected as well as technique. Additionally it can be an opportunity to learn new tricks from your supervisor who has more experience in that field.

Remember to ask your supervisor to explain their reasoning. That way you will learn how they think about research and you can check if their reasoning is logical and defensible. Always explain your reasoning to others so that they can check your logic and evidence and either confirm that you have a strong case or give you corrective feedback before you go too far off-course.

Be sceptical until there is a logical case plus sufficient evidence. This is actually, in many ways, part of your ultimate job description – healthy scepticism. Research is all about gathering proof that addresses your particular question, interpreting (without bias!) that data into meaningful conclusions and communicating your case to others.

When It's Time To Move On ...

There is variation between countries and disciplines in terms of how long a degree should take. You will need to check what is usual for your discipline, institution and country. For example, in the UK, a PhD is officially 3 years (paid) however a substantial proportion of postgraduates find themselves spending an additional year (unpaid) in order to complete their PhD. In the US and Canada, PhDs are more open-ended in terms of length but at least you still get paid while you are working on it. In these cases it will involve negotiating with your supervisor/principal investigator about when enough is enough. They will often want you to continue working on your degree because you will be producing results at a relatively low cost to them. However, at some point you will need to leave the nest – both to pursue your independent research goals and also to start making a better salary – because let's face it, postgraduates don't get paid much! (Not that any of us went into research to get rich!) It's a good thing that research can be so interesting. Enjoy it as much as you can!

Thinking About Your Research

- 2 -
What Is Your Research Question?

Postgraduates often become *busy* with doing their research (experiments, measurements, surveys and everything else) before they have a clear idea of what is the overall aim or purpose of their research project.

In our opinion, research questions fall into one of three categories:

1) **Exploration/Discovery**: *what* happens in given conditions?
2) **Explanation**: *why* or *how* does ⟨...⟩ happen?
3) **Application**: *how* can knowledge of ⟨...⟩ be used in some way?

So the first question Ted asks postgraduates is:

"What is the aim or purpose of your research project?"

If they look at him blankly or ask what he means, then he asks:

"What will you have to show if you are successful?"

Ted usually gets one of three responses:

1) They imitate a fish breathing.
2) They tell him all the things they are *doing* or going to do.

   After the long list of activities, Ted asks them *why* they are *doing* all these things and then they resort to the fish-breathing imitation. To help them out, he asks if they are trying to:

   - Find what happens or if something happens? (Exploration)
   - Explain why or how something happens? (Explanation)
   - Decide if ⟨...⟩ is feasible/possible? (Application)
   - Use what is known to ⟨...⟩? (Application)
3) They give Ted a collection of apparently disconnected questions they want to answer. So he asks:
   - Do these questions have a common aim or theme?
   - Are these questions part of a larger question/problem?
   - Can these questions be grouped into larger categories or classes?

Once the postgraduate students have clarified the aim of their research project, then Ted asks them to explain why this is important.

- Why do we need to know what happens?
- Why do we need to explain why or how ⟨...⟩ happens?
- Why do we need something which does ⟨...⟩?
- How is ⟨...⟩ worthwhile?

In one workshop, a postgraduate student came up to Ted at the coffee break and said that she didn't have a research question but the *subject* of her research was eco-tourism. So he asked "Who cares about eco-tourism?"

This then provoked a vigorous explanation about how the increasing levels of tourism were affecting the environment and the tourist sites themselves. There were increasing levels of pollution from the air travel and the sites of historical interest or natural beauty were being eroded from the thousands to millions of visitors!

Ted then said "So it's a problem. So what?"

She responded that the world needed ecologically/environmentally responsible tourism, but no one even knew if such a thing was possible. [Bingo – the primary research question had surfaced!] And if ecologically responsible tourism was possible, then how could it be implemented? [A follow-up question had appeared!]

At this point he asked if she had noticed how she had just identified the ***problem***, its ***importance*** and the principal ***research questions*** that she wanted to answer with respect to that problem.

- A serious weakness in a dissertation/thesis is the lack of a clear thread or theme – it reads like a collection of results with nothing tying it all together. This is why defining your research question is so important.
- Your research question defines the information that is relevant, necessary and sufficient to answering it convincingly.
- Explaining why your research question is useful will require defining the larger context in which the research fits.
- You are awarded an advanced degree because your research is ***relevant***, ***useful***, (hopefully) ***novel*** and ***timely***. You won't be awarded your degree simply because you showed up and were busy.

- 3 -
How To Answer Your Research Question

In *Chapter 2* you defined your primary research question. How do you turn this question into the specific research tasks that you need to execute?

Cutting Your Research Question Down To Size

Top-Down Approach

The *top-down* process converts a larger, more general question into a set of progressively smaller, more specific sub-questions until you reach the point where you have identified the specific pieces of information required to answer each question. The information required then defines the actions/tasks needed to obtain it.

Top-Down Approach To Defining Research Tasks

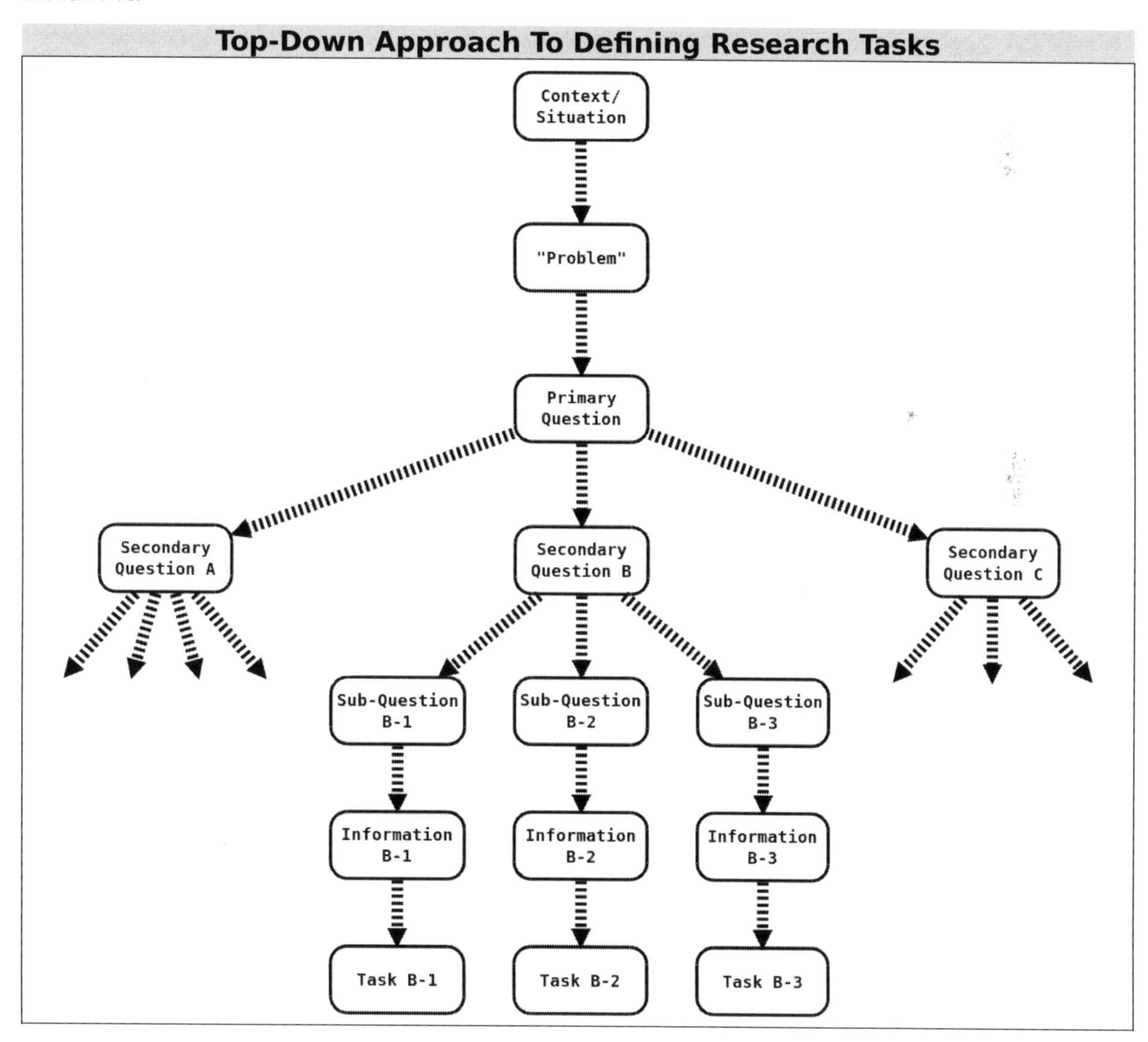

In the above diagram, the collected answers to the secondary questions A, B and C will either let you answer the primary question or will indicate additional secondary questions that need to be resolved (areas that require more work).

Remember that you are doing the research activities/tasks because they provide information that is relevant and useful in answering your research question(s)!

Questions And Possible Explanations (Hypotheses)

A research question that seeks an explanation may have several *possible* answers. Each possible answer is called a *hypothesis* and it may be either true/correct or false/incorrect. Your research will be to find information that supports or contradicts each hypothesis. Let's look at a simple example to illustrate this idea.

You're at home and you have put a CD in your stereo and it doesn't play. Before you can fix this situation, you need to know why it won't play.

Question of Explanation: Why won't the CD play?

Possible hypotheses (explanations) include:

→ There is a problem with the CD (blank or faulty).

→ There is no electrical power to the wall outlet.

→ The stereo is set on another function.

→ The CD laser lens is dirty.

→ The stereo has an electronic fault.

From our experience, we find it is more natural for people to think in terms of questions and the information that is required to answer them rather than thinking in terms of provisional statements (hypotheses) that must be proven true or false. This is why we recommend converting hypotheses into corresponding questions and working with the questions.

Turning the above hypotheses into questions and using the top-down approach, you can draw the following diagram.

Top-Down Summary Of The CD Problem

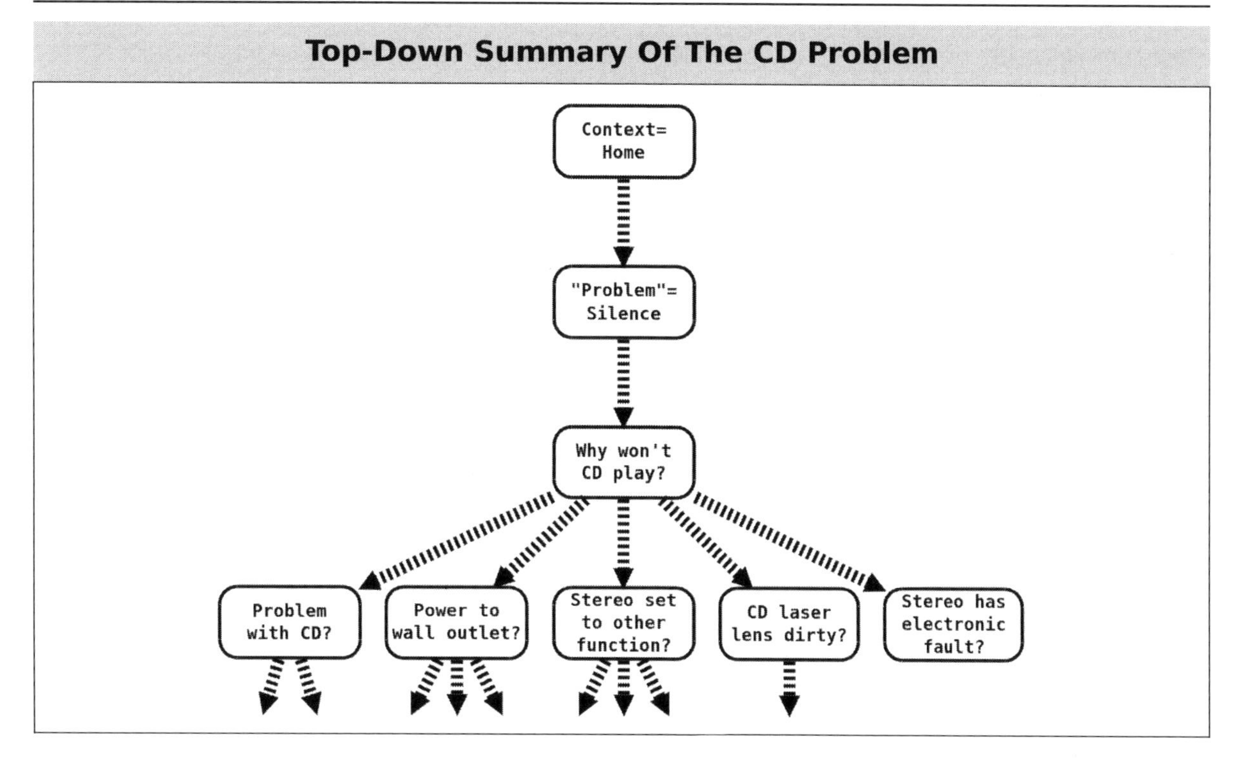

The primary question "Why won't the CD play?" has been broken down into a set of secondary questions. Taking each secondary question in turn, you can define the relevant sub-question(s) that need to be answered and the tasks required to obtain the relevant information. For example:

Hypothesis 1: There is a problem with the CD.
Question 1: Is there a problem with the CD?

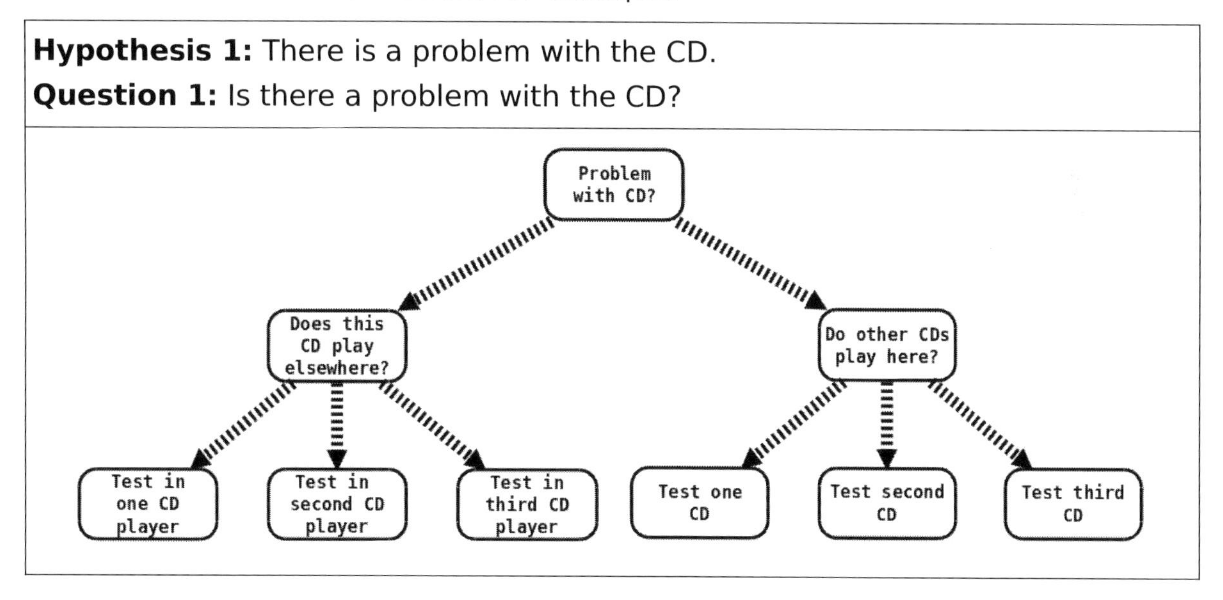

If this CD plays elsewhere then this disproves the idea that there is a problem with the CD.

If this CD doesn't play elsewhere and other CDs play here, then this indicates that the problem is with the CD.

If no CDs play here, then you need to check the hypotheses involving the electrical outlet and the stereo.

Hypothesis 2: There is no electrical power to the wall outlet.
Question 2: Is there power in the wall outlet?

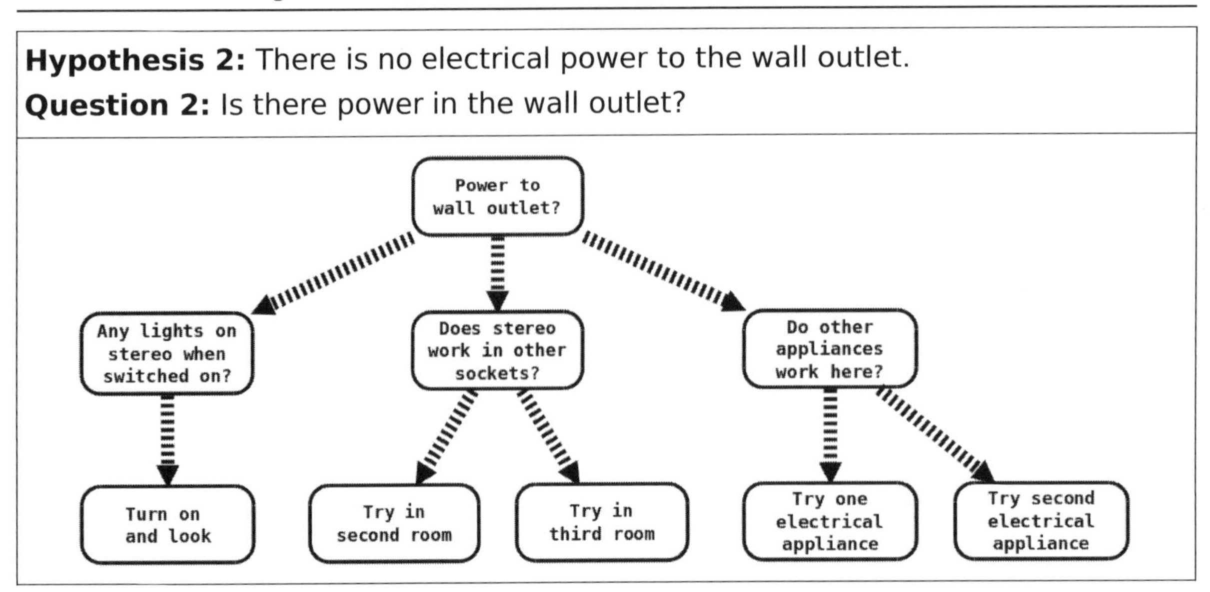

The same process could be applied to the remaining hypotheses.

Hypothesis 3: The stereo is set on another function.

Question 3: Is the stereo set on another function?

→ Are any indicators lit on the front panel?

→ Does any sound come from speakers when volume is increased?

→ Does tuning the radio reveal radio stations?

Hypothesis 4: The CD laser lens is dirty.

Question 4: Is the CD laser lens dirty?

→ Does the CD in question play properly after a CD cleaning disc has been used?

Hypothesis 5: The stereo has an electronic fault.

Question 5: Is there an electronic fault with the stereo?

This hypothesis is more complicated to address and should only be considered after the simpler hypotheses have been eliminated. If this hypothesis is correct, then you may need to find someone with expertise in electronics to help you troubleshoot the problem further. This would be similar to a research collaboration where you work with someone else whose skills complement your lack of expertise in that area.

NOTE

Notice how you eliminate simpler explanations/hypotheses before moving to more complex ones. Of course, in this simple example you would probably do these steps automatically, without thinking.

For a research project which is longer and more complicated, it is essential to work through these steps systematically, because otherwise you might miss something important.

You need to ***consider multiple hypotheses*** at the beginning of your research.

If you consider only one hypothesis, then you run the risk of coming to incorrect and/or irrelevant conclusions!

For example, in the simple example above, if you fixate on no electrical power as the *only* explanation, no amount of electrical testing will solve the problem if it turns out that the CD is actually blank or faulty!

Creative Thinking Required First

How can you come up with new ideas or hypotheses? The principal creative approach is to break out of the boundaries that are defined by your current habits of thinking and behaving.

- *Challenge – Doubt – Question what you currently do or think you know.*
- *Pretend that you don't know or that you may even have it wrong!*
  What are the arguments and evidence *against* your current position? Play *Devil's Advocate*. Ask yourself: "What if my understanding about this is wrong? How else could this be explained or interpreted?
- *Imagine what else might be possible.*
  Just because you think it's implausible or improbable, doesn't mean the universe will agree with you.
  - "Rail travel at high speed is not possible because passengers, unable to breathe, would die of asphyxia. " Dionysys Lardner, *Professor of Natural Philosophy and Astronomy*, *University College London*, in 1830.
  - "Heavier-than-air flying machines are impossible." Lord Kelvin, mathematician, physicist and founder of the *Royal Society* in 1895.
- *Beware of overconfidence!*
  - Research psychologists have shown in numerous studies that human beings are notoriously *overconfident.* Even experts claiming 100% certainty, typically have a 20% error rate. Are you *really* as certain as you think you are?
  - What additional information would allow you to increase your level of confidence?
  - Can you realistically express your level of confidence as a percentage? Would you be willing to bet your life upon it?
- *Encourage and explore alternative, diverse and/or contrary views.*
  Often other viewpoints have accurately captured aspects of the situation that your viewpoint might have missed. And talking to people outside your field can be a useful source of new ideas.
- Survey and read material from a wide variety of sources and fields because you never know where your next idea will come from.

- *Explore what is presupposed by a hypothesis.*
  - If a given hypothesis is correct/true, then:
    - What *else* must also be true?
    - What *else* (if anything) must be false?
  - If a given hypothesis is incorrect/false, then:
    - What *else* must also be false?
    - What *else* (if anything) must be true?
- *Beware of point estimates!*
  When we represent a distribution with a single value, such as an average, we obscure the complexity of the situation and mislead ourselves into thinking we know something better than we really do.

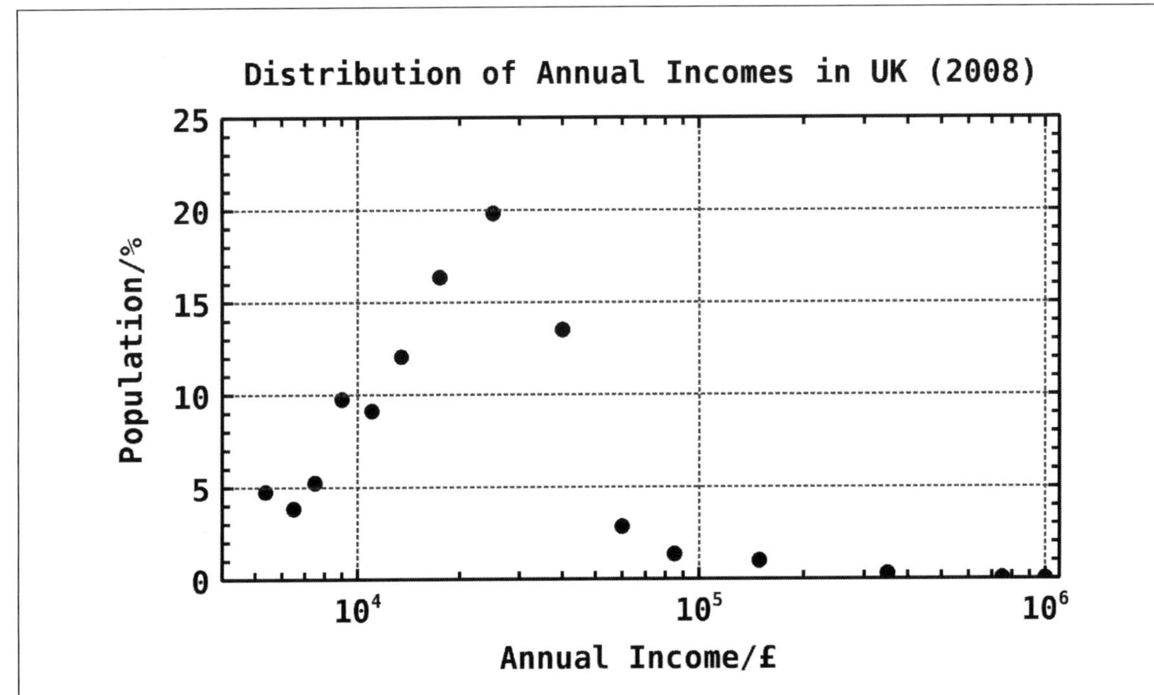

Depending upon which point estimate you choose, you will get different results. For example, in the above distribution of incomes:

- *Mean* income is approximately £24,000 per year.
- *Median* income is approximately £15,000.
- *Modal* income is approximately £25,000.
- 80% of the population has an income below £25,000.

Can any single point estimate be considered to be more correct than the others? Does any single number accurately represent the complexity of this situation?

Visually Representing Complex Situations And Systems

Cognitive psychology tells us that when we *know* something, we actually have an interconnected network of ideas in our mind. Mapping what we think onto a piece of paper is a useful approach to building up a picture of a research area, since it can:

- show how ideas are connected;
- reveal gaps in what you know; and
- stimulate ideas.

This process of *concept mapping* is flexible and has only a few guidelines, so it can be readily adapted to suit yourself.

- ***Nodes*** contain ideas/items/issues/etc.
- ***Arrows*** indicate the presence of some form of interaction between the two *entities* that are connected. The interaction could be:
    - a *transfer* or *transformation* of something from the first node to the second;
    - that the first node *causes* or *leads to* the second;
    - that the first node *affects* or *influences* the second.
    - that the first node *occurs sequentially* before the second.

Let's look at an example. *Human Activities* on this planet are known to affect:

- the use of fossil fuels;
- the forestation of the planet; and
- the amount of concrete produced.

These effects can be represented by the following simple diagram.

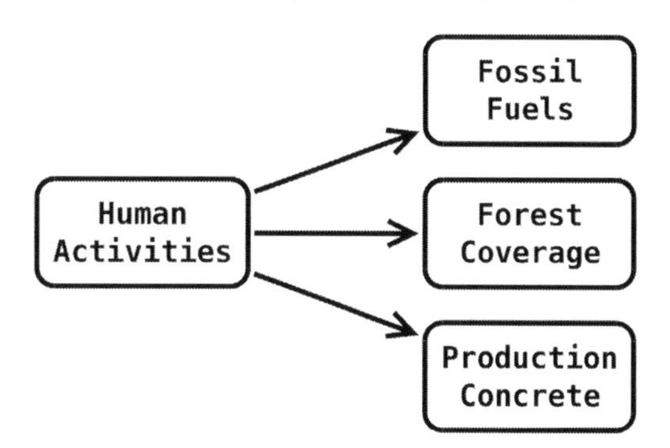

Fossil fuels, forestation and concrete production will in turn affect the amount of carbon dioxide in the atmosphere.

This concept map illustrates a student's explanation of their research project involving oceanography and CO_2 to other students in a workshop. When they had finished drawing the diagram, they realised that the logical place to start was *Human Activities* and the finishing point was the effects on *Seawater Organisms*.

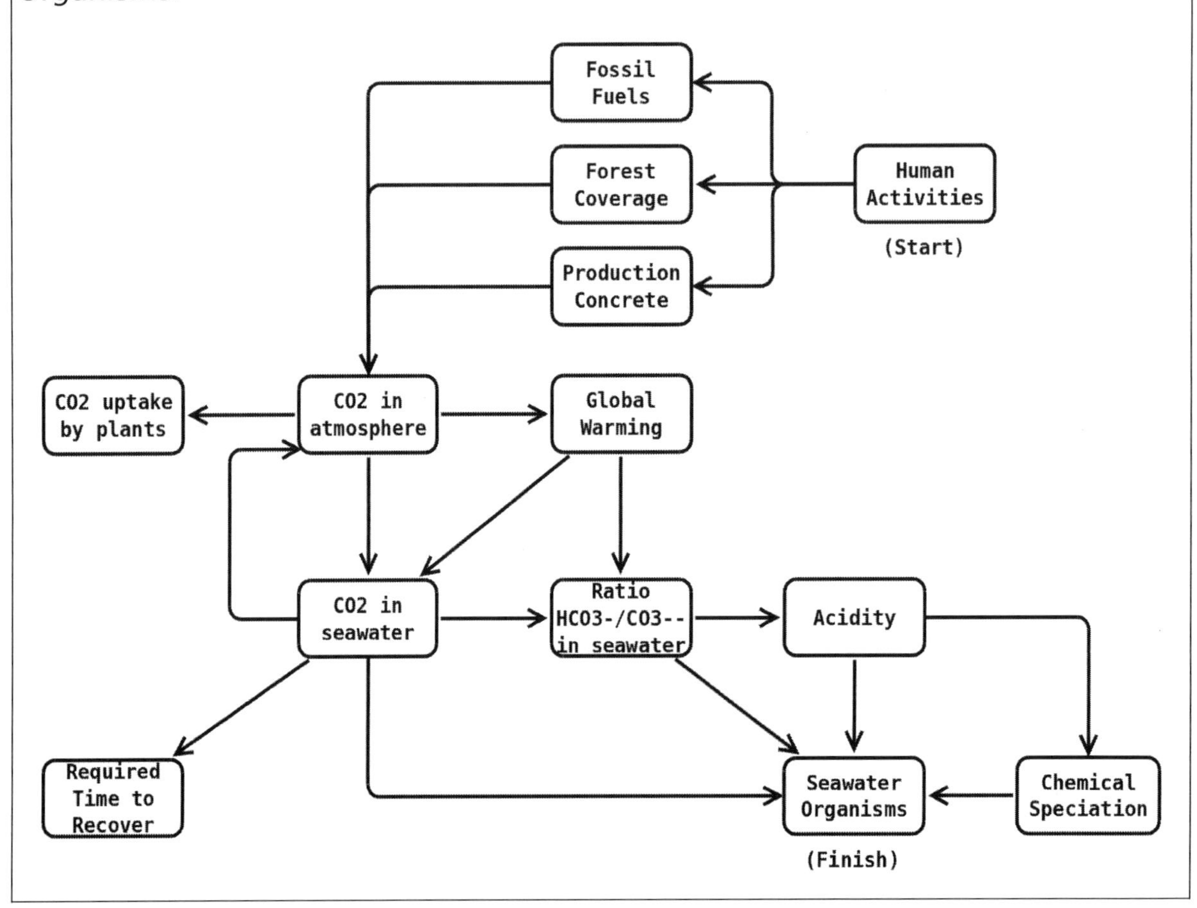

Causal Flow Diagram

This is a more specific form of visual mapping that aims to represent the cause and effect interactions, sometimes as a prelude to computer simulation.

- If one factor has no *direct* effect on another then no arrow connects them!
- If a change in one factor (B) changes another factor (C) in the ***same*** direction, then this relationship is indicated by a ***plus (+) sign***:
  if B ↑ then C ↑ ... or ... if B ↓ then C ↓.
- If a change in one factor (A) changes another factor (B) in the **opposite** direction (*inverse or reciprocal)* manner, then this relationship is indicated by a ***minus (–) sign***:
  if A ↑ then B ↓ ... or ... if A ↓ then B ↑.

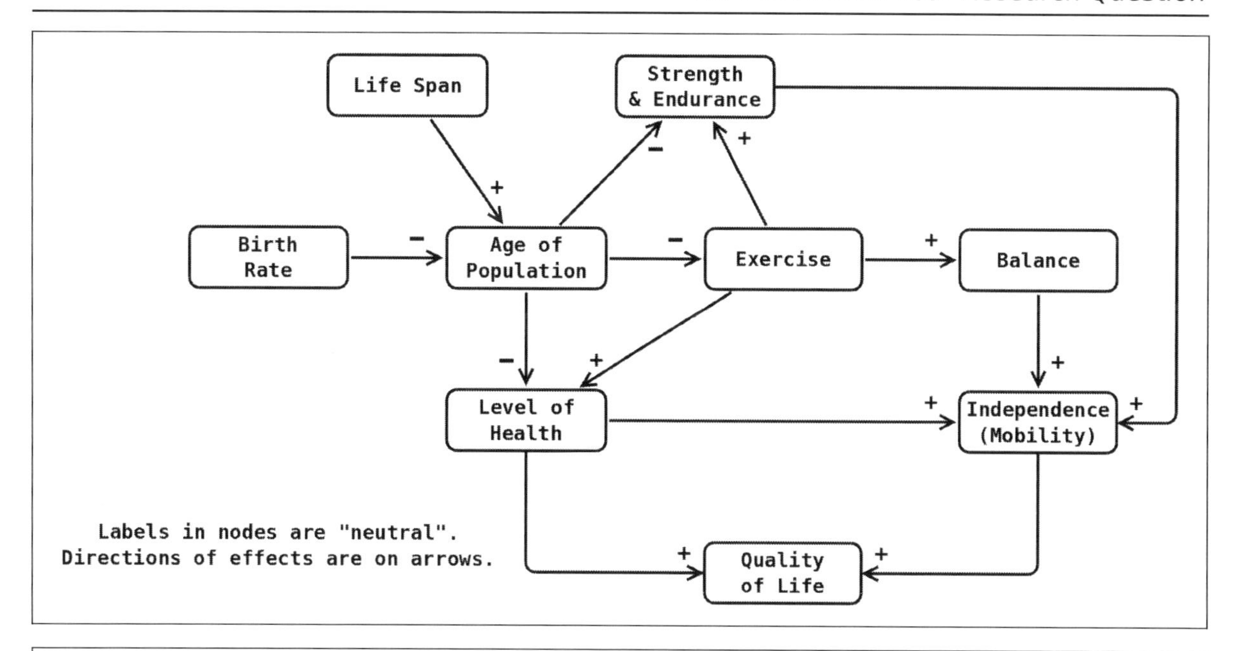

If the birth rate *increases* then there will be more children and the average age of the population will *decrease*.

If the birth rate *decreases* then there will be more adults and the average age of the population will *increase*.

In both cases, the effects are in the *opposite* direction to the birth rate, hence a *negative* sign on the arrow.

Note that *Birth Rate* and *Age of Population* are *neutral* labels because they don't indicate a direction.

If the life span of individuals *increases* then the average age of the population will *increase* because there will be more elderly people still alive.

If the life span of individuals *decreases* then the average age of the population will *decrease* because there will be fewer elderly people still alive.

In both cases, the effects are in the *same* direction to the life span, hence a *positive* sign on the arrow.

Again, *Life Span* and *Age of Population* are neutral labels.

Evidence And Logic Required Next

Once you've defined the set of possible hypotheses, or the questions which represent them, then you need to obtain the information that will let you answer them.

When you consider a particular hypothesis or question, ask yourself:

- What information would be most useful in answering this?
  - What is ***necessary*** and ***sufficient*** to definitively answer this question?
    - Information that is *definitive* in answering a question is ***high-value***.
    - Information that is *consistent* with several hypotheses or is *circumstantial* (indirect) is ***low-value***.
    - Are you collecting information that is *useful* or are you collecting information because you *can* collect it?
- Which methods or techniques are required to obtain the required information?
- Research is a cycle of continuous development and refinement. It is always a work-in-progress.
  - From some data or evidence ...
  - We propose (guess) possible explanations (hypotheses) ...
  - Each hypothesis/question logically implies other facts.
  - The research tasks check the accuracy (correctness) of these logical implications.
  - The new information then helps us to eliminate some hypotheses and revise the set of remaining hypotheses.

Avoid becoming fixated on a single technique or a single idea.

- If you are fixated upon one idea, then you are more likely to *rationalise* (distort) your reasoning and results to fit with your preconceived idea.
- When the only tool you have is a hammer, then you will tend to look at everything as if it is a nail.
- Everything is part of a larger system and nothing happens in isolation. One method/technique will have difficulty capturing the richness (complexity) of a real situation, with the associated risk of missing important factors/connections.

NOTE

If you have experience with primarily one technique or approach, then:

- What parts of your research question can you address?
- Do you need to find additional techniques or approaches to address other aspects of your research question? This might indicate that you need to collaborate with someone else who has the necessary expertise and equipment.
- Do you need to choose a related but different research question that can be answered by the techniques you do have at your disposal?

Danger Ahead: Confusion Of Correlation And Causation

One of the most dangerous errors in research reasoning is mistaking a *correlation* for a cause and effect link. For example, we've all heard in the media (TV, radio, magazines and newspapers) about the fact that high blood-cholesterol levels are *correlated* with cardiovascular disease. A correlation indicates that two quantities move together. We can draw a diagram indicating the *correlation* between blood-cholesterol levels and cardiovascular disease.

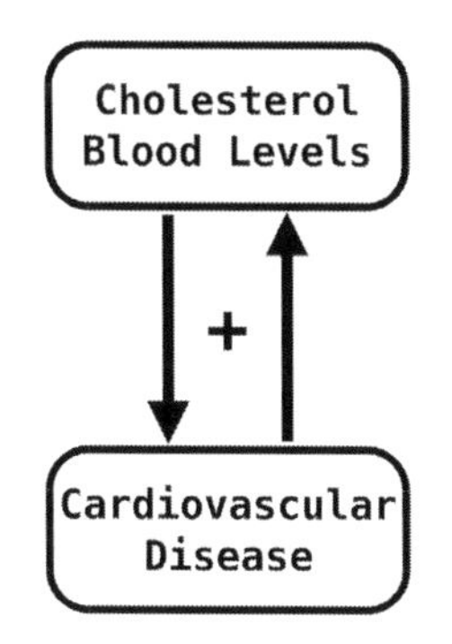

Do high blood-cholesterol levels *cause* cardiovascular disease?

Or ...

Does cardiovascular disease *cause* high blood-cholesterol levels as a side-effect?

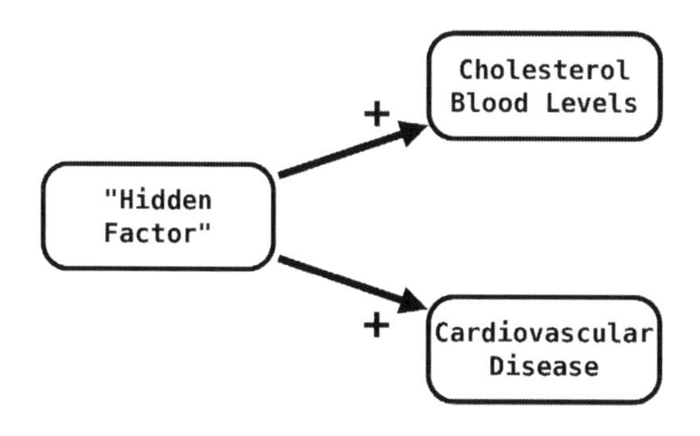

Or perhaps there is some other factor that causes both high blood-cholesterol levels and cardiovascular disease.

What are the consequences of these possibilities? If someone were to visit their doctor and found their blood-cholesterol level was elevated, their doctor might prescribe drugs to control cholesterol levels.

- If blood-cholesterol *causes* cardiovascular disease, then this is a sensible course of action.

- If blood-cholesterol levels are a side-effect of cardiovascular disease, then the drug will be treating a side-effect, but not the cause. The patient and doctor will assume the cause has been dealt with.
- If some other factor is responsible for causing *both* high blood-cholesterol levels *and* cardiovascular disease, then the drugs will again be treating a side-effect and not the cause. Once again, the patient and doctor will be assuming the cause has been dealt with.

So, the next time you see a correlation between two factors, ask yourself if you have really tested and examined all the possibilities or are you simply assuming one possibility to be true without considering and checking the others?

Appendix 1 has *Guidelines For Concept-/Causal-Mapping*.

– 4 –
Planning Your Research Project

You have broken your overall research question down into sub-questions and eventually the tasks that need to be performed to obtain the information needed to answer them. Now it's time to plan the sequence in which the research tasks are performed.

Planning A Project

A guideline is that planning should take a *minimum* of 1% of the time period involved. Planning an eight hour work day, would require at least five minutes. Planning a three year research project *ought* to take at least ten days! Studies have consistently shown that few projects are planned this carefully and as a result approximately 70% of projects (public and private) take longer than planned and cost more than estimated. Don't let your research degree become another statistic.

The required research tasks will define what is needed in terms of time, techniques, people, equipment and resources (including money).

Time

When does each task need to be done?

- Some tasks will take a long time and will need to be started early. For example, collection of samples, construction of equipment and development of new techniques all take time.
- Some tasks may only be partially successful and will require additional work or clean-up to complete. For example, if your research requires you to send out questionnaires or surveys, you will never get a 100% return rate, even if you pay well! And people have a tendency to take their time in completing questionnaires. So you may need to send a second or third batch to obtain the required total number of replies which will take longer than you might have imagined.
- Some tasks are *independent* of each other and can be done in *parallel* or *concurrently* with other tasks.
- Other tasks are *dependent* and must be done serially/sequentially. For example, if you have sent out questionnaires, then you can't do any statistical analysis until the required number have been returned.

How do you estimate the time you should allow for completing a task? For a given task, estimate a range of possible times for completion:

- shortest possible time if everything works perfectly;
- longest possible time if everything goes wrong.

Often the *worst-case scenario* can easily take two to five times as long as the *best-case scenario*. Although the worst-case scenario may be less likely, it is still useful to make the estimate, if for no other reason than it avoids slipping into a fantasy of expecting everything to work perfectly. From the best and worst-case estimates, calculate the difference and add two thirds of the difference to the best-case estimate as a ***buffer*** or ***safety-margin***. For example:

Best-case estimate = 1 day

Worst-case estimate = 5 days (Let's face it, when things go wrong, they *really* go wrong!)

Difference = 4 days

2/3 x difference = 2.67 days (This is the buffer or safety-margin to be added to the best-case estimate.)

Working estimate for scheduling purposes = 1 + 2.67 = 3.67 days

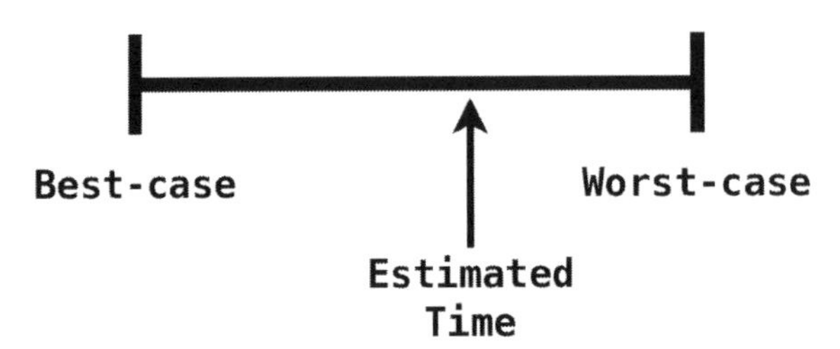

Before you start thinking we're being overly pessimistic, remember the statistics concerning how many projects are over-time and over-budget. What would have happened if the planners had been more realistic? As an example from daily life, think of some journey you have made many times (perhaps commuting to school or work). What is the fastest you have ever made the journey? What is the longest time it has taken you, when things have gone wrong? When Ted was commuting daily in London, he typically had a twenty minute journey to work (when everything was working perfectly). When the *London Underground* had major disruptions, it would take him three hours to walk home (nine times longer than the best-case time)!

Even if your research project has already been planned by your supervisor, it won't do any harm to go through the planning of the project to:

- understand the thinking behind the project and the plan;
- identify any new skills you will need to learn;
- check that you can actually do what is required in the time allocated.

It's better to find out early that there might not be enough time because you can then take steps to cope with this. If you find out later, then you have less time and fewer options for coping with it effectively.

Techniques And Equipment/Services

Shared services may need to be booked in advance, so you will need to know:

- How much you have that needs to be processed by the service?
- How long it will take you to prepare this amount? (Earliest date you can show up.)
- How quickly the service works at processing things?
- When does the service have availability?

Once you have booked a service in advance, then you must make sure that the other bits are completed in time. So put in a safety buffer/margin before the scheduled booking of the service.

People

You may require the assistance/consultation of experts or technicians in other fields, departments, or institutions, such as statisticians, electronic engineers, or computer/database experts. When will these people be available? Will they have travel plans that will affect your timetable or work? For example, if they are planning a 6 month sabbatical, then this could seriously affect your project depending upon when their sabbatical is scheduled.

Resources

Once you have defined the above aspects of the project, then you are in a position to estimate the resources (budget) required for completion according to the schedule. You estimate the budget at the end because the speed at which you want to complete the project will have cost implications. For example, if a project needs to be completed more quickly, then some staff may need to work overtime or extra staff may even need to be hired. Completing tasks or projects quicker *always* costs more money and more effort. Never, never guess what budget is needed without working through the planning steps!

In the case of your PhD project, the budget and resources have probably been predefined for you. Nevertheless, by going through the project planning, you will understand the project better and you will be able to use the resources you have more wisely.

Planning Diagrams

One of the best ways to begin planning is to use a diagrammatic technique. There are various forms of diagrams and corresponding software that can be used in project planning. We want to emphasise that using a piece of software that draws pretty pictures is not a substitute for doing the thinking!

Ted's preference is to use ***PERT*** (Process Evaluation and Review Technique) diagrams because he finds these more helpful for thinking about tasks and sequencing. They visually indicate sequence as well as serial and parallel branches. They are also easy to draw and redraw as your thinking develops.

There are two common variations that you will encounter:

- *Process on Arrow (POA)*
- *Process on Node (PON)* which is more common

Use whichever you feel more comfortable with. For the examples which follow, we will use *Process on Node* (each box is an activity/task) and the results of the task flow to the next task in the chain. Let's begin with the simple example of making an omelette ...

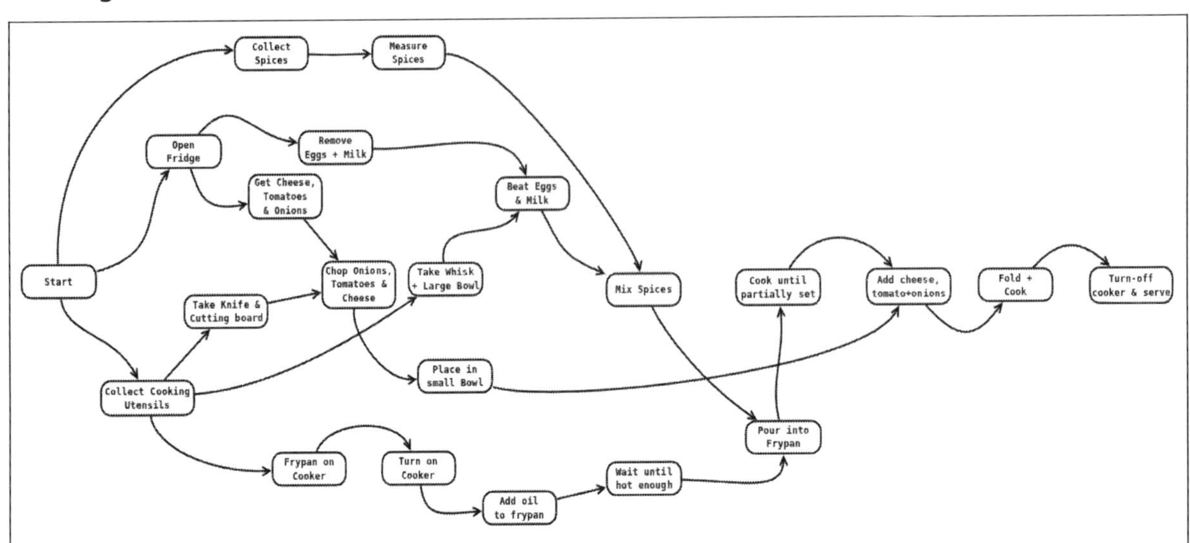

Here is the first draft when Ted started thinking about how to make an omelette. His aim was to get something on paper that more or less captured the various parts of the overall process, even if the result was messy or incomplete.

(A larger version of this diagram is in *Appendix 6*.)

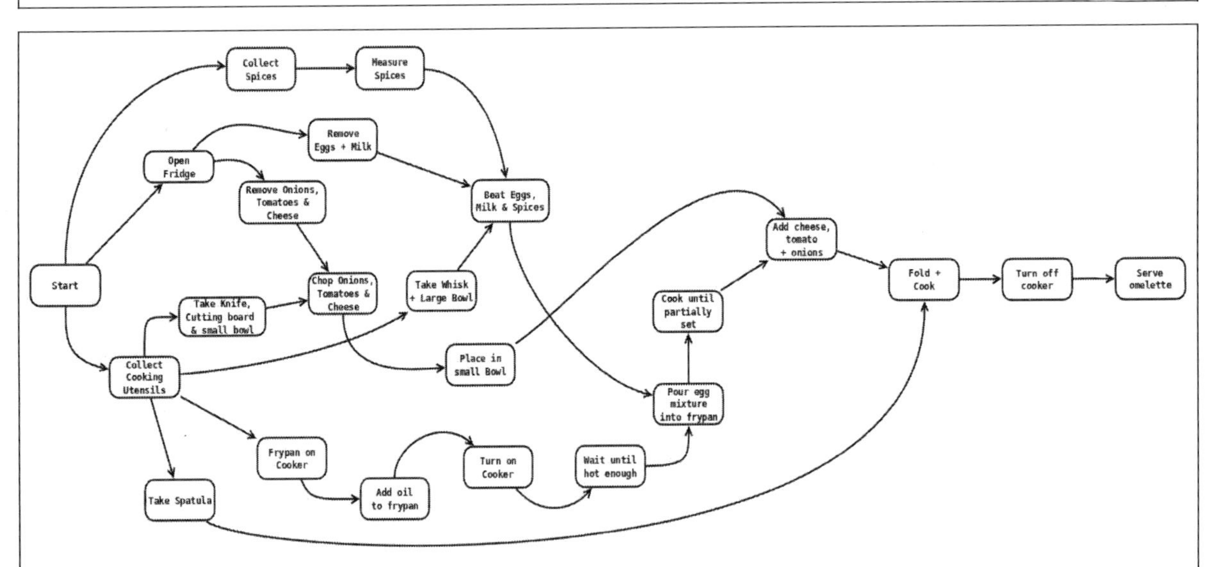

Here is the second draft. It's somewhat neater and the relationships and sequence are beginning to be sorted out. It's still a work-in-progress. Redrawing the diagram also provides additional time to think about what tasks are involved and how they need to be sequenced.

(A larger version of this diagram is in *Appendix 6*.)

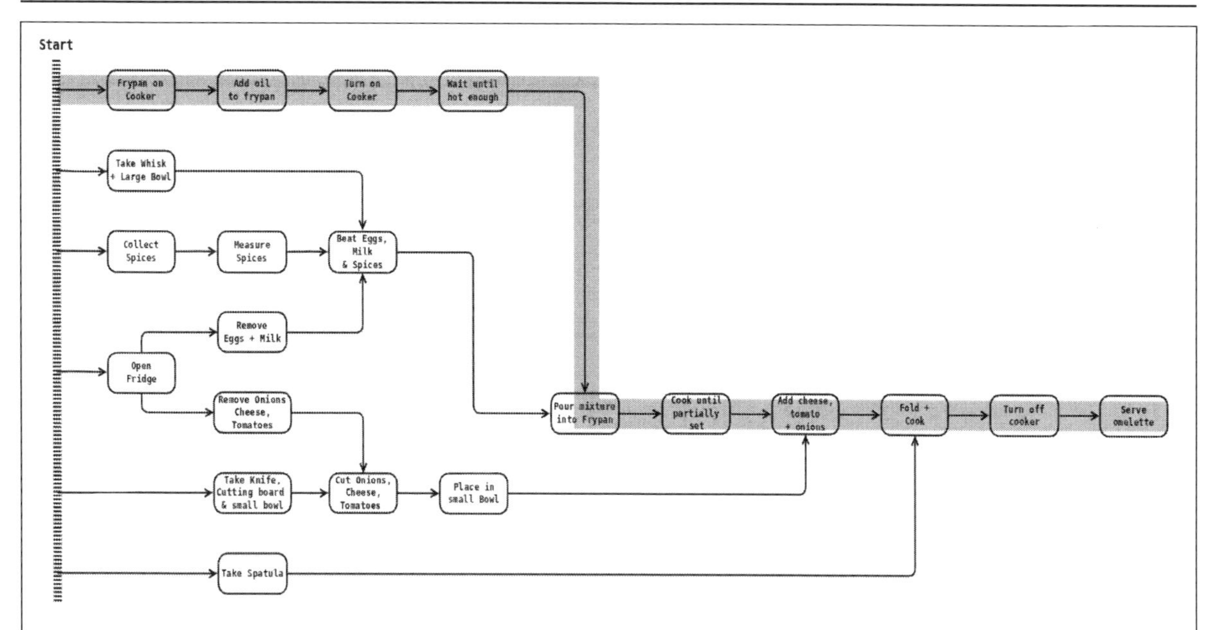

Here's the third draft. It now clearly shows the required tasks and their relationships. The *Start box* from the first two drafts has been replaced by a *Start line* in this diagram because it makes the parallel branches easier to see.
(A larger version of this diagram is in *Appendix 6*.)

The ***parallel branches*** indicate tasks that can be done ***independently*** of one another. Later in the process of making the omelette, these independent branches will join when the results of the different streams are combined.

All of the tasks need to be done at some point if the omelette is to be completed successfully. How long will the omelette take to prepare?

- **If Ted has some people helping him in the kitchen**, then they can work independently *carrying out the different branches concurrently (at the same time)*. In this case, the most time-consuming branch is the one that is shaded in grey. In this particular example of cooking an omelette, the grey path also happens to be a branch that shouldn't be interrupted once the omelette mixture is in the frying pan.
  The *branch that takes the longest time to complete* (the grey branch) determines the minimum time that the group could hope to cook the omelette if everything works perfectly. This *slowest path to completion* or *path of maximum duration* is referred to as the ***critical path*** in project management. The word *critical* does not refer to the importance of the tasks (they all need to be done), rather it is used in the sense of emphasising the best-case time to completion. The omelette cannot be completed quicker than this, so this is the critical time in any planning or scheduling.
- **If Ted has no one helping him in the kitchen**, then he will need to complete all the branches himself. For this example of cooking an omelette, the branches that feed into the grey-shaded critical path will need to be completed first and set aside to be added later. If any of these parallel branches is delayed, then the whole process will be delayed. The time it will take to cook the omelette will be the sum of the times it takes Ted to

complete all the branches on his own. And again this estimate assumes that everything works perfectly.

- **If the cooker breaks while cooking the omelette**, then the omelette could take substantially longer than planned!
  What is the contingency plan if the cooker stops working? (Eat a sandwich and then go to the shops to buy a new cooker!)

Finally, it took three iterations to remember and sequence the tasks for making an omelette. So imagine how much extra thinking and planning a 3 – 4 year *research* project will need!!!

Remember to account for unexpected (some would say inevitable!) delays by calculating and adding buffers as mentioned earlier. The fact that many projects take longer than estimated indicates that people underestimate both the buffers required and the likelihood of problems!

Exercise: Mapping And Scheduling Production Of A Film

This exercise is to draft a *PERT–PON* chart. The example is for making a single-set film, such as *Phonebooth* which was filmed in ten days in one city location. A list of the tasks with estimated durations follows the instructions.

- For reference purposes, each task has been arbitrarily assigned an *Identifier* which has no necessary relationship to the sequence of tasks. The *Identifier* is simply to label the tasks so that we can tell them apart.
- The *Prerequisite* column indicates the other tasks which *must be completed* before the given task can be started.
- Remember that each task is meant to produce a result which is then necessary for the following stages.

Step 1: Sequence/Schedule the tasks and draft a PERT–PON diagram.

- Which tasks are *independent* of other tasks? These can be done concurrently (in parallel).
- Which tasks are *dependent* or *contingent* upon the completion of other tasks? These tasks must be done sequentially.
- Which tasks are once only?
- Which tasks are recurring or ongoing?

Step 2: Find the ***critical path*** for the film project.

- What is the minimum possible time to completion (film première) if everything works perfectly?
- Which branches feed into the critical path?

Step 3: Check your diagram and critical path with the answer in *Appendix 2*.

Identifier	Activity	Duration	Prerequisite
Start	Producer has financial backing for the film.		
A	Find Director	4 weeks	Start
B1	Find Screenwriter	4 weeks	Start
B2	Produce Screenplay	12 weeks	B1
C	Legal: Insurance	1 week	Start
D	Accounting	ongoing	Start
E1	Find Composer	4 weeks	B2
E2	Produce Musical Score	8 weeks	E1
E3	Find Orchestra/band	4 weeks	E2
F	Storyboard the screenplay	8 weeks	A, B2
G1	Cast principal actors/actresses	8 weeks	B2
G2	Cast supporting actors/actresses	8 weeks	B2
G3	Cast extras	2 weeks	B2
H	Legal: Negotiate contracts	8 weeks	G1, G2
I	Advertising/Marketing	ongoing	H, M
J	Find & negotiate city exterior location	8 weeks	F
K	Legal: Permits & Permissions	12 weeks	J
L	Arrange accommodation for film cast & crew.	2 weeks	H, K
M	Costumes: Design & Preparation	8 weeks	H, G3
N1	Props: Preparation & Transportation	8 days	K
N2	Costumes: Transportation	3 days	K, M
N3	Lighting: Preparation & Transportation	4 days	K
N4	Cameras: Preparation & Transportation	9 days	K
N5	Sound: Preparation & Transportation	2 days	K
O	Catering: Arrange catering	1 week	K
P	Filming	10 days	N1 – N5, O, L
Q1	Props: Re-packing & Transportation	3 days	P
Q2	Costumes: Re-packing & Transportation	2 days	P
Q3	Lighting: Re-packing & Transportation	4 days	P
Q4	Cameras: Re-packing & Transportation	4 days	P
Q5	Sound: Re-packing & Transportation	2 days	P
R	Studio: Editing film	12 weeks	P
S	Studio: Recording soundtrack	1 week	E3, R
T	Studio: Editing soundtrack	3 weeks	S
U	Studio: Titles & Credits	3 weeks	T
V	Distribution	3 weeks	U
Finish	**Film Première**		

Notes:

- Many of the large tasks (*e.g.* ten days of filming) could be expanded and presented as separate PERT charts. This would follow the same principles and practices as this exercise and would be an example of *drilling down* from general to more specific actions and details.
- The ten days of filming may be the exciting part, but the preparation before filming and the processing after filming are equally important. Furthermore, the pre-filming and post-filming processes are much more time-consuming than the filming itself! If we translate this example to the context of doing a PhD, the research activities might be the exciting bits, but do not underestimate the importance or time taken in doing preparation and processing. And writing a thesis always takes longer than postgraduates imagine.
- Never underestimate the amount of thinking and planning it takes to organise a research project. We're reminded of a quote from General Dwight D. Eisenhower who said that "Plans are nothing; planning is everything." The plan will inevitably change but the thought put into planning will serve you well. When your PERT diagram is complete, it will indicate the flow of tasks, the deadlines, as well as the deliverables from each task.

In this movie example, the ten days of filming is what is called a *bottleneck* or *choke-point* or *critical junction*. It is called this because a set of parallel branches must come together and pass through this point successfully before the project can continue. There are no alternative pathways that can bypass this bottleneck and still produce the required result (the film).

In a research project, this might occur if you have booked time at some large national facility or service. All the various strands will have to come together and be ready for your booked appointment.

If your project has a bottleneck, then you will need to account for it in your planning. Make sure you include slack in your time estimates!

In research, especially research proposals, you may come across something called a ***GANTT*** diagram. The advantage of a *GANTT* diagram is that its bar format clearly illustrates start times, durations and deadlines. This makes it useful as an overall *summary* of the project timing. However, we find its disadvantage is that it tends to obscure the connections and flow of the processes, which we think is the most important information. Ted never used *GANTT* diagrams unless he was preparing a grant application. If you need a *GANTT* diagram for some reason, then you can easily create one from your *PERT* diagram.

Plan B: The Contingency Plan

Once you have a project plan, then it's time to think about your contingency plan. Anticipate things that could go wrong and think of alternatives in case they happen. The first step is to look for weak points in the plan, processes or equipment. For each aspect or task in your plan, ask:

- How *vulnerable* is this part/process to breakage, interference or disruption?
    - Where could it fail or break or be delayed?
    - How could it fail/break/be delayed ... ?
- What are the *consequences* for the project if a particular part, process or task doesn't work as expected?
    - How seriously will this affect the results?
    - How serious will it be if it can't be rectified?

Once you have identified the various weak points, the next step is to ask yourself: "If something went wrong with ⟨...⟩, then what are my options for coping with this?"

- If ⟨...⟩ doesn't work as planned then:
    - Can it be fixed? Or do you need to shift to your Plan B?
    - What would be the time-scale for the part or process to be fixed or replaced? For large pieces of equipment, this can be several months!
    - What is the cost of fixing it? What is the cost to the project if it isn't fixed? How much money is available in the budget to cope with this?
    - Could you find the same equipment, facilities or service elsewhere? How much would they charge? If it is a substantial amount, then this should have been included in the budget as a contingency item.
- If you can't do a high-value task ⟨...⟩ then what can you do that's almost as valuable while you wait for ⟨...⟩ to be repaired/replaced?
- If you can't do ⟨...⟩ at all, then what else could be done? How else might you achieve all or most of the important results of your research?
- What is your ***cut-off point***? How do you decide when something is unlikely to succeed and that it's time to give up and move on to your backup plan?
- If you are forced to abandon a particular approach or path, then what alternative approach or path would have the next highest degree of interest and value?

When military operations are planned, they often make use of a *counter-measures team* whose function is to identify all the different ways that a plan could be stopped, delayed, disrupted or circumvented. Their job is to identify weaknesses and the tactics necessary to exploit the weaknesses. This is then fed-back to the planners so that the plan can be made more bullet-proof.

- 5 -
Task-Management And Troubleshooting

Your project plan defines your overall strategy for completing your research. It is your route-map for the research journey. However, in addition to your research, you will have other demands upon your time.

If we use juggling as an analogy, then you will have some research balls (tasks) and some non-research balls (tasks) which need to be juggled. Task-management is concerned with which balls and how many balls do you juggle today? And when balls start falling on the floor or breaking, then it's time for troubleshooting!

What we call task-management some people call *time-management*, but this is a misnomer. You don't manage time, it flows on relentlessly. You manage your choices and tasks within the time you have available.

Task-Management

In our opinion, there are three important considerations within task-management:

1) Finite Resources
   a) How many balls are you capable of juggling today?
   b) How long can you juggle before becoming tired?
2) Value Of A Task = Importance Of Its Outcomes
   a) Which balls should be juggled today?
3) Time-Scale And Tempo
   a) When do you need to start juggling a particular ball?
   b) How long will this ball need to be juggled?
   c) When do you need to finish juggling this ball?

Finite Resources

Your personal resources (time, energy, concentration, ...) are limited and have to be managed like any limited resource.

Mentally, there is a limit to how many things people can juggle at one time. If people try to juggle more than that, then not only do they become stressed and overloaded, but the chance of making mistakes increases.

Multi-tasking is a dangerous myth in our opinion. Each activity takes a part of your mental processing power. If you are trying to do two things at the *same time*, for example plan your project and type emails, then each activity gets 50% of your brainpower.

Do you really think a surgeon could perform an operation while reading medical journals and texting colleagues?

In the same vein, it's important to realise that each time you change from one task to another, there is a mental cost in terms of switching between tasks, which can be as high as 15% depending upon the activity. Have you noticed when you change from one thing to another, it takes a while for your brain to get in the groove? Each time you interrupt what you're doing to check your emails or answer you mobile telephone, you delay how quickly you can recover your train-of-thought.

(Before you say "What about your juggling metaphor?", a juggler is only handling one ball at a time while waiting for the other balls to finish their trajectories. And they aren't texting friends while they are juggling!)

NOTE

When the project plan has parallel tasks, this does not mean they are done simultaneously. The parallel tasks may all be in-progress at the same time, but you are only working on one task at a time. For example you might work on one task until:

- you reach a convenient point to pause; or
- you have to wait for some reason.

In this case, while you are waiting for the first task to be ready to continue, you can switch your full attention to another task and work on that, for example working on your literature survey.

So several tasks may be *progressing in parallel*, but you are only working on one thing at a time, often when there is a waiting period in the other branches.

The number of workable hours in each day is limited as is your ability to concentrate. For example, two commonly encountered types are:

- The *Early-bird*: These people are full of life in the morning and fade as the day progresses. By evening, they're yawning and ready for bed.
- The *Night-owl*: These people have difficulty waking up in the morning and they haven't fully warmed up until the afternoon. And in the evening, they are full of life.

Value Of A Task = Importance Of Its Outcomes

In *Chapter 3*, we mentioned high-value (definitive) and low-value (circumstantial) information with regard to answering your research questions. High-value tasks will produce the high-value information that is required to answer your research question(s).

We want to extend that idea to *all* your other activities. An activity/task is important because of its positive or negative consequences. Are you spending your time and effort wisely?

Get in the habit of asking yourself questions such as:

- "What is the most useful/valuable thing I can be doing in these circumstances?"
- "What will have positive consequences if it is done?"
- "What will have negative consequences if it is not done?"

Concentrate on the tasks with high-value consequences and reduce, postpone or avoid the low-value tasks. Unfortunately, we've seen students waste time on low-value activities such as fiddling with the margins on a quarterly report, but not backing-up their thesis which is high-value and potentially catastrophic! (Repeat after us: "I will backup my files today. I will backup my files today. I will backup my files today ...")

Distinguish whether some task is *important* or simply *urgent.*

Important means that a task produces a valuable result for you or your research.

Urgent means the deadline is very close and someone is jumping up and down impatiently!

- For *whom* is it urgent?
- Why did they leave it so late?
- What happens to *you* if that deadline isn't met?
- If there are no positive consequences for doing it quickly and/ or no negative consequences if it isn't done at all, then why are you wasting your time on it?

Just because some task is urgent does not necessarily mean that it is also important. Beware of other people dumping on you tasks that are urgent and/or important to them. Just because it is urgent and/or important to *them* does not necessarily mean it is urgent and/or important for *you.*

Although we're emphasising the need to focus on what's important to your research degree, you can't be completely selfish – there is some give and take required to get along with your colleagues, friends and family. Help others when you can, just make sure to maintain a balance.

Time-scale And Tempo

Some tasks develop at their own pace and can't be rushed (*e.g.* growing plants). Other tasks can't be delayed beyond a deadline (*e.g.* tax return).

Some tasks are routine and need to be scheduled consistently, such as meeting your supervisor, writing quarterly reports, backing up your files, *etc.*

Complex tasks will require many stages or steps and hence a longer time to complete. You need to begin working on larger tasks *as soon as possible* so that they *can* be finished on time later. Just because a large task has a deadline that is months or years away, doesn't mean that it is unimportant or that you can postpone it indefinitely. If a farmer doesn't plant the seeds in the spring and cultivate them during the summer, there will be no harvest in the autumn.

Procrastination most commonly results from one of two motivations: perfectionism or avoidance. If you are a perfectionist, then I suggest you get over it. The universe seems to take a perverse delight in frustrating perfectionists. And only some things, such as brain surgery and bomb-disposal, are really worth the extra time and effort to make them perfect. And if you are avoiding a task, then why are you avoiding it? Matters rarely improve or disappear with postponement, so delaying is not normally a wise choice.

Because of the inevitability of the unexpected, it's also important to have *slack* in your project plan (spare time and spare resources) so that you have the flexibility to cope with the altered circumstances. This is where the buffers become important! (You did add them like we suggested didn't you?)

How Do You Combine The Three Considerations?

Many time-management experts recommend ranking tasks according to the value of the consequences and the time-frame involved. The table below shows the sort of ranking scheme we recommend.

	Short-term	**Medium-term**	**Long-term**
High-value	A	B	C
Medium-value	B	C	D
Low-value	E	Avoid?	Avoid?

You would do your (A) tasks when you are at your best, your (B) tasks when you are at medium-strength and your (C) tasks when you are at low-strength. (D) and (E) tasks would be postponed until a time when you're twiddling your thumbs with boredom. And remember to update/revise this table as tasks are completed!

In the cases of *Early-birds* or *Night-owls* that we mentioned previously, their daily timetables for dealing with tasks might look like the following:

	Early-bird	**Night-owl**
Morning	A	C
Afternoon	B	B
Evening	C	A

Troubleshooting:
(When The Biologically-Derived Excremental Fertiliser Hits The Rotational Air Displacement Device)

You have your research plan and you have anticipated possible problems and developed possible responses (Contingency Plan). Then you begin your research work. It may go smoothly (lucky you!) or something might happen ...

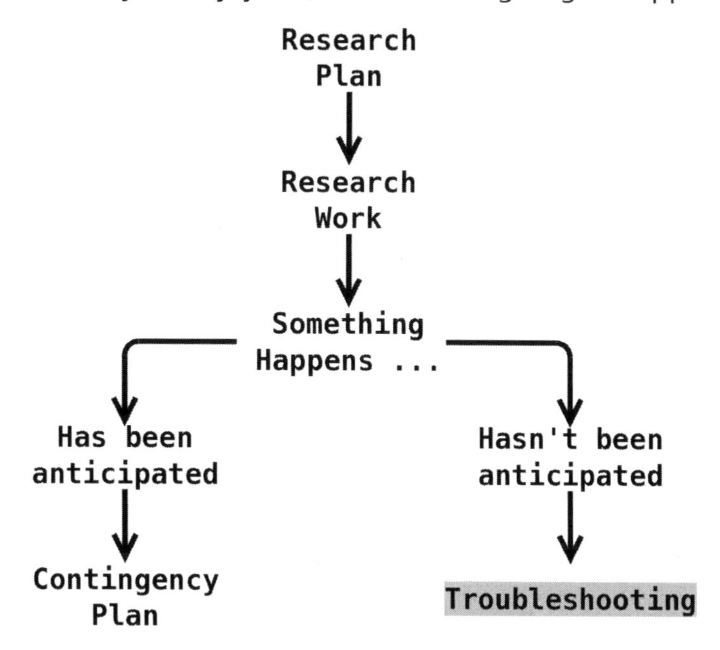

Useful Troubleshooting Questions

Troubleshooting uses the same kind of thinking that you used when you developed your Contingency Plan, except that you are now thinking on your feet with the clock ticking. The experience you gained while thinking about your Contingency Plan will help you here and may be a source of useful ideas.

- ***Why isn't (...) working?***
  - Check the simple things first before looking for more complicated causes. There is a reason that computer helplines always start with asking "Is it plugged in?" and "Is it switched on?"
    - Could it be a *hardware* problem? Failing hard drives and power-supply-units often cause erratic behaviour in computers, especially after they have been on for a while and have warmed up. USB memory sticks have a tendency to fail suddenly and completely. One day they are working, the next day they are a useless piece of plastic. (If your data and/or thesis are on a USB stick, then you did back them up today didn't you?)
    - Could it be a *software* problem? If a program was working before and has stopped working since the last set of software updates, then it might be the most recent updates. Or perhaps someone has changed the default settings?

    - If you use equipment, when was the last time it was calibrated? When was the last time it had maintenance?
    - If you use chemicals, could there be an impurity in the previous or current batch that explains the change in behaviour?
    - Could it be a problem involving *people*? Has someone failed to do something they should have done?
  - If at first you don't succeed, then try, try again to see if *some* practice helps. Then take a different approach! If ⟨...⟩ isn't working after a few attempts, then repeating things indefinitely is unlikely to magically start working later.
  - Talk to people! Maybe someone else has had a similar problem and has suggestions concerning the cause and/or how to fix it.
  - Keep notes of what has been checked or tried. For more complex problems it is easy to lose track of what has been done and what hasn't been checked/tried yet.
- ***What can you do about ⟨...⟩?***
  - If ⟨...⟩ can be fixed or replaced in a reasonable time-frame and within budget, then this is the solution.
  - If ⟨...⟩ can't be fixed/replaced, then what are the alternatives? How else might you be able to accomplish this task?
    - Does someone else have the same piece of equipment or software?
    - Could a different measurement or method provide similar information?
  - If ⟨...⟩ can't be fixed/replaced and there aren't any alternatives, then you must limit the damage to the overall project. What else can be accomplished from the remaining parts of the project which are still working? From the tasks that can still be done, what are the most important deliverables?

Even though ⟨...⟩ has stopped working, you won't be able to spend 100% of your time troubleshooting the problem. You may reach a point where you have (temporarily) run out of ideas of what to check next or you may be waiting for someone else to check something or call you back with information. So when you aren't involved in troubleshooting, continue working on other tasks that still need to be done and can be done.

Saying things like the following will accomplish nothing.

- "The ⟨...⟩ was working fine last week!" (Things break or wear out. Fuses blow. CD lens get dirty. People unplug equipment to vacuum.)
- "I haven't changed any settings!" (Well *someone else* might have because it's not working now!)
- "I'm doing *exactly* the same thing I did last time!" (Well it's not working *exactly* like last time is it!)

- 6 -

Research Reasoning: Making Sense Of The Results

In earlier chapters, we looked at:

- how to define your research question;
- how to define the information and tasks that would be required to answer you research question(s);
- how to plan your research project;
- how to manage the tasks on a daily basis and troubleshoot difficulties.

Once you have some results and you are thinking about what they mean, there are two things to keep in mind:

- facts don't speak for themselves; and
- a collection of facts and assumptions is not a logical argument.

The Facts Never Speak For Themselves!

There seems to be a myth that the facts speak for themselves. Apart from being a faulty metaphor (facts aren't people and they can't speak), facts are just facts.

As an example, at the time this book was being written, there was a lot of media discussion in the UK concerning how the UK universities compared to the rest of the world. One frequently quoted statistic was:

> Out of the top 20 universities in the world, 13 were in the US and *only 4 were in the UK*.

The frequent interpretation was that the UK university system was declining as a result of cuts in UK government funding.

But does this *interpretation* really follow from this one fact? This statistic by itself, doesn't really justify *any* conclusion, because it is isolated from any context or relevant comparisons. What follows are questions we would ask or comments that we would make before we were willing to accept any conclusion about the decline of the UK university system. There may be others that occur to you which we've missed.

- Why did they choose to consider the top 20? If they had considered the top 10, then the UK would still have had 4 compared to only 6 for the US.
- Since we are talking about 13 US universities and 4 UK universities, we are talking about a small sample of the best universities in each country. This statistic provides no information concerning the majority of US and UK universities!
- What are the relative populations of the US and the UK? Assuming all other factors are equal (or irrelevant), one might reasonably expect that a country with a smaller population (the UK) would have fewer universities in the top 20 than a country with a larger population (US). In this case, Switzerland did well to have even 1 university in the top 20!

- What are the levels at which the different university systems are funded? How are they funded? This will affect the majority of universities in each country.
- How do we assess *quality* of a university? What *measures* or *criteria* do we choose?
    - Do we count only undergraduates or do we count both undergraduates + postgraduates?
    - Do we include some measure of how flexible the degree program is? Or how much support there is for students?
    - Do we consider only full-time students or do we also include part-time and/or returning students?
    - Do we look at staff/student ratios?
    - Do we look at the percentage of students who find a job after graduating?
    - Do we look at the starting salary of graduating students?
    - Do we look at number of research publications by staff? Or number of patents? Or number of prizes? Or grant income? Or consulting income? Or some combination of all of these?
    - Do we measure (somehow) the general public's brand awareness? In this case, older universities will have an advantage compared to younger institutions.
    - Do we look at *value-for-money*? If a particular institution charges twice as much, is its degree twice as good? Are its graduates twice as likely to find a job or will their lifetime earnings be twice as much?
    - Do we consider the *efficiency* of the institution and normalise any results by number of staff and expenditure so that we find a quality-measure per unit member of staff and unit expenditure?
    - Which disciplines or subjects do we consider?
- Once we've decided which criteria we want to consider, then how much *weight* do we assign to each factor? For example a ranking where research publications are weighted 50% will give radically different results than one where research publications are weighted 15%.
- How do we account for differences in the educational systems preceding the university degree?

With this many questions, does that single statistic really justify any conclusion?

A Collection Of Facts And Assumptions Is Not A Logical Argument

Please note that when we use the word *argument,* we don't mean a situation where people are shouting at each other! We're using the word argument in its logical sense – it is a reasoned case that what is being claimed is true.

A disconnected collection of data, assumptions and speculations does not constitute a reasoned, logical case. You cannot expect other researchers to make sense of your data for you. They are busy with their own research!

Missing steps in the logic can hide potential errors in your reasoning and/or can make it harder for others to understand your case.

For example, let's imagine that a politician makes a statement that the increasing number of people on sickness benefit is adversely affecting the national economy, which we will assume means that the economy is declining. We could represent this statement by a simple diagram:

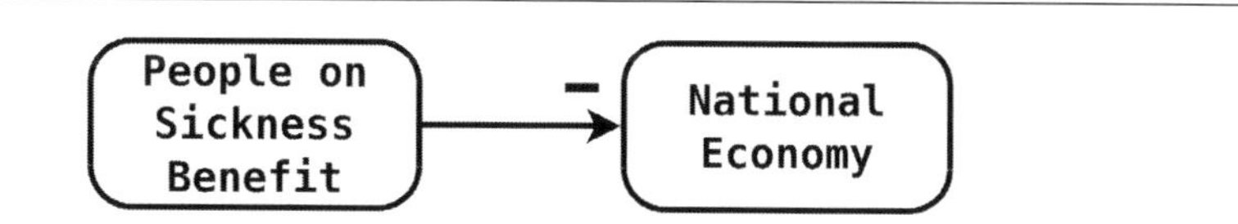

Remember from previously:

- A ***plus*** sign on an arrow indicates that two quantities move in the ***same direction***.
- A ***minus*** sign on an arrow indicates that the two quantities move in ***opposite directions***.

Because the increasing number of *People on Sickness Benefit* leads to a decline in the *National Economy*, we use a minus sign on the arrow.

We're neither politicians nor economists but we're sure that the above statement is a *large* jump in logic and that a lot of stuff has been *hidden beneath the arrow*. The following diagram is what resulted when we mapped it out.

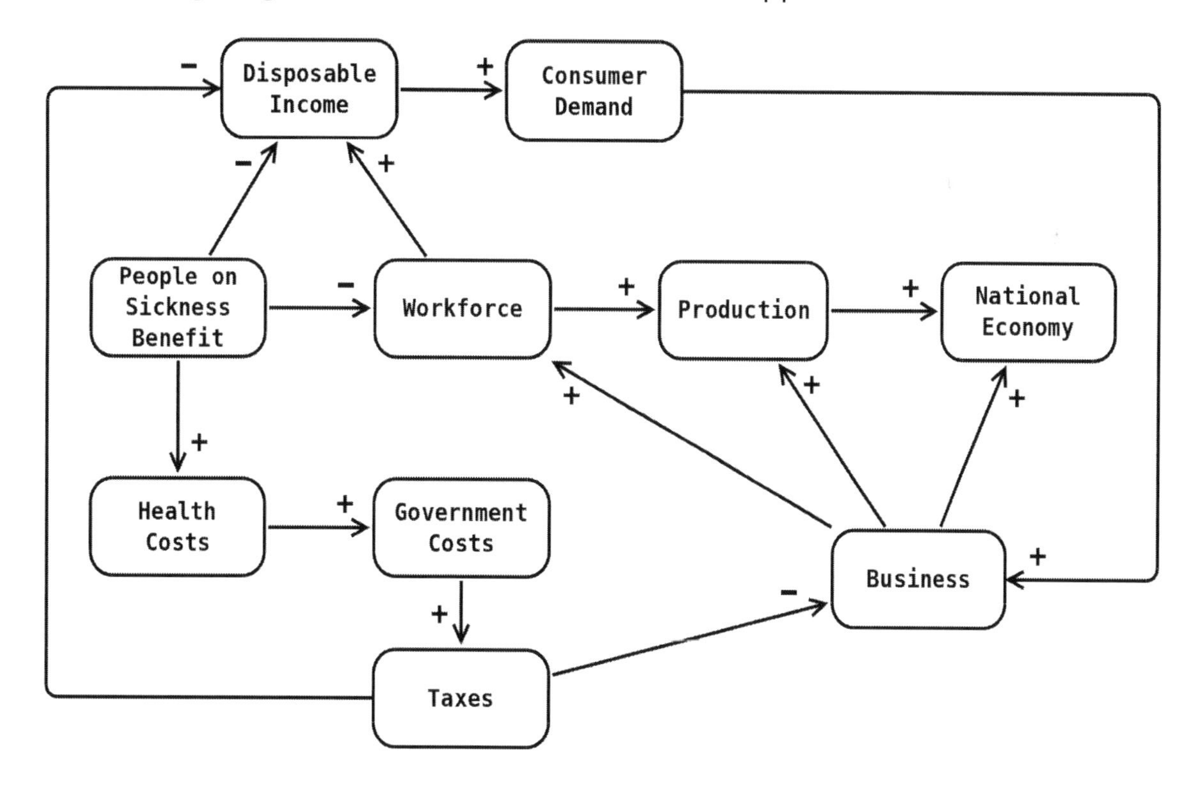

In mapping it out, we can see that the situation is much more complex than the politician's simple statement would lead us to believe (and possibly more complex than what we've drawn)! The number of people on sickness benefit only affects the national economy *indirectly*, through its effects on other factors.

The morals of this example are:

- beware of what is hidden within single steps in arguments; and
- not all arguments are simple and linear. They will often involve interconnected networks or patterns of ideas.

In more general terms, arguments can be flawed in several ways:

- *Poorly connected/linked;*
- *Inaccurate/misrepresentative;*
- *Ill-defined/imprecise evidence*;
- *Incomplete/insufficient evidence*;
- *Irrelevant/unnecessary conclusions and/or evidence*;
- *Indirect/implicit/circumstantial conclusions and/or evidence.*

To avoid making the above mistakes, your evidence must be connected to form a larger pattern that means something. If your facts were pieces of a jigsaw puzzle, then what would be the larger picture they create? How do the pieces connect?

Techniques For Structuring A Case/Argument

Meaning comes from:

- the *context*; plus
- the *selection* of *relevant* information; plus
- their *connection* to form a *pattern*.

We recommend that you build your case/argument by mapping the relationships between its elements. There are several advantages to this approach:

- Aids in structuring the logic.
- Makes it easy to see if there are any gaps or missing steps.
- Makes links, transitions or changes in direction more obvious.
- Prevents repetition, digressions and omissions.
- Makes the flow/sequence of the argument more obvious.

How do you lay out your reasoning to avoid the kind of problem we saw in the example of questionable political-economic logic? There are two principal techniques that we recommend:

- *Concept Maps* and *Argument Trees*, where you map out the ideas, conclusions, evidence and their relationships; or
- *Structure Tables*, where the ideas, conclusions and evidence are arranged within a structured tabular framework.

Concept Maps and Argument Trees tend to appeal to people who are more visual. These diagrams emphasise how facts and ideas connect without worrying about words. Structure Tables tend to appeal to people who are more verbal and prefer lists. Use whichever technique you prefer.

Argument Trees

If you recall in *Chapter 3*, we used a Top-Down process for drilling-down from the biggest question(s) to smaller sub-questions and eventually the specific information that was required to answer each question. The required information then defined the research tasks which have been omitted in the diagram below.

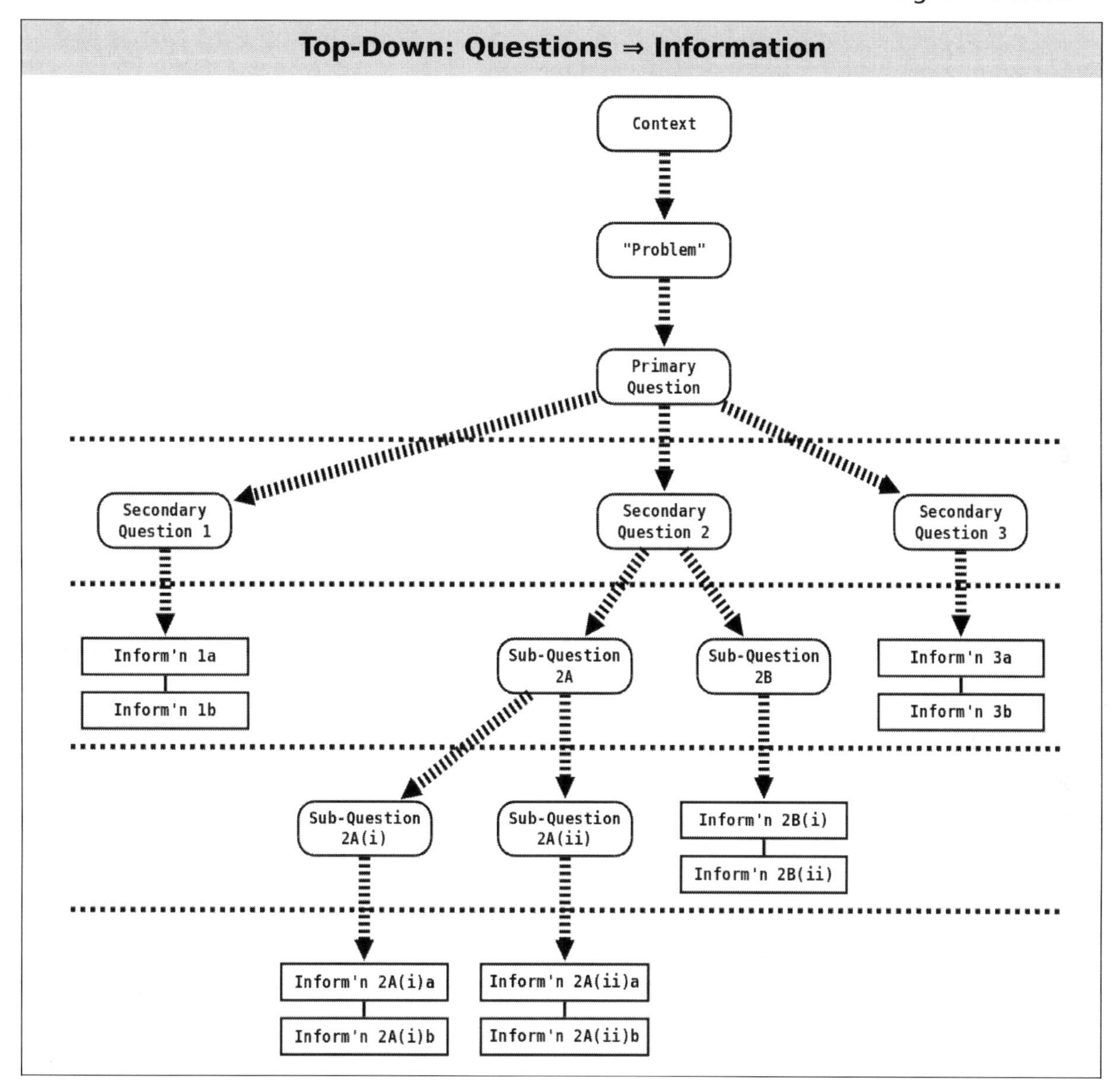

Having this Top-Down map of your research is helpful because you can use it as the basis for creating your logical argument/case. Assuming the tasks have been completed as planned with no unexpected results, then you can work upwards from the information to answering the questions at each level. Each answer to a question is a conclusion. This Bottom-Up approach, working from information to conclusions is known as an argument tree.

The *information* used to support each conclusion may come from your research results or data from relevant literature citations or assumptions.

NOTE

A conclusion from the literature that is *consistent* with your conclusion or that is *interesting* can be mentioned elsewhere, but it does not count as *evidence* in support of your conclusion.

Consistency does not count as evidence in a logical argument, because two things which are consistent could both be incorrect.

Let's look at the Bottom-Up Argument Tree that would correspond to the earlier Top-Down map.

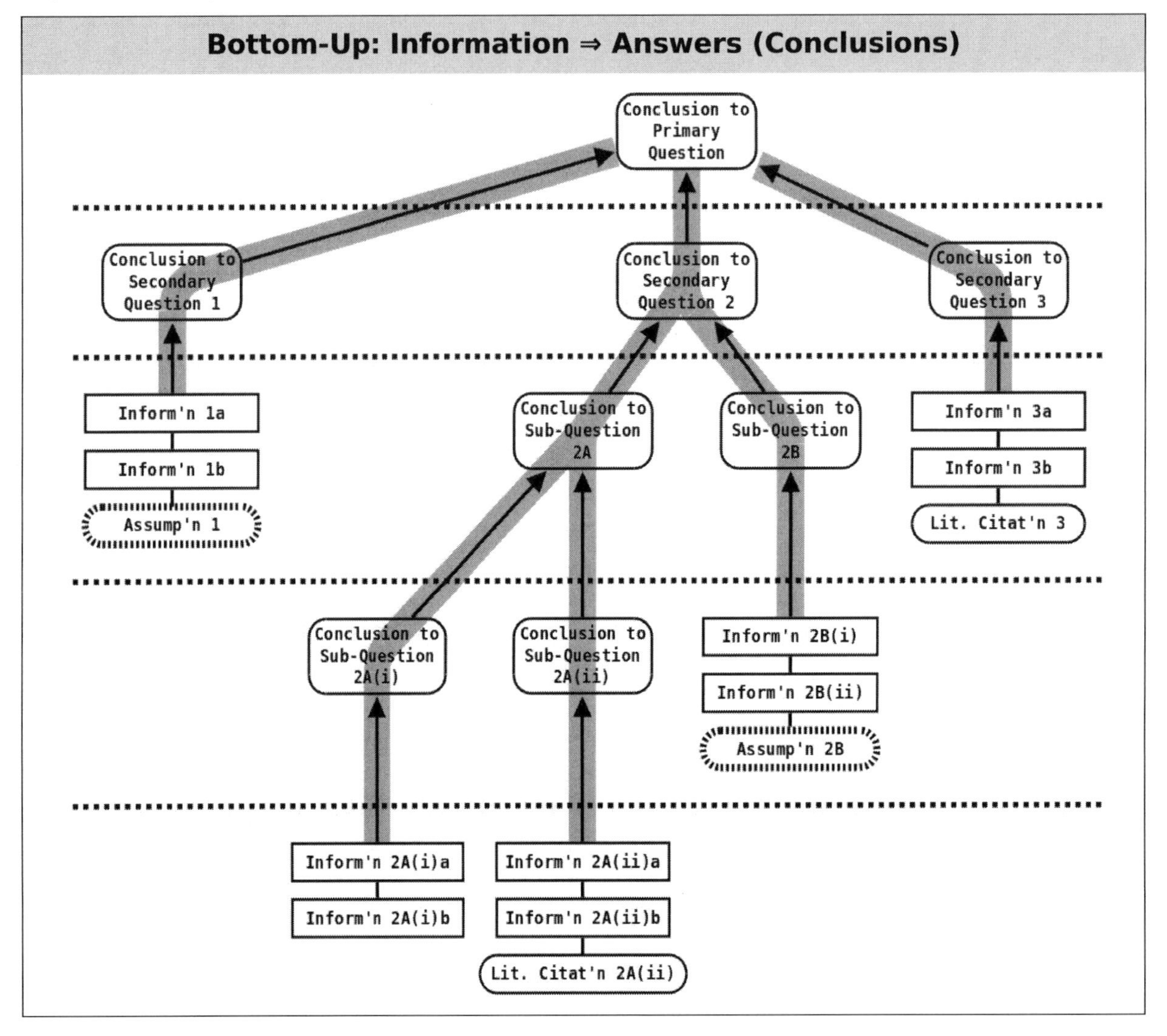

Notice how this ***argument tree*** illustrates the logical relationships between information and conclusions. This *argument tree* has four ***layers*** below the main conclusion which shows the depth of the argument.

If some things don't work as planned or there are unexpected results, then you will need to identify additional questions that need to be answered. These additional questions will require additional work to produce the information required to answer them.

As a result of the additional questions and information, you will need to revise your Top-Down map, which in turn will lead to a revised Bottom-Up argument tree.

Remember, you may need to adapt your plans and your logic as your research progresses.

Structure Tables For Planning/Analysing Logical Arguments

Ted created *Structure Tables* for students as a way of organising information and reasoning so that these can be assessed critically without the distraction of the writing style. Using a Structure Table forces you to explicitly define:

- Context - What is the larger context within which this fits?
- Audience - Who is the intended audience? What is their connection with this matter? What is their background knowledge in this area?
  (This will only be relevant when you are involved in communicating your research.)
- Importance/Value - What is the importance or value in the larger context? What is the importance to this specific audience? Why would they care?
- Claim or Conclusion or Recommendation - In one sentence what is claimed to be true or worth doing?
- Logic/Reasoning - What are the steps in the argument that lead to the final conclusion/recommendation?
- Assumptions, Suppositions and Speculations - What is being treated *as if it is true*, but proof has not been provided for it? If someone states something without support, then be sceptical and treat it as an assumption.
- Literature Citations - What is being quoted from the results or conclusions of other researchers?
- Data/Evidence - What is the objective/measurable data?

<table>
<tr><th colspan="6">Structure Table – Deconstructing The Argument/Case</th></tr>
<tr><td colspan="3">Context:</td><td colspan="3">Audience:</td></tr>
<tr><td colspan="3">Importance/Value:</td><td colspan="3">Claim/Conclusion/Recommendation:</td></tr>
<tr><td colspan="6">Logic/Reasoning:
1) .....
2) .....
3) .....
4) .....
5) .....</td></tr>
<tr><td colspan="2">Assumptions, Suppositions and Speculations:</td><td colspan="2">Literature Citations:</td><td colspan="2">Data/Facts/Evidence:</td></tr>
</table>

The approach of using Structure Tables categorises what has been offered as evidence in an argument.

- Assumptions, suppositions and speculations are subjective and conceptual. If you wouldn't be willing to wager a *large* sum of money on something being true, then it is probably an assumption.
- Literature citations are intermediate in quality.
  - The original authors could be wrong either in their results and/or their interpretation. Mistakes happen and get published!
  - The people citing the paper could have misunderstood or misrepresented it.
  - Exactly what is being cited? Objective, measurable data is most reliable. Conclusions from the literature are less reliable and more subjective because they involve interpretation. And assumptions/speculations are completely unreliable!
- Research data is objective and factual.

When a Structure Table has been completed, check for:

- Insufficient evidence
- Data which is unnecessary and/or irrelevant
- Assumptions which are used as evidence within the argument

- The balance between data, literature and assumptions. The less actual data, the weaker the argument.

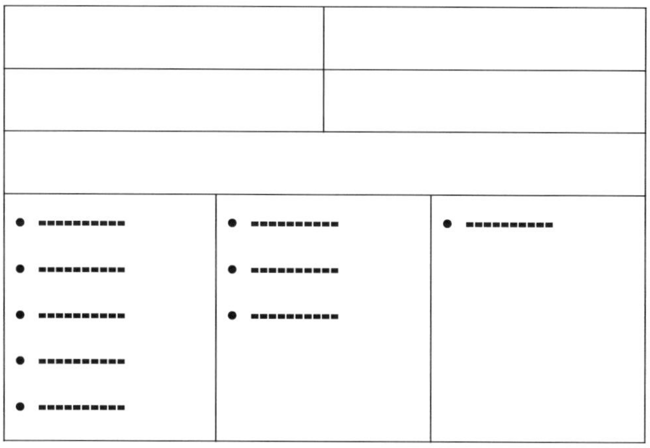

<table>
<tr><td colspan="3"></td><td colspan="3"></td></tr>
<tr><td colspan="3"></td><td colspan="3"></td></tr>
<tr><td colspan="6"></td></tr>
<tr><td colspan="2">• ----------
• ----------
• ----------
• ----------
• ----------</td><td colspan="2">• ----------
• ----------
• ----------</td><td colspan="2">• ----------</td></tr>
</table>

This distribution would correspond to an argument that is poorly substantiated. There are lots of assumptions, some literature citations and only one piece of data!

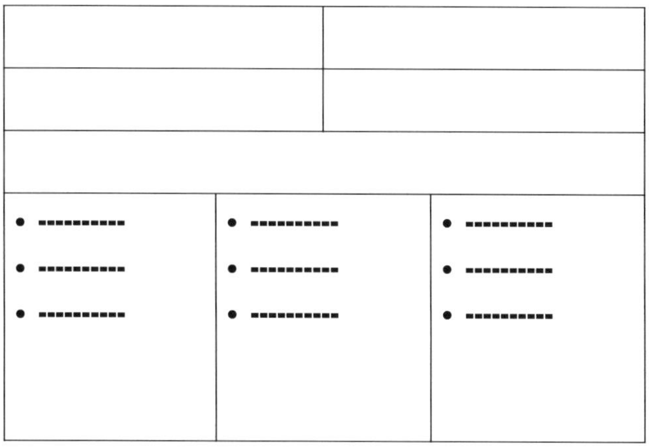

<table>
<tr><td colspan="3"></td><td colspan="3"></td></tr>
<tr><td colspan="3"></td><td colspan="3"></td></tr>
<tr><td colspan="6"></td></tr>
<tr><td colspan="2">• ----------
• ----------
• ----------</td><td colspan="2">• ----------
• ----------
• ----------</td><td colspan="2">• ----------
• ----------
• ----------</td></tr>
</table>

This distribution would correspond to an argument that has mediocre support. There are equal proportions of assumption, literature citation and data.

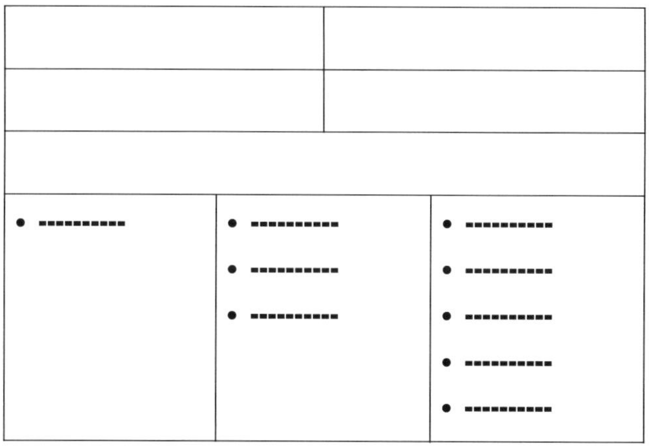

<table>
<tr><td colspan="3"></td><td colspan="3"></td></tr>
<tr><td colspan="3"></td><td colspan="3"></td></tr>
<tr><td colspan="6"></td></tr>
<tr><td colspan="2">• ----------</td><td colspan="2">• ----------
• ----------
• ----------</td><td colspan="2">• ----------
• ----------
• ----------
• ----------
• ----------</td></tr>
</table>

This distribution would correspond to an argument that is well supported. There is one assumption, some literature citations and lots of relevant data.

Using Structure Tables to analyse or deconstruct other people's arguments:

- What evidence would you need to see to be convinced of their overall conclusion?
- What evidence do they actually offer in support of their overall conclusion?
- Do these two sets match?

Using Structure Tables to prepare your own argument:

- What evidence would your audience need to see to be convinced of your overall conclusion?
- What evidence can you offer in support of your overall conclusion?
- Do these two sets match?

When working with larger arguments (more reasoning plus evidence), you can use a sheet of paper to represent each cell (or panel) in the Structure Table. This gives you more space to work with.

Research: Buyer Beware

- Research is done by human beings who can exhibit all the same human failings (deceit, greed, laziness, prejudice, pride, carelessness, ...) which appear in any other human endeavour.
- Research as a human endeavour is *conservative.* It tends to progress gradually and incrementally rather than suddenly or discontinuously. Even sudden breakthroughs had their beginnings ten or twenty years previously.
  - Researchers often consider only what fits within their existing *paradigm* (research belief-system). Because of this, there is a tendency to resist, selectively exclude or reject new data that is inconsistent with existing ideas.
  - The danger of collective belief is that everyone may be believing and acting upon an incorrect idea!
- Knowledge is always conditional/provisional which is to say that it's a work-in-progress. And research also has *fads* and *fashions* like any other human activity.

Data/evidence is more objective and tends to be longer-lasting than concepts. So be willing to discard a concept more quickly than data which contradicts it.

Communicating Your Research

– 7 –
Purpose, Point And Persuasion

After you have been working and have some results, eventually you will need to communicate your research to others. Typical ways will include:

- presenting to your group or department;
- writing a progress report to a corporate sponsor or funding agency;
- transfer viva (MPhil → PhD);
- attending a conference (local, national or international);
- writing a research paper;
- writing and defending a thesis.

Some of the above may be assigned by your supervisor for practice whereas others will be for real at conferences or other institutions. Our advice is always get as much practice as you can before you face a presentation that matters.

Remember the times when you have been on the receiving end of someone else's communication efforts and you thought one or more of the following:

- "Who cares? I certainly don't!"
- "Where does this fit?"
- "I can't believe someone funded this."
- "What does it all mean?"
- "What am I supposed to do?"
- "Where is this going?"
- "OK, I'm officially confused now!"
- "I am so bored! I wonder if I can sleep without anyone noticing ..."
- "Whoa! This is way too much!"

All of these thoughts are symptoms of poor communication by the presenter/writer. How can you avoid this happening when *you* communicate with others?

Effective Communication

Communication is about:

- changing/influencing what people think, feel or do;
- causing something to happen/change;
- producing a response or result.

Think about it, if you didn't want or need anything, then why would you talk to anyone? (And if you say because you're lonely, then you *want* companionship.) Ask yourself the following questions:

- "What do I want to accomplish? Why is this important to me?"
- "Who can help me accomplish what I want?" This defines your audience – *the people you need to convince*.

- "What do I need to say to them in order to convince them or gain their cooperation?"
- "How do I need to say it so they will understand quickly, easily and correctly?"

We find it useful to think of communication (spoken or written) as being composed of layers. The first (surface) layer that an audience will encounter is the ***style*** of your communication. If you are presenting, then this will consist of your slides and your delivery. If you are writing, then this will consist of how your document is formatted and your writing style. If it is too difficult for the audience to cope with your style of communicating, then they will give up.

If the audience can cope with your style, then the next and deeper layer in your message is the ***structure***. The structure is concerned with the overall meaning, which is a result of your logic and evidence. Once again, if this layer is too difficult to make sense of, then the audience will switch off.

Assuming the audience can cope with how you deliver your message (style) and can also make sense of your reasoning and evidence (structure), then they will want to know about your message's ***significance***. How or why is this important or useful?

When preparing presentations for example, too often people begin by collecting and fiddling with their slides *before* they have a clear idea of the meaning and significance of their message. Then they are surprised when the audience doesn't understand the meaning or importance of the presentation. To have an effective and persuasive message, our suggestion is to design and construct it in reverse order:

- What is the larger context/background where this work fits?
- Why is this important and/or useful and to whom?
- What is the reasoning, evidence and overall conclusion or recommendation?
- How can this message best be delivered to my intended audience?

Purpose, Audience And Approach

We recommend four steps in planning and preparing an effective message.

Step 1: Define the response or result you want.
What is supposed to *happen* after you communicate?

Researchers communicate for a variety of reasons, which include:

- Contributing to the knowledge-base or skills-base of their research field
    - New information or techniques
    - Confirm information or techniques
    - Indicate problems with information or techniques
- Gaining comments, feedback, ideas, suggestions on their work
- Testing ideas or conclusions in public before submitting for publication
- Recognition/Publicity and Networking

   - Gaining recognition/reputation
   - Winning a competition
   - Finding collaborators
   - Attracting staff or students
   - Attracting clients
- Achieving a qualification or degree
- Finding employment
   - Selling themselves and their skills
   - Gaining promotion
- Funding and Revenue
   - Securing funds for a new project
   - Maintaining funding for an ongoing project or service
   - Justifying a cut in funding level
   - Selling their employer's products or services
- Approval or authorisation to proceed or to change direction of the work.
- Safety or Liability Issues ("Don't do this or it will explode and we will be sued!")

All of the above require a response from someone, namely your intended audience. The response can be categorised as either ***agreement*** or ***action*** of some kind. You need to be crystal clear in your mind:

What do you want your audience to *do* when you have finished?

Your audience will need to *understand* as a necessary step towards getting what you want, but understanding should never be your *only* or final objective. Ask yourself questions like:

- "*Why* do they need to *understand*? What happens then?"
- "If they understand, then what would I expect/want/need them to do?"
- "What would be the visible signs of their agreement or cooperation?"

In preparing a one hour presentation, people will spend on average 20 – 30 hours thinking, making slides and rehearsing. Are you going to spend all this time and effort so that nothing useful happens? This would be like spending a week working on something that you knew would be a complete waste of time!

Written reports are equally time-consuming.

Step 2: Define the people whose cooperation is essential to achieving your result.

Who can give you the response you want?

How is this relevant and important to them?

→ Why should they pay attention?

→ Why should they agree with what you propose?

→ Why should they cooperate?

If your audience has been pre-assigned for you, for instance by your supervisor, then what useful result could you achieve from communicating with them? (*e.g.* comments, suggestions, help, ...)

Your audience are the people who:

- can (potentially) understand your request; and
- can give you the response you want; or
- control the resources you require; or
- might be interested in what you can offer; or
- might be affected if you accomplish your objective(s).

What are their interests? How can *they* benefit from your message?

- Why should they pay attention, be convinced and then cooperate?
- How is it relevant or useful or novel or beneficial to them? Why does it matter to them?
- What can you offer to make it worth their time and effort?
- Does your message threaten or conflict with their interests?
- Will they need to change what they think or do? If so, why and how much and how quickly?

What do they currently believe and do?

- People believe they have excellent reasons for thinking and acting as they already do.
- People prefer information which is compatible with their existing beliefs and values.
  - Will your message challenge their beliefs or values?
  - Will your conclusions or recommendations pose difficulties for them?
  - Will they be sufficiently open-minded?
- What is your credibility with your audience?

People are busy. They want maximum value for minimum time and effort.

Ask yourself: "From my audience's point-of-view, what is **relevant, useful**, **novel** and **timely** in this?"

Step 3: What is the most appropriate way to communicate your message to your intended audience?

Where, when and how can you reach your intended audience?

- Possibilities include:
  - Papers and reports
  - Articles or reviews in trade/professional journals
  - Seminars or conferences
  - Trade-shows
  - Professional training courses
  - Telephone
  - Email
- While you are a student, you often won't have a choice and you will be told whether it will be a presentation, poster or a written report. If this is the case, then do what you can to make the best of the experience and the audience.
- As your career progresses, you will have more freedom to choose the method of communication that is best suited to your purpose, intended audience and message. Papers, posters and presentations have different strengths and weaknesses, some of which are listed below.
- **Papers and Reports**
  - *Advantages*
    - Permanent record of work that can be searched and/or cited globally.
    - Reader is in control of *pace* and they can pause, reread, or get help. The reader can take as much time as they need to understand the material.
    - Reader can select sections *they* want and skip what isn't of interest.
    - Papers count heavily towards career advancement in academic environments.
  - *Disadvantages*
    - No interaction with audience – you can't explain and they can't ask.
    - Rejection rates can reach 95% for some journals.
    - Many journals charge a fee per page plus additional charges for photos or colour. This can make publishing in these journals costly.
    - Journals place limits on the number of words, pages, figures, tables, photos, which they will normally allow.
    - Journals have a bias for positive results, so it can be difficult to report negative results.
    - Your critics (referees/reviewers) are anonymous.

- **Presentations**
  - *Advantages*
    - Quicker to prepare and present than a paper, so more timely.
    - More interactive which can be useful to both sides: questions, comments, suggestions and criticism.
    - Your critics aren't anonymous – it's all public.
    - Format and content are flexible *e.g.* video or audio clips, demonstrations or audience participation.
    - Invited lectures count as much as a paper.
    - Excellent for networking and collaboration!
    - Can report work-in-progress, provisional conclusions or even negative results.
    - Visit nice places in the world.
  - *Disadvantages*
    - Presentation has more limited accessibility since it is one-time only.
    - Presenter is in control of pace, so there is a risk of too much and/or too fast for the audience.
    - Presentation is dependent upon hardware and software working correctly.
    - Anxiety and stage-fright
    - Hostile questions

NOTE

Posters are much more like presentations than papers/reports.

- The audience will be viewing your poster from a distance of approximately two metres, so it's much more like a projected slide than a page of a report.
- You will probably be available to answer questions.
- The extra advantage of a poster compared to a presentation is that the audience is in control of the pace which makes it easier for them.
- Posters full of text and small print are *not* appealing and guarantee that people will keep walking past you and your poster. Why prepare a poster only to have people ignore it and you?

Structure And Significance: Making Your Case

Step 4: From *their* point-of-view, what case would *they* find convincing? What is *necessary and sufficient* to make your case to them?

- The structure of your case will be developed from both your desired outcome and your intended audience.

  Outcome + Audience ⇒ Structured Case + Supporting Evidence
- In designing a structure suited to your outcome and audience you will need to answer many of the following questions:
  - What was the ***context*** and background for the research?
  - What was the ***issue***, hypothesis, problem or question to be addressed?
    - What were the assumptions about this issue?
    - What were the criteria for success?
  - Why was this issue ***important*** or worth resolving?
    - Why was it *relevant*, *useful*, *novel* and *timely* for the various parties involved?
    - What were the consequences or implications if this issue wasn't addressed?
    - Did the benefits outweigh the time, effort and costs involved?
  - Why was the chosen research ***approach/method*** considered appropriate, suitable or likely to succeed?
    - What were the advantages of this approach/method?
    - What were the disadvantages or limitations of this approach/method?
  - What was the ***conclusion***, interpretation or recommendation?
  - What were the reasoning + evidence that led to the conclusion?
- If you are speaking to experts in the same field as you, then much of the above might already be mutually understood, so you can dive into the details.
- If you are speaking to a mixed audience or to people from outside your field, then you will need to provide more of the background so that they will be able to understand. They will need more of the big picture and less of the details.

Just because someone isn't an expert in your field, doesn't mean that they won't have a vote in whether or not you are hired, funded, promoted, ...

Meaning Comes From The Pattern Formed By The Information!

- Meaning doesn't come from a pile of unrelated bits of data. The human brain makes sense (creates meaning) by finding a pattern that relates the individual pieces of information. That is why structuring your message is essential if you want your audience to be convinced and to cooperate.
- The more pieces of information you have, the more complex the possible patterns and consequently the more difficult to understand. As an example, why do you think the difficulty of jigsaw puzzles is partly determined by the number of pieces?
- As the ***number of pieces, n,*** in your message increases, the ***number of possible relationships, n(n – 1)/2,*** will increase faster. This is why we recommend keeping messages composed of approximately 5 major pieces because otherwise you risk overloading your audience's ability to make sense of the relationships. It is possible to exceed 5 major pieces but this requires more planning and more skill in the delivery.
- Don't dump your information on your audience and expect *them* to make sense of it. From our experience, they won't. They are busy with their own work and they have little incentive to do the thinking that you were apparently too lazy to do yourself.
- In preparing a logical case for consideration by your intended audience, you need to work backwards from the conclusion to what is ***necessary*** and ***sufficient*** to support it. This is called ***Reverse-Design***.
  - What is the context and importance?
  - What is your principal conclusion or recommendation?
    - What is the essence of your message in one sentence (or approximately 12 seconds)?
    - This gives a unifying theme to your message.
    - This will influence your choice of title and introduction.
  - What are the reasons and supporting evidence for this conclusion?
    - If you had another 3 – 5 sentences (or approximately 60 seconds), then what would you say? These would be your main supporting points.
  - How do these reasons + evidence logically lead to the conclusion?
    - Make the connections, transitions or changes in direction easy to follow.

Representing Knowledge By Concept Mapping

As we have seen in earlier chapters, concept mapping can be a useful first step in designing your argument when there is a network of interrelated ideas which must be understood as a whole pattern.

As an example from one of Ted's workshops, an engineering PhD student began explaining his research project in mobile telephones to PhD students from other departments. He dove into what he was *doing* and started explaining the optimisation technique he was using. Unsurprisingly, the other students were immediately confused and asked "Why?". The diagram which follows traces the sequence of their questions and the answers that he provided at each stage.

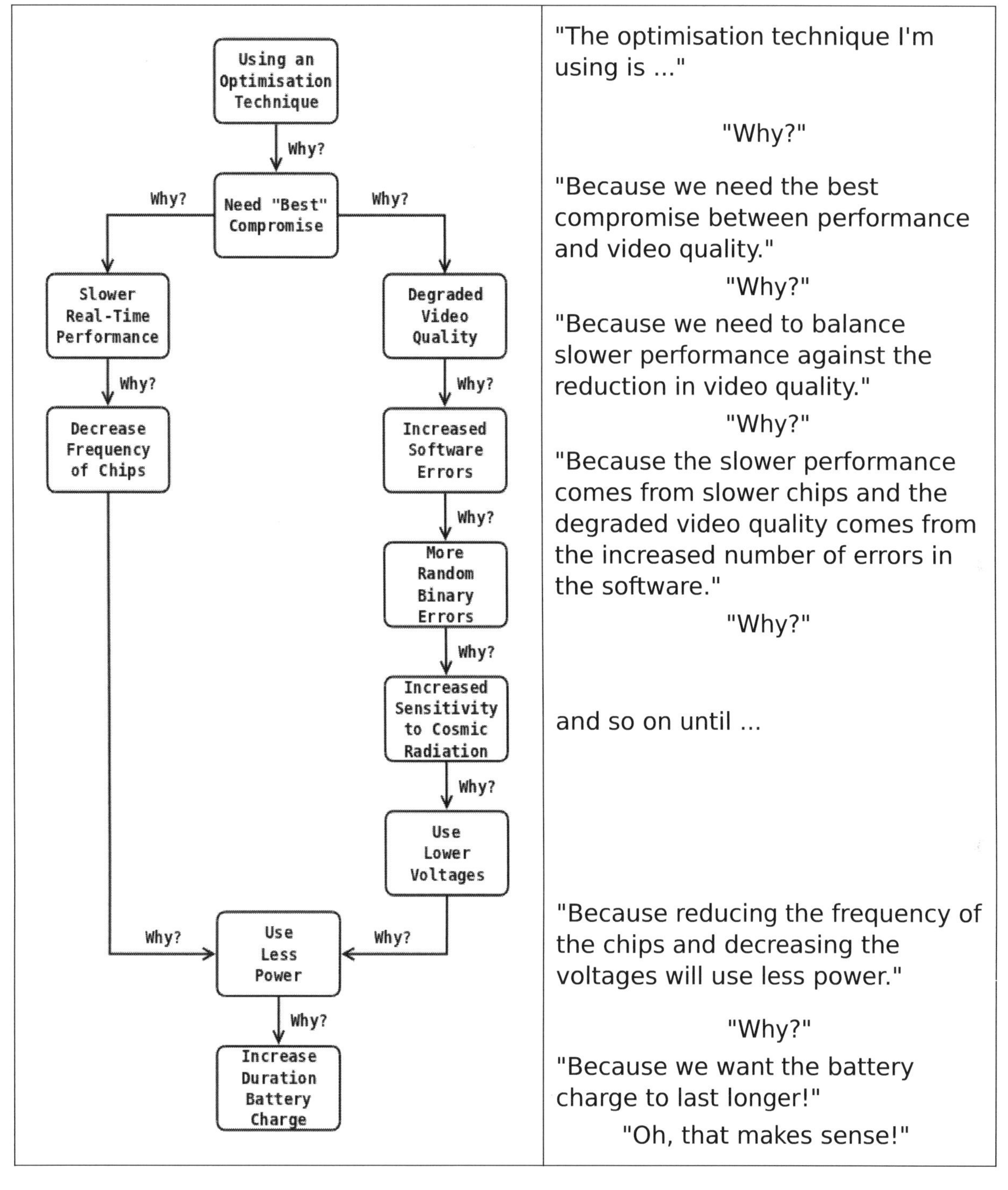

Notice how the series of *whys* worked backwards (or *upstream*) from what he was *doing* (the optimisation technique) to the reasons and circumstances that initiated the work. Once the group of students had done the exercise and produced this diagram, the logic for the research project was obvious, even to the students from other research fields!

This diagram was then redrawn and while redrawing it, the students realised that an alternative to reducing power usage would be to improve the battery itself, so that it held a larger charge in the first place. However developing a better battery involved another field of research and was outside the scope of the engineering student's PhD. The redrawn diagram looked like the following:

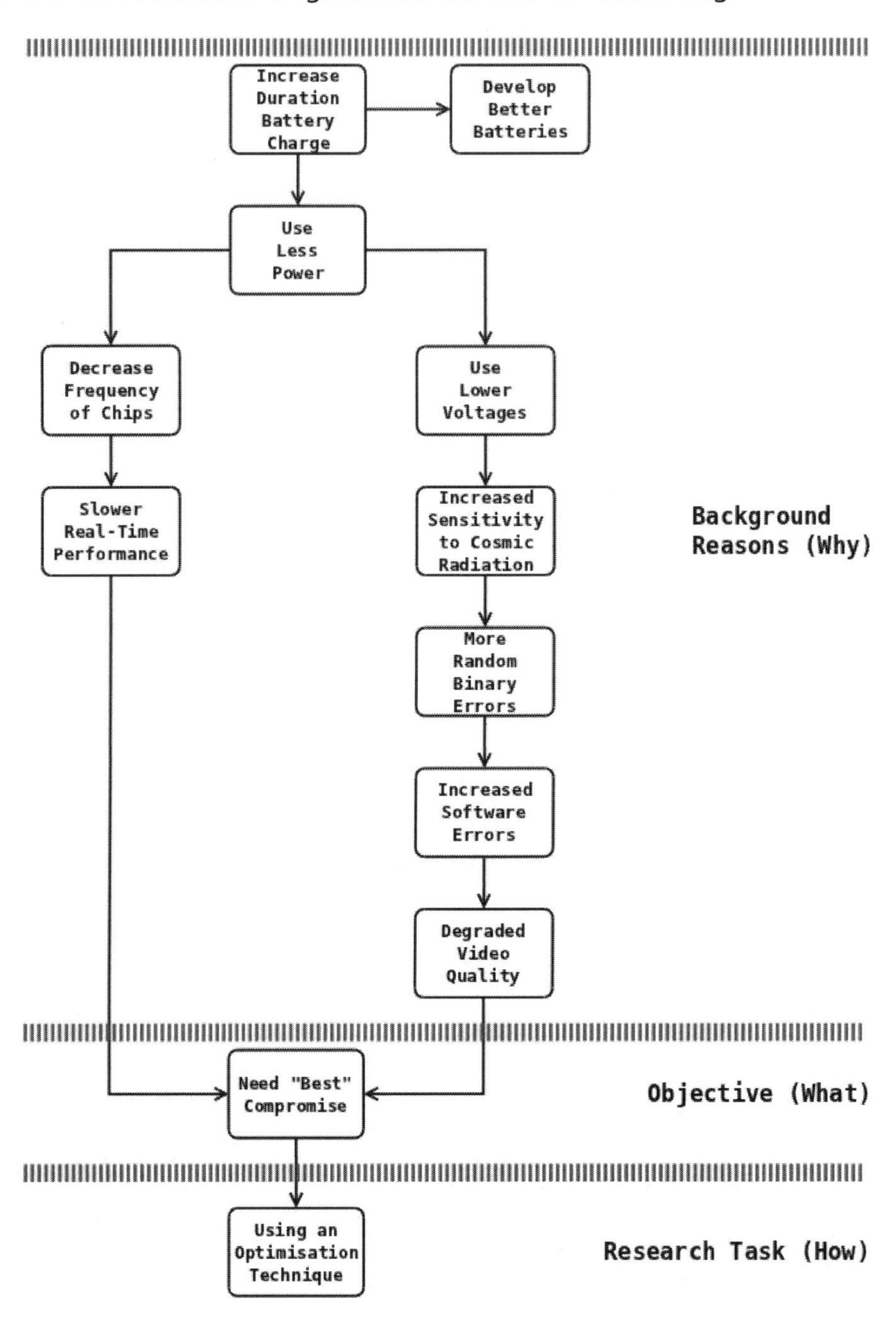

There are several points to notice about this diagram:

- It is now obviously divided into sections indicating the *background issues*, the *objective of the research* and *how this objective will be approached*.
- Notice how the background context or back-story was necessary to explain:
    - what he was doing;
    - why this approach was reasonable; and
    - why it was necessary/important.

- The desire for longer battery life in mobile telephones is an obvious place to begin and it is understandable to anyone. Aside from improving the battery, the other option is to reduce the power consumption, which can be achieved in two ways, each with consequences:
  - Decrease the frequency of the chips which will lead to slower performance;
  - Decrease the voltage which will make the telephone more susceptible to errors and consequently degraded video quality.
- This logical flow of ideas would make an excellent introduction to the engineering student's PhD thesis, since it defines the context and importance of the work. It then gives the logic for the approach that was chosen.

The classical definition of an *Introduction* is a logically argued case that:

- a piece of research was worth doing; and
- the approach chosen was appropriate/suitable to address it.

An introduction is not the same thing as a literature review of everything that has been done in the past twenty years.

Flow = Directed Sequence + Obvious Links

- **Where do you start from?** Points that have only leaving arrows typically make good places to start.
- **Where do you finish?** Points where arrows terminate (entering arrows only) make logical places to finish. Hopefully, this is the same point as your conclusion/recommendation. If it isn't, then you will need to go back and do some more thinking!
- **What is the sequence of ideas?**
  - What steps are required to connect the starting point to the finishing point?
  - How large or small do the steps in logic need to be for this particular audience?
  - Are there any decision points where the reasoning could take more than one direction? If you chose one direction over another, can you explain why?
  - How does one idea lead to the next? What is the logical connection or transition? Explaining the relationships will improve comprehension by your audience. It can help to:
    - *review* where you have been; and
    - *preview* where you are going next and how this follows from what has come before.

Aim for a connected sequence of ideas with manageable steps. Smaller steps are more digestible.

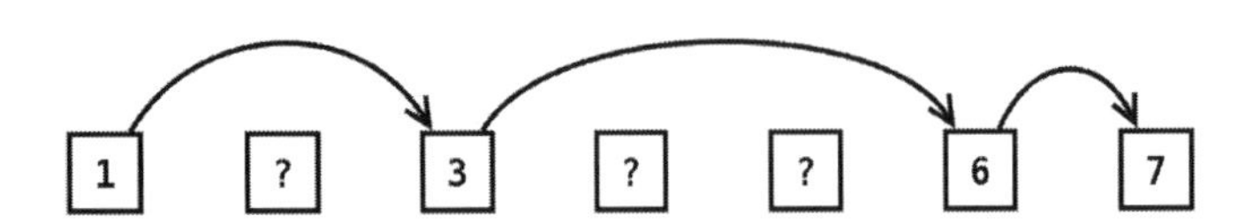

This sequence jumps over some steps in the argument. The missing steps will make it harder to follow and comprehend. Eventually the audience will give up because sleeping is an easier alternative!

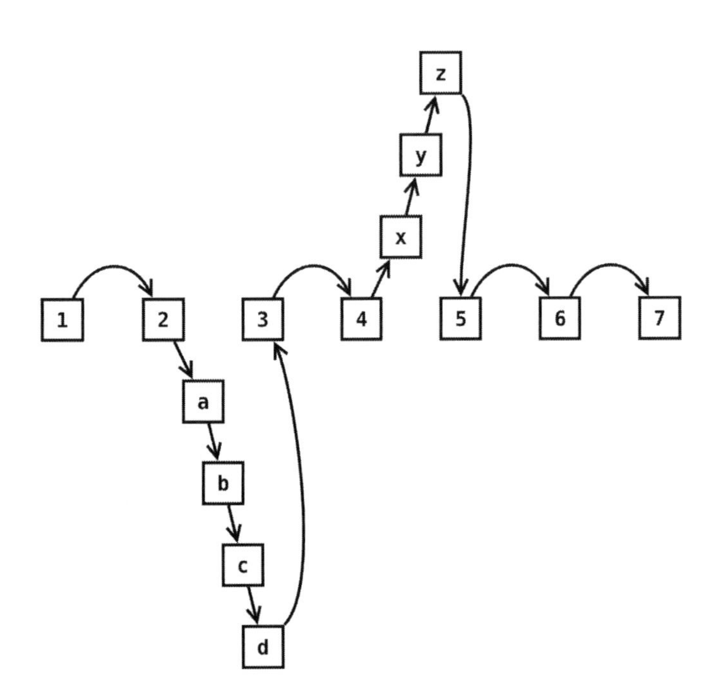

Avoid *digressing* from the sequence of the argument. The audience will become distracted or confused when you wander off onto side-topics.

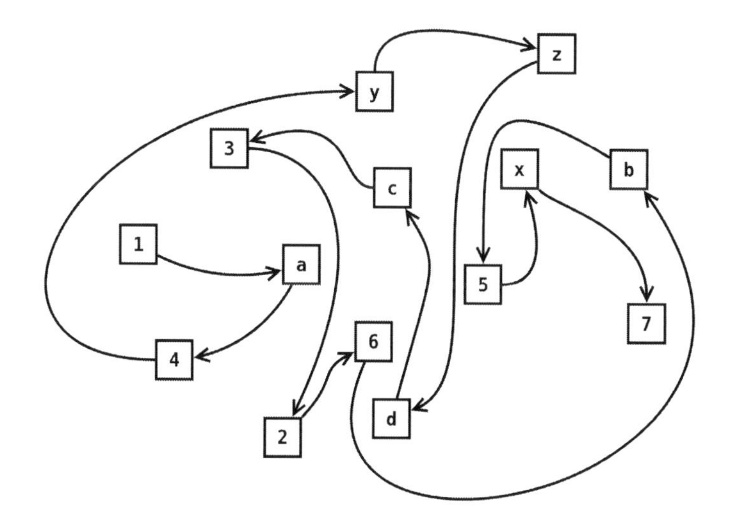

Avoid a random sequence of ideas. The audience will become confused and lost, possibly even annoyed!

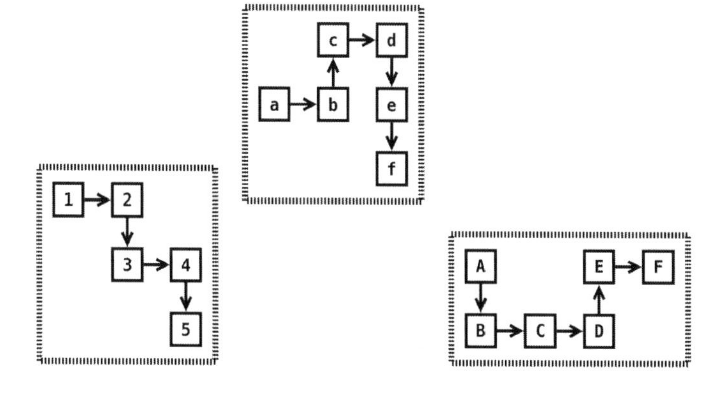

Avoid disjointed sets of subject areas. The audience will become confused and lost when they can't see how the different sets are connected.

Most presenters/writers presume that their audience is as expert in their subject as they are! Thus the presenter/writer omits important ideas and explanations, such as the background story that explain why the work was undertaken.

How Much Information And Detail?

More is not better! Your audience needs a manageable message, so ask yourself:

- "What background story is necessary and sufficient to place my research in context and define its importance?"
- "What is the *essential* information necessary and relevant to defending my conclusion/recommendation?"
- "What is novel or important about this material?"

Unnecessary or irrelevant information makes it more confusing and therefore unconvincing. Too much information makes your reasoning mentally indigestible.

Special Considerations When Planning a Presentation:

- **Your audience has no control over your presentation and only one chance to get your message.** They can't pause your presentation to think about something or go check a reference. They can't rewind to hear something again.
- **Their pace of reception will be slower than your pace of transmission!** They will need extra time to see, hear, possibly translate into their native tongue, make sense of it and then do the mental filing in preparation for the next piece. This means that you won't be able to pack your presentation full of data because they won't be able to handle the pace.
- Because of the above points, the total amount of material that they can handle is limited, especially in comparison to a paper or report. Remember how many times you have felt overwhelmed with information during a presentation. It's not enjoyable.
    - Aim to fill only 75% of the time allotted with talking. This means:
        - You won't need to rush in order to squeeze all the information in.
        - The ***slack*** will give you a safety margin to cope with the unexpected.
- Explain the meaning and importance of your research to the audience rather than telling them a seemingly endless list of facts.
- The audience has a limited ***capacity*** in terms of attention and memory.
    - Their attention is highest at the beginning when they are fresh and at the end when escape seems imminent. Use these times to state your core message and summarise the important steps in your argument/reasoning.
    - Research has shown that the attention span for oral communication is about 18 minutes! Longer than that and their attention declines.
    - They will miss things. They may be tired, hungry, distracted, ...
    - One week after the presentation, they will remember 1 or possibly 2 ideas. There is no point cramming your presentation full of facts that no one will remember.
    - Only include details that are essential to the explanation of your case. If they want to know more details, they can and will ask.

Scripting shorter talks is a useful exercise to learn the relationship between time and amount of material that can be covered. A guideline of 100 words-per-minute is a reasonable conversational pace to assume when writing your script. If you have slides, then these will slow you down even further because it will take additional time for changing slides and pointing at things. **If you can't fit your message into a script of the correct length, then you have too much information.** Focus on the essential and cut excess material until you can say what must be said within the word limit.

Remember this is an exercise during your preparation, so ***do not***:

- Memorise and recite your script to your audience;
- Put your script on your slides as bullet points.

Either of the above would be incredibly boring!

Avoid personalising negative events (disease, death, financial problems, attacks by criminals, ...) and/or projecting them onto your audience. Your audience will psychologically resist or reject your message if you do.

I attended one talk by a cancer researcher who spent the whole talk saying things like:

- "When *you* are diagnosed with cancer ..."
- "... as the tumour is growing inside *your* body ..."
- "... the effects of chemotherapy on *your* body will be that *your* hair falls out, *you* feel nauseous all the time and ..."
- "The radiation may cause *you* to vomit ... "

No wonder people were feeling uncomfortable and walking out!

– 8 –
Presenting Clearly

Now that you have prepared the structure of your message, how should you deliver it so that the importance, reasoning and evidence come across clearly and correctly?

Because this is a research (professional) presentation, there is no need to be fancy, flashy or entertaining. Entertainment is not expected and is no substitute for a meaningful and important message that is clearly presented.

Which Slides Do You Really Need?

Typical Presentation Slides

Title Slide

- The title is the most important part of your poster/presentation, since it is the advertisement for your presentation.
- Is the title ***accurate and representative***?
  - Can the audience accurately predict what they will see and hear if they turn up?
    (Remember how annoyed you feel when the title leads you to think the presentation will be about one thing and it is about something completely unexpected!)
  - Ask yourself: What does my title *mean*? If your title is a collection of keywords that doesn't mean anything or if it doesn't contain a verb, then do it again!

Let's consider three ***completely fictitious*** titles below:

"*The Role of Hydroxy-methyl-cellulose Waste in the Epigenetic Expression of Multiple Cranial Phenotypes in Tepuihyla luteolabris*"
This is a vague and generic title (sometimes called a *descriptive* title) which linguistically means nothing because it's a sentence fragment. This collection of keywords tells us that if we show up the presenter will say: – something about a role; – something about hydroxy-methyl-cellulose waste; – something about epigenetic expression; – something about multiple cranial phenotypes; and – something about *Tepuihyla luteolabris* (whatever that is!). How these various topics are related is vague and ambiguous. To make sense of this title, we would need more specific information, such as what is the role?

"Hydroxy-methyl-cellulose Waste Is Correlated With Multiple Cranial Phenotypes in a Species of Amazonian Tree Frogs."
This title is more specific and *informative*. This title also has *meaning* because it is a complete sentence and the presenter is *claiming* that there is a correlation between the Hydroxy-methyl-cellulose waste and multi-headed frogs. If we were to attend this presentation, then we would rightly expect the presenter to explore/explain the relationship.

"Is Hydroxy-methyl-cellulose Pollution Responsible for the Increase in Two-Headed Amazonian Tree Frogs?"
This is an informative/specific title for less expert audiences.

(**Note:** No Amazonian Tree Frogs were harmed in the making of these titles.)

- What is the conclusion you are claiming is correct? Or what is the question your presentation will answer?
- Titles serve to pre-filter the audience. With a good title you are more likely to get people who will find your presentation relevant and interesting.
- Include your name and contact details (*e.g.* email). Your full postal address is not necessary, especially since sending letters is no longer common.

Overview/Outline Slide

- What will be the major steps in the logic of your argument? If you show these steps to the audience, it will give them a road-map of your presentation which will help to orient them as you progress.
- Alternatively, the sequence of questions you will address can serve as an effective road-map of your presentation logic.
- Slide titles such as *Introduction, Objectives, Methods, Results, Conclusions* are ***not*** steps in a logical argument! These slide titles are simply vague labels.

Slides Showing Your Evidence

- What diagrams, figures, images, graphs will illustrate/show the points you want to make? Review the structure of your message to find the ideas that can be illustrated by drawings, graphs, photographs, ...
- Individual slide titles:
  - Questions make excellent titles for each slide. The title question creates a desire to know the answer. The content of the slide should then answer the question!
  - Alternatively, the conclusion, meaning or point of each slide makes a strong title.

Summary Slide

- This is essentially a repetition of the *Overview* slide, reminding them of the steps in your reasoning leading to your conclusion.

Conclusion Slide

- This is where you state your single main conclusion. Don't state several minor or possible conclusions, because the audience won't remember them all. The audience will also wonder if you actually know for certain.

Acknowledgement Slide

- This is where you thank anyone who helped but isn't responsible for the work and its conclusions.
- Thank people or organisations for any significant and substantial assistance you received.
  - Financial support (*e.g.* funding councils)
  - Samples or materials
  - Loan or use of equipment
  - Help with the analysis (*e.g.* statistics)
  - Useful discussions

References Slide (optional)

- This is where you list the important references you mentioned in your presentation.
- If you must put references, then they must be:
  - sufficiently complete,
  - large enough to read; and
  - left on the screen long enough for people in the audience to write them down.
- Alternatively, offer either to provide a handout of references or to email the references to anyone who wishes.

Title Slide

- This is a repetition of your first slide, which marks the official end of your presentation. This reminds them of your title and makes your contact details available in case they didn't get them at the beginning.
- It can be left on the screen while you answer questions.
  Alternatively, some people blank the screen during the question-period.

Supplemental Slides

- These can be prepared and placed after the ending title slide, for anticipated questions or points of discussion.
  - In some cases, you may require your employer's approval for all slides that you are considering to show in public, including supplemental slides.
  - In other cases, conference organisers insist on having copies of all slides that you intend to use.

Both of the above can place restrictions on the supplemental slides which you might wish to bring in case you get a certain question.

Slides are ***visual aids*** and *not your speaking notes!*

If you have too much to remember without notes, then you have too much! Reading your slides to the audience is mind-numbing and will not impress them. And very few of us have sufficiently wonderful backsides that the audience will happily watch our rear-ends while we face the screen for the entire presentation!

Plan for less than one slide per minute.

A reasonable estimate for the number of slides is to take the number of minutes and multiply by 60%. So for a 50 minute talk, you would have approximately 30 slides. (This number *includes* your title, overview, summary/conclusion and acknowledgement slides!)

Adhering to this self-discipline also prevents you from attempting to include too much information and it forces you to focus on what is important and essential! It also means that when you come to present, you won't have to rush through your slides.

Keep your slides simple, direct and meaningful.

- Find out what equipment the venue uses and then prepare accordingly. Prepare or at least check your presentation on whatever hardware the venue will use. Alternatively, bring your laptop.
- Beware of problems caused by hardware and software incompatibilities for both preparation and playback.
    - *Windows®* v Mac v Linux v BSD
    - different versions of *Windows®*
    - different versions of *PowerPoint®*
- Take copies of your presentation in multiple formats: USB memory stick, CD, email it to yourself, bring hardcopy, ...
- Some people use PDF files in presentation mode, since these display correctly under almost all conditions.

We can guarantee you that at some point in your career, there will be a catastrophic hardware and/or software failure and it may not even be your fault!

At this point you will have two options:

1) You can give up and go home; or
2) You can present your material without slides to the best of your ability. It may not be perfect, but it will get the job done.

Guess which option will do more for your reputation? So, the sooner you start practising without using slides, the easier it will be when it happens.

(We're not joking about this, we've seen it happen to others and it's happened to us!)

Prepare your talk as if you couldn't use any slides, for whatever reason.

→ You will concentrate on explaining the big story.
→ You will keep it simple and conversational.
→ You won't get lost in a sea of details.
→ This will prepare you in case disaster strikes!

Then, being optimistic and assuming that the hardware/software will work, add slides with the pictures/images that would be helpful to telling your story.

→ This will avoid slides filled with text and bullet-points which are rarely essential and never interesting.

How Do You Design Your Slides?

We have not included examples of good and bad slides. When you start attending seminars, talks and conferences, you will see enough examples of poorly designed (dreadful!) slides. Start paying attention to your reactions when someone puts up slides like the following:

- full paragraphs of text;
- full of bullet-points;
- has 4 or 5 small graphs, charts or diagrams crammed into one slide;
- has a graph with 8 or 9 lines on it;
- has a dreadful colour scheme;
- everything is too small to see.

If a slide annoys, bores or confuses you when you are in the audience, then it will have the same effect if you try to use something similar when you are presenting!

To design slides that will be helpful rather than annoying, boring and confusing, you need to be aware of two truths plus some other considerations.

The First Truth: Projection

What you see on your computer screen is *not* what the audience will see projected on the screen! The reason is ...

	PC/Laptop Screen	Projected Slide
Aspect Ratio	Typically widescreen 16:10	Sometimes widescreen, sometimes older 4:3
Resolution	1680x1050 1920x1080 3840x2160 Historically, PC/laptop resolutions have been consistently 40 – 60% higher than projectors.	800x600 (SVGA) 1280x720 (720p) 1920x1080 (1080p) *Note:* Projector resolutions higher than these are less common at the time of the 2nd printing.
Contrast Ratio	1000:1 to 3000:1	≈ 600:1 (projector output) 250:1 (on-screen)
Illumination	Direct	Indirect / Reflected
Apparent Screen Size Expressed As A Viewing Angle	≈60°	≈30°

- Many projectors have improperly adjusted brightness and contrast levels.
- Larger projection screens will have even lower brightness and contrast levels because the projector's beam will be spread over a larger surface area.

Because of the above facts, your projected slides *WILL* appear:

- *smaller* than on your PC screen;
- *less defined/sharp* than on the PC screen;
- *faded* (lower contrast) compared to your PC screen.

There is no useful reason to have high resolution images in a presentation slide when the projector has a lower resolution than your PC/laptop. The audience will see the images at the resolution of the projector. So, resize any images you will use in a presentation so that they are comparable to the resolution of the projector. This will also reduce the file size of your presentation without affecting the visibility of any details.

- Project your slides and check their visibility from the back of an auditorium. **You cannot trust what you see on your PC screen. You must project them to check!** Book a large seminar room in your institution for an hour if necessary.
- Up to 25% of your audience can have some degree of vision-impairment, such as colour-blindness, astigmatism, *etc.* Ask yourself – how would this look to someone with poor eyesight sitting at the back of a 300 seat auditorium?

The Second Truth: Slide Backgrounds And Foregrounds

A projected slide does not perform under the same conditions as a piece of paper!

	Printed page	**Projected slide**
Angle of Viewing	↑ Directly in front	↗↑↖ From sides as well
Distance	Approximately 35 cm	Variable distances up to 10 metres or more depending on the size of the room!
Lighting conditions	Daylight	Daylight, Dimmed or Dark

Because projected slides must be legible under different conditions than a piece of paper, the effects of slide background, foreground images and room lighting upon the audience's eyes must be considered carefully and rationally.

If the ...	Then the pupils of the audience's eyes will ...
Image is dark.	need to ***Dilate*** (↑) in order to see the details.
Slide background is dark.	***Dilate*** (↑)
Slide background is white.	***Contract*** (↓) because of the bright light from the white screen. With white backgrounds, all images and text are essentially backlit, which reduces visibility.
Room is dark.	***Dilate*** (↑)
Room is well-lit.	***Contract*** (↓)

- **Why would you design your slides so that your audience's eyes must perform contradictory actions?**
  - white backgrounds (pupils ↓) in a darkened room (pupils ↑); or
  - white backgrounds (pupils ↓) with dark images (pupils need to ↑); or even worse
  - dark images (pupils need to ↑) on white backgrounds (pupils ↓) and darkened room (pupils ↑)!

If you want maximum visibility of the content of your slides, then your images, slide background and room lighting must be mutually consistent in terms of what is required from the eyes of the audience.

- If you have ***dark images*** (*e.g.* X-rays, MRI scans, fluorescence photos, *etc.*), then you will need a ***dark background*** for your slides and preferably a ***dim or darkened room***.
- If you have *only* ***light images***, then you can use a ***light background*** for your slides in a room with the ***lights turned on***. Do not use light backgrounds in darkened rooms; it's illogical and will tire their eyes!
- If you have ***dark images***, and you use a ***white or light-coloured background***, then your images won't be easily visible.
  Remember the last time it was a bright sunny day and you were inside your home. If someone was standing in the doorway, you could see their silhouette but you couldn't see the details of their face. It's the same principle: it is difficult to see details in dark areas against a bright background.
- Remember, how it looks on your computer screen in normal room illumination is not how it will look to your audience when projected as a slide.

The images you have will determine the slide background that you must use for maximum visibility. The slide background forms the largest area on the slide and this is why the choice of background is so important. A poorly chosen background can render your slides difficult if not impossible to see.

Once you have chosen the background, then any text you use must be **BIG!** with strong **CONTRAST** against the background.

- Remember, a lot of people like to sit at the back of the auditorium (so they can make a quick getaway if you turn out to be boring!).

Black Foreground **80% Grey Foreground** **60% Grey Foreground** **40% Foreground** **20% Foreground**	**White Background** You need maximum contrast for visibility. This will be legible but tiring for the eyes in darkened rooms.

Black Foreground **80% Grey Foreground** **60% Grey Foreground** **40% Grey Foreground** **20% Grey Foreground** **White Foreground**	**Black Background** You need maximum contrast for visibility. Dark backgrounds are less tiring for the eyes.

- **Avoid using:**
  - backgrounds that are middle grey in terms of saturation. Everything on the slide will appear dull and faded because of the reduced contrast.

Black Foreground **80% Grey Foreground** **60% Grey Foreground** **40% Grey Foreground** **20% Grey Foreground** **White Foreground**	**Middle-Grey Background** This gives limited contrast to black and white. Everything looks dull and faded when projected.

  - gradient backgrounds, since text can disappear in certain regions of the slide.

Black Foreground	**Gradient Background**
80% Grey Foreground	**Gradient Background**
60% Grey Foreground	**Gradient Background**
40% Grey Foreground	**Gradient Background**
20% Grey Foreground	**Gradient Background**
White Foreground	**Gradient Background**

  - patterned or textured backgrounds! These interfere with visual recognition of letters.

It takes 1 – 3 minutes for people's eyes to adapt to darkness.

Do not alternate slides with light- and dark-coloured backgrounds because:

- The audience will have difficulty seeing any dark slides that follow a light-coloured slide; and
- Alternating light- and dark-coloured slides will tire the audience's eyes even quicker than a continuous light-coloured background.

Once you have designed and prepared your slides, when you come to deliver your presentation, check if it is possible to control the lighting level (dimmed rather than on/off).

If you *can* control the lighting level then balance the light level for the room with the brightness of your projected slides on the screen.
Neither should appear to be brighter than the other. This minimises eye-strain while retaining maximum visibility of the slides.

Colour Schemes

- Approximately 10% of men are Red-Green colour-blind and they have difficulty distinguishing these colours. (Women are genetically less prone to colour-blindness.)
- Approximately 1% of the population is Blue-Yellow colour-blind, which means they can't distinguish blue and green.
- Everyone has trouble distinguishing foreground/background combinations of Red + Black.
- Different colours are brought into focus at slightly differing distances in front of and behind the retina. Red (long wavelength) and blue (short wavelength) is one of the worst combinations for this!
- Certain combinations of colours cause after-images which can linger for several seconds. This leads to what is perceived as visual vibration or movement.
  Do not use the following combinations:
  - Red-Green
  - Blue-Orange
  - Green-Magenta (Purple)
  - Yellow-Cyan (sky blue)
  - Blue-Magenta
  - Orange-Yellow
  - Blue-Green

Your department or institution may have an official presentation template that you are expected to use for all your presentations. We have seen some good ones, some terrible ones and many in-between. Just because it's the official template, doesn't mean it's a well-designed template! We recommend that you use your own judgement and modify the template if necessary. It would also be useful to send your comments/changes to the people who prepared it.

Diagrams And Figures

You are there to provide the words. The slides are there to provide the images.

Research has shown that speaking to people while they are trying to read is the worst combination for comprehension and retention.

- **Pictures are remembered, text isn't!**
  - The next time you attend a presentation, when it has finished, close your eyes and see which slides you can remember. Most people remember the pictures and can't remember any of the text.
  - Pictures also don't require the presenter to keep looking at the screen to read the next thing to say!
- For many people in the audience English will be a second or third language. Pictures are more universally and more easily understood.
- Each diagram or figure should make a single point.
  - Diagrams and figures with too many items or curves can be too complicated to understand.
  - Avoid linking the data points with a line or curve unless you have established that there is a mathematical or functional relationship which exists between the points.
- Use major grid lines to help the audience to see the relative position of things. Minor grid lines are not usually necessary and only clutter the diagram.
- File Formats for images:
  - Graphs, bar charts, pie charts, drawings and diagrams (any figure which has areas of the same colour) are most efficiently saved as *.gif, *.png or *.svg files. This is because the algorithms for these formats presume that there will be areas of uniform colour.
  - Photographs or diagrams which have variations in colour, pattern or shading are most efficiently saved as *.jpg files.
  - Avoid *.bmp and *.tif file-formats which are inefficient and result in larger files than the other formats.
- If copying and pasting from a PDF, enlarge/zoom in before screen capture. That way you capture the image at the maximum resolution of the PDF. Depending upon how you plan to use the screen captured image, you may also need to check if there are any issues with regard to copyright or plagiarism.
- If you need to indicate something on an image or photograph, then we recommend using ***block arrows*** (in *PowerPoint®* look for *Autoshape > Block Arrows*) with opposite fill and line colours. When your arrow crosses the border between light and dark regions it remains visible.

Notice how the block arrows below have opposite colours (black and white) for the outline and the fill so they are visible on both light and dark backgrounds.

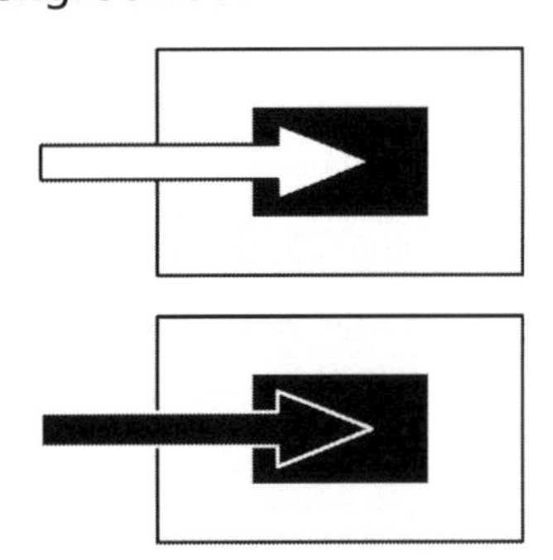

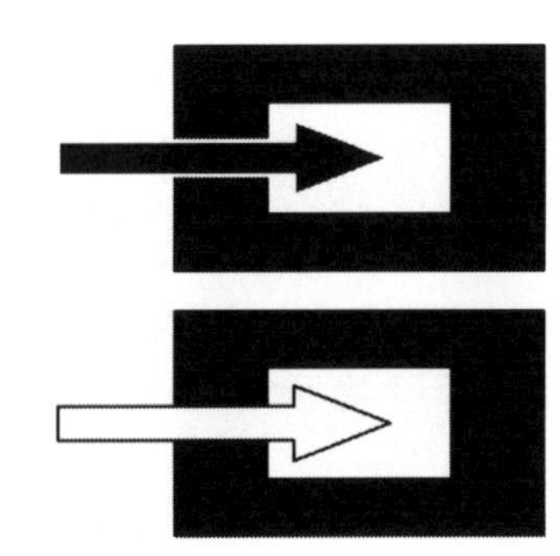

Figures for print are unsuitable for use in projected slides unless they have been modified. In particular, font sizes, arrow-lines and arrow-heads will need to be increased in size.

The default settings for graphics and plotting software are for print (paper) and these default settings will produce fonts, lines, markers that are too small (or thin) for practical use in projected slides.

Create a separate *Presentation Template* for any software which you use to prepare diagrams or graphs. This template will contain default settings (font size, line thickness, arrowhead size, *etc.*) that are suitable for use in projected slides.

Start keeping a separate collection of drawings, graphs, photographs that you have prepared for use in presentation slides.

Data Markers, Lines And Arrows In Charts, Graphs And Diagrams

- Data markers should be large enough and any lines thick enough to see easily in the final figure, even from the back of a large auditorium.
- **3 point is the *minimum* line thickness you should use in preparing any figure or diagram.** 5 point is better. Thin lines won't be visible to those sitting at the back of the room.
- Arrow-heads should also be larger than you think. Arrow-heads that are acceptably visible on your computer screen, will be too small when projected.

Font Styling (When You Must Have Words)

Size

- 40+ point for titles;
- 30+ point for text.
- ***Never use anything smaller than 24 point!***

- Turn off *shadowing* and *underlining* both of which make it more difficult to read in the projected slide. And if you have a dark-coloured background, then shadowing on your text doesn't make a lot of sense since no one will see a dark shadow on the dark background!
- Avoid excessive variations in font sizes and font styles (bold, italics, upper case). In particular, *PowerPoint®* has the unfortunate habit of resizing your fonts so that regardless of how much you type, it *all* fits in the one slide. Not only does this encourage people to put more on a slide than they should, but different slides will have varying font sizes!
- NEVER USE ALL CAPITALS. IT MAKES IT HARDER TO READ AND IT CAN COME ACROSS AS THE VISUAL EQUIVALENT OF SHOUTING.

Font Face

- ***Serif*** fonts, which have the little *serifs* at the ends, are considered formal. The variable thickness of the strokes can make them more difficult to read when projected. Making serif fonts **bold** will help. This bullet-point is in a serif font.
- ***Sans-serif*** fonts are semi-formal. These fonts have a consistent stroke thickness which makes them easier to read when projected. Sans-serif fonts which have a thin stroke (such as *Arial*), are poorly suited for projection. Prefer sans-serif fonts with a thicker stroke (such as *Verdana).* This bullet-point is in a sans-serif font.
- ***Artistic fonts*** are informal. Some people have strong reactions to non-traditional fonts: "It's childish!", "It's unprofessional!", "I hate it!"
  Use these only if you have a valid reason – for example if you are speaking to schoolchildren or you want to emphasise the informal nature of your presentation. This bullet-point is in an artistic font (ITC Kristen).
- Avoid using more than two different fonts in one presentation. One font for titles and another one for text is common.

Justification

- Left justified text is easiest to read because the spacing between each word is constant.
- Fully-justified text has even margin lines at the expense of creating uneven spacing between words which makes it harder to read. Sometimes, the uneven spacing can look quite absurd.
- A slide full of centred text is also more difficult to read than left justified text.

Animation Effects:

- Use animation only when you have a relevant and useful reason!
  Animation is not a cure for boring text slides. Making the text move, doesn't make it more interesting, just harder to read. And if you ever see a presentation where the bullet-points are animated *and* have sound-effects, then please walk out before you are driven insane!

Print your slides – ***two per page*** – on A4 paper (or comparable size 8½ inches x 11 inches in North America) and then look at them from arm's length. This approximates the size and viewing angle of the slide that many of the audience will see. If you can't see everything on your slides, then it's too small!

If you can afford the cost of printing them in colour, then printing them on A4 sheets (or comparable size in North America) will give you an accurate idea of how the colour scheme will work when projected. The contrast ratios of a printed page and a projected slide are similar, and both are substantially lower than the contrast ratio of a PC/laptop screen.

Never use the timer function to advance the slides, even during rehearsal. The funniest talk Ted ever attended was when the presenter was trying to catch up with his slides, which were happily advancing without him!

And if you are giving an interactive or open-forum style of presentation, then you definitely won't want to use the timer function.

***If* you use *PowerPoint®*, then save your presentation as a *PowerPoint* Show (*.pps or *.ppsx).**

- It opens in slideshow mode when you click on the file icon.
- To edit slides, start *PowerPoint®* first and use *PowerPoint®* to open and edit your *.pps as normally.

***PowerPoint®* keyboard shortcuts:**

A or = keys hide the mouse cursor.

Ctrl+H to *permanently* hide the mouse cursor.

B or **.** key will toggle between the slide and a black screen.

W or **,** key will toggle between the slide and a white screen.

Typing a **number** and pressing **Enter** will jump to that slide.

Home jumps to the *first* slide.

End jumps to the *last* slide.

Ctrl+P to annotate displayed slide with an on-screen pen. A right-click will let you change options for the pen.

E to erase the annotations.

Delivering The Poster/Presentation

This is your audience's first and only chance to understand your message. They cannot control the pace of your presentation. They cannot pause or rewind. They have to keep going at the pace you set. Or they can fall asleep.

Common presentation faults include:

- too much information;
- too detailed;
- too many parts or sections;
- too complicated;
- too fast;
- too vague/generic;
- too much jargon.

You can deliver the information faster than they can absorb it. And continuous fast-talking is a technique that professional hypnotists use to put people asleep.

- If the audience doesn't know you then they will unconsciously use the following weightings when assessing your credibility:
  - 60% Body Language
  - 30% Voice
  - 10% Words
- If the audience does know you and thinks you are credible then their unconscious weightings will be more like:
  - 30% Body Language
  - 20% Voice
  - 50% Words

Body Language (Visual)

Dress And Appearance

- Dress better than your audience, but not too much better. This is a sign of respect and demonstrates that you take this presentation seriously.
- Make sure your clothing fits and is comfortable. You don't want to be adjusting your clothing while you are presenting because initially it will distract them and if it continues it will become annoying.
- Check all zippers, buttons, snaps, clasps, *etc.* before you walk up to the front. You don't want to hear later that they liked the Mickey Mouse pattern on your undies!
- Make sure your hair is also under control. When presenters are always fidgeting with their hair, this can become annoying for the audience. We can think of more than one presentation where we've had a nearly irresistible

urge to shout "Get a haircut!" when someone has been fussing with their hair endlessly during the presentation.

Eye Contact

- Look at people's eyes but don't shift your gaze back and forth from one eye to the other because you'll look shifty. If you look at the bridge of their nose, then this gives you a steady gaze.
- Unless you are directly addressing someone (listening or speaking to them) don't look at someone longer than approximately a second or they can find it very unsettling/disturbing. This especially applies to anyone who is smiling, don't look at them too much or they will become uncomfortable and stop smiling!

Facial Expression

- People pay attention to the *facial triangle* which covers the central part of the face from the eyebrows to the chin.
- ***Smile!*** It's more attractive for the audience and it helps calm you down, since it's neurologically more difficult to be nervous and smile at the same time.
  Use discretion and good judgement though – if you are talking about death or suffering, then don't smile because it is inappropriate for the serious nature of the material.
- **Lip Reading:** *Everyone* lip-reads when listening – even people with perfect hearing! This is why it is important to face the audience as much as possible. People unconsciously compare the shape the mouth is making with the word they are hearing as a way to check that they are hearing correctly. This is why badly dubbed foreign films are funny, because the movements of the actors' mouths don't match the words.

Gestures

- Need to be larger and slower than you would usually make them, so that they appear normal to the audience sitting some distance away. Otherwise you will come across as hyperactive.
- Meaningfully act out what you are talking about. Use your gestures to reinforce what you are saying. It helps get your message across and gives you something more useful to do with your hands than fidget with the pointer.
- If you designate/indicate someone in the audience, use a full hand (fingers together) held on-edge or with the palm up. A full hand is easier to see and avoids pointing which is rude in some cultures.
- Elicit questions from the audience by raising your hand.

Stance And Movement

- Face the audience with your whole body – hips and shoulders. Avoid twisting your body.

- If something is on the other side of the screen, *you may cross to the other side and point to it from the nearer side.* Never stretch across the screen.

Pointers And Pointing

- **Most presenters point too much.** It may give them a feeling of doing something important, but it distracts the audience!
- If the slides are well-designed then there should be little or no need to point, since it will be obvious what you are referring to.
  - Excessive pointing is often a symptom of overcrowded slides.

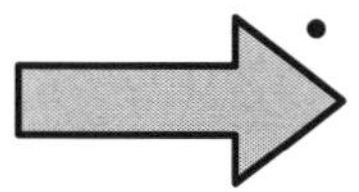

- **Use block arrows, ellipses and rectangles to indicate areas on the slide to notice.** These can be animated to appear when you click.
  - This is the best option in our opinion. The audience will see what you are referring to, even if you don't point at it.
  - The disadvantage is that it will require a 'mouse click' for each animation and this may tie you to the computer, unless you have a remote control.
- **Pointers and Sticks**
  - The tip can be touched against the screen allowing the presenter to turn back and face the audience without losing their place.
  - Risk of hitting the screen or fidgeting with the pointer.
- **Laser Pointers**
  - **These are potentially dangerous toys.** Depending upon the power levels, **they can cause *permanent* eye damage, for which you will be legally responsible.**
  - The small red or green dot which is moving will be difficult to see at the back of an auditorium.
  - When pointing, use the laser dot to SLOWLY underline or circle the item.
  - When not pointing, hold the laser behind your back or point it at the floor beside you.
  - **Never aim the laser pointer towards the audience.** It is rude and makes them nervous. If you fidget with your hands and/or have poor awareness of what you are doing with your hands, then it might be safer to avoid using laser pointers altogether.
  - The sale and use of laser pointers are legally controlled in various countries. For example, at the time of writing, in the UK, only Class 2 (< 1mW) laser devices of any kind are legally permitted for use in public areas.

Before you begin your presentation, decide on which side of the screen you will be standing.

- Point with the hand that is closer to the screen. This way you keep your body angled towards the audience, rather than turning your back to them.
- If you are using a microphone attached to your shirt collar or jacket lapel, then clip it on the collar or lapel that is closer to the screen. That way, when you turn towards the screen you will still be speaking into the microphone. If you clip the microphone on the collar or lapel that is further from the screen, then when you turn your head towards the screen, you will be turning your head away from the microphone and your voice will fade.

Vocal Characteristics (Auditory)

- It can take an audience 2 – 3 minutes to 'tune in' to the sound of your voice.
- Vocal characteristics to pay attention to:
  - volume
  - pace
  - pronunciation + juncture
  - pauses
  - pitch
- In general people find accents interesting. However if your accent is interfering with getting your message across, then you might need to get some help with pronunciation.

1) People in your audience can be hearing impaired.
2) English is becoming the international language of research, so English can be a foreign language for either you as the presenter and/or many in your audience.

Therefore, when you are presenting:

⇒ Speak louder and more slowly than normal. (How loudly you speak will depend upon the size of the room.)

⇒ Pronounce your words more carefully.

⇒ Separate words and sentences clearly rather than running them altogether.

⇒ Pause more often and speak in shorter phrases.

⇒ Use pictures as much as possible. Avoid using text unless it is an important keyword.

English is less musical than many other languages and is in some sense more like percussion because it relies more on consonants, rhythm and pauses.

Words (Verbal)

- Make it easy for them to mentally process your message.
- Express one idea at a time and pause frequently. Remember the audience needs to:
    - watch you;
    - watch the screen;
    - listen to what you are saying;
    - make sense of it;
    - do the mental filing (this is where your conclusion and structure help them) and/or make any notes on paper; and
    - get ready for the next part.

  The last three items are done during the pauses when you aren't speaking.
- Natural variety in sentence length helps to maintain attention and interest.
- Verbs (actions) are more interesting than nouns (things). Don't suffocate your sentences with nouns.
- Descriptive and sensory-rich words are more interesting and vivid than abstract or conceptual words.

- Use simple words – they are easier to pronounce and easier to hear.
- Minimise the use of technical terms and acronyms which can be different in other languages or other subjects.
  In English it is *DNA* and in French it is *ADN.*
  In Chemistry and Physics, *ESR* stands for *Electron Spin Resonance* and in Medicine it stands for *Erythrocyte Sedimentation Rate*.
  When you use a technical term or acronym for the first time, make sure you define it for the audience.
- International audiences won't be familiar with many colloquial or idiomatic expressions which may be in common use where you live.

If 10% or less of your audience is bored, asleep, distracted or walking out then you are probably doing OK.

If 30% or more of your audience is bored, asleep, distracted or walking out then it is probably what you are doing.

By random chance, you will occasionally have a difficult audience. It's just bad luck. Don't take it personally. But if your audiences *always* seem difficult then maybe it is something you are doing wrong!

Nerves → Confidence

- Everyone suffers from the fight/flight/freeze response to the stress of a presentation.
- In opinion polls, speaking-in-public is often the number one fear of people. Death is usually fourth or fifth on the list. Fortunately, presentations seldom prove fatal.
- Anxiety and nervousness usually result from:
  - self-criticism;
  - self-doubt;
  - unpredictability with the risk of embarrassment or failure;
  - imagination of all kinds of scary stuff.
- Additionally, Ted often hears presenters tell him that they are nervous because they are afraid their audience "might not remember it all".
  - If this is the case, then cut it down! If *you* have trouble remembering it all, then it's a sign that either you have too much detail and/or your storyline is weak.
  - The audience doesn't have a check-list of what you are planning to say and most times the audience doesn't notice that you forgot something.
  - And on the rare occasion when someone does notice, they will ask you a question. And you respond: "Good point! I didn't mention that in my presentation, but since you've brought it up ... " and then you tell them what you forgot to tell them before!

- Nervousness decreases with practice.
- You look better on the outside than you feel inside. In most cases, you look perfectly normal to the audience. So, your *internal* feelings are not a reliable guide to how you appear *externally* to the audience. When you present, stop being preoccupied with how you feel. Most people in the audience don't really care how *you* feel anyway plus most people won't notice any signs of your nervousness.
- It is tricky to eliminate an emotion you don't want. It is easier to increase another emotion instead. What can you do that will boost your confidence?
- Presenters can copy a trick used by competitive athletes. Before a competition, athletes will visualise and mentally rehearse **positive** actions and results. They imagine performing well and winning. **They never visualise performing badly and losing!**
- Your hobbies might be a source of useful skills or preparatory routines (rituals) that you can use before presenting. For example:
  - If your hobby requires you to perform in public (music, dance, theatre, comedy) then you may have a routine that you use

before you go on stage.
  - If your hobby involves competitive sports, then you might have a routine that you go through before you compete in public.

Ted was running one workshop and there was a young man who was very nervous when presenting – one of the rare cases where you could actually see his shaking from the audience!

At the lunch break Ted asked him what he did as a hobby and he answered that he was a member of the competitive amateur British Rifle Team. He was quite enthusiastic about travelling all over the world and competing against the best marksmen from other countries.

Needless to say Ted was surprised and asked him:

"When you're competing against the best marksmen from around the world, how do you manage to get a tiny bullet in the centre of a target that's several hundred metres away while you're shaking so much?"

He smiled at Ted like he was being a bit thick and answered that he didn't shake when shooting because he had a mental routine that he used to put himself into a "calm zone" for shooting. [Bingo!]

Ted then asked him if he ever thought of using that pre-shooting mental routine before presenting and he responded that he didn't know you could do that!

Just before his next presentation, the postgraduate went through his pre-shooting mental routine and the effect was spectacular! The audience could see the nervousness draining from his body while they watched. And the presentation itself was steady and on-target.

How Do You Handle Questions?

- One common reason people fear the question period is that questions in research can be critical and the questioners can also be confrontational or rude!
- There are cultural differences and issues in styles of listening, discussing and questioning. For example, universities in the former Soviet Republic have what we in the UK would consider a confrontational style of discussion. To them, it's not personal, it's just their habit to have a good rousing discussion before they make up their minds.
- Another reason people fear the question period is that they feel exposed at the front.

Preparing a *defensive* presentation based upon fear and imagined worst-case scenarios doesn't work. There is no way to prepare a presentation that will protect you from every possible question from every possible person in the audience.

Don't set yourself impossible standards by expecting to be able to answer every question perfectly.

Focus on delivering a strong case and then deal with the questions to the best of your ability.

Psychological research indicates that one way people can be classified is according to their receptivity to new ideas or new products/services. The numbers below aren't exact but they are accurate enough for our purposes.

- **20% of people are positive and receptive.** They will:
  - be curious;
  - offer or request advice/help/suggestions.
- **60% are neutral** and they will wait to see what happens. They will:
  - check facts, interpretations, reasoning, ...;
  - assess your knowledge or skill;
  - discuss the matter to achieve a more thorough understanding.
- **20% are critical and/or resistant.** They will:
  - be prejudiced or biased;
  - disagree with your findings for some reason;
  - prefer some other model or interpretation;
  - possibly be bad-tempered, impolite, sarcastic or even rude!

This means that you have a reasonable chance of persuading approximately 80% of your audience. Don't waste your time worrying about trying to achieve 100%, it rarely happens.

The remaining 20% of your audience are unlikely to be persuaded by a single presentation and question-period. If these people are difficult then realise that it's not your fault, it's simply the way they are.

Receiving Questions

- **Ask** if there are any questions and raise your hand to demonstrate what you expect.
- **Select** someone in the audience using your open hand.
- **Listen** to the whole question.
- **Repeat** their question, echoing key words or phrases.
  - The person asking the question then knows that s/he has been heard.
  - The rest of the audience clearly hears what the question is. This is important because the acoustics of an auditorium favour the stage and presenter, rather than the audience.
  - The repetition gives you some time to think.

- **Clarify** their question if necessary. Ask them to rephrase or to provide further details.
- **Answer** to *both* the person *and* the rest of the audience.

Responding To Questions

- If the question comes from the 80% of the audience that are receptive or neutral, then their question will typically be polite and will focus upon the reasoning and evidence of your case.
  - If they question your conclusion, then the actual source of disagreement will lie further upstream. Identify the specific area either by asking them to be more specific or by asking a series of questions like the following:
    - "Do you agree that this was an important research question?"
    - "Do you agree with my/our reasoning?"
    - "Do you agree with the methods and analysis I/we used?"
  - Once you've identified the specific point, then you can discuss it.
    - Keep the discussion short, since the rest of the audience may not be sufficiently interested that they want to listen to this for the whole question-period.
    - Deal with the facts and reasoning. Don't let it become personal.
    - Accept the possibility that you could be mistaken. You won't be correct 100% of the time.
- If the question comes from the cranky 20% of the audience, then you need to resort to special tactics.
  - Their questions can sound critical and even rude. For example, the questions below are often brought up in workshops when Ted asks for samples of questions that would scare workshop participants:
    - "Have you ever thought of taking up a different career?"
    - "Is your supervisor aware of how you've been wasting the last three years?"
    - "Do you really enjoy wasting time and money?"
    - "Don't you know that Blogs *et al.* have already done this?"
    - "Your whole argument is completely specious."
    - "We did the very same experiments and they didn't work, so you couldn't possibly be correct."
    - "Isn't this a vast oversimplification of the multi-factorial complexity of the real situation?"
    - "Why did you do it this way when it is well known that this method is ineffective/obsolete/has been replaced by ..."
    - "What about the paper by ...?"
    - "What implications do your results on genetic defects in elephants have for the Chinese Rice fly?"
    - "Do you still continue to falsify your lab results or have you been fired for it at last?"

There are some important points to notice about these cranky questions:

- **The question *is personal*.**
  - The attitude (voice and body language) is aggressive, insulting, sarcastic, provocative or confrontational.
  - They attempt to create an unpleasant feeling in the presenter (you) such as doubt, uncertainty, anxiety, fear, embarrassment, ...
- **It is subjective criticism/opinion masquerading as objective fact.**
  - These are opinions, interpretations or value-judgements about you or your work presented *as if* they were obvious and objective truth.
- **The questions are often vague and/or hint at what they mean.**
  - The questions often use unspecified qualifiers (adjectives and adverbs) such as: *really*, *quite*, *somewhat*, *very*, ...
  - They hint or imply their meaning rather than stating it plainly. *e.g.* "Have you ever thought of taking up a different career?" is implying that either you or your work (or both!) are substandard.
    - They don't provide the reasons for their opinion. It's easy to be critical when you don't back it up with facts and logic!
- **The question distorts the situation.**
  - They polarise things, events or situations to an extreme using words such as *all*, *none*, *never*, *each*, *every*, *completely*, *extremely*, *totally*, ...
  - They misrepresent what you said or "put words in your mouth" by rephrasing your statements.
- **The question may be irrelevant.**
  - The question or statement may raise some aspect that is actually irrelevant to what you talked about and the person asking the question hasn't indicated how it is supposedly connected with your presentation.
  - The question or statement may even refer to something that wasn't mentioned in your presentation at all!

The trick to handling difficult questions is to do your homework in advance. Anticipate difficult questions, prepare and practise possible responses. The preparation means that you don't need to think on your feet.

- When you hear (or imagine) a horrible question, write it down.
- Then think of as many ways as possible in which you could respond to it. As long as it doesn't violate the *Laws of Physics* or require a divine miracle, it's allowed as a *possible* response! Even rude, sarcastic answers that you would only dream of saying are allowed!
  - You *will* need to empty your head of the sarcastic answers before you can start thinking of the more professional and polite responses.
  - Getting the sarcastic answers out of your system also feels good and is fun when a workshop group compares their answers.
  - Another advantage of capturing the sarcastic responses is that they often contain the seed of a good idea that can be developed into a more polite and professional response.

- In Ted's workshops, he tells students that they aren't even warmed up until they have at least ten possible responses and twenty is better.
- Always remember that you have more options than you imagine you do.
- With more experience, you will create a "data-bank" of possible polite answers in your mind and all you need to do will be to choose which one you want to use in a given situation.
- The person asking the question can't force you to respond a particular way. You get to choose how you respond and you can choose one they won't like! (No sense encouraging them to do this again.)
- Often these people are "Show-offs" or "Bullies" who never learned how to "play nice with the other children". Like all bullies, they are hoping you will give up without a fight.
    - So you need to "fight" them (politely and professionally) every single step. Make them sweat for each point, and above all, make it take as long as possible. They want a quick, cheap thrill at your expense. The longer it takes and the more effort it costs them, the less willing they will be to pick on you or anyone next time.
    - **Certain people are known to be consistently cranky, critical or bullying so the rest of the audience will be on your side.**

Appendix 3 has some horrible questions with possible responses that students have thought of during Ted's workshops.

- 9 -
Writing Clearly And Concisely

Writing For Research

Writing for research is a specialised form of communication:

- It is a professional communication of facts, reasoning and conclusions. It is not intended to be artistic or entertaining.
- It occurs within complex and specialist disciplines or fields.
- It has an international audience, a large proportion of whom have English as a second or third language.

During the course of your research career, you will have to read many, many, many papers, articles and reviews. Unfortunately you will come across numerous examples that are badly written. Just because something has been published, does not *necessarily* mean that it was well written or even useful. You will need to learn to critically assess each paper on its merits and decide if it is good, marginal or "rubbish".

In our experience, poor writing style is often a symptom of one or more of the following. The writers:

- Are struggling to write in English which is their second or third language;
- Haven't come to a definite conclusion;
- Have a poorly reasoned and/or substantiated case;
- Are too lazy to do the work needed to confirm their reasoning;
- Have made assumptions in their reasoning that they have not explicitly defined;
- Are trying to "cover up" weak research by making it difficult to understand;
- Are trying to "show off" by using big words and complex sentence constructions.

So, when you read a published paper ***do not*** assume that:

- It's well written.
- The research tasks were appropriately chosen and/or well executed.
- It's well reasoned and well supported.
- It's relevant and/or useful.
- Your English skills are poor.
- You don't know your subject well enough.

When you are reading a poorly written paper which is annoying, boring, confusing or making your brain melt, you will need to get beneath the superficial writing style to uncover the reasoning and evidence that (hopefully) lie below.

Remember that structure tables and/or concept-mapping can help you to reveal the logical connections between ideas and assess the balance of evidence.

What Are The Various Faults In Writing Style?

Based upon Ted's experience with teaching postgraduates and postdoctoral fellows, there are six (6) categories (or classes) of stylistic fault in research writing:

- **Vague or Ambiguous**
- **Irrelevant or Unnecessary**
- **Indirect, Implicit or Evasive**
- **Complicated or Confusing Sentences**
- **Inaccurate, Distorted or Misrepresented**
- **Connection and Continuity**

These suggested classifications of stylistic fault serve as guidelines and are not rigid rules. The important thing is to realise that *stylistic faults* interfere with clarity and brevity. The fewer stylistic faults there are, the more clear and concise your writing will become.

In this chapter, we will only be considering the first five topics. We'll omit *Connection and Continuity* because if you have structured your reasoning, then this will be less likely to be a problem compared to the first five faults.

Vague Or Ambiguous

Many times what people write or say is vague (poorly specified) or could have more than one meaning (ambiguous). The information presented is insufficient for the reader to be certain of what is meant.

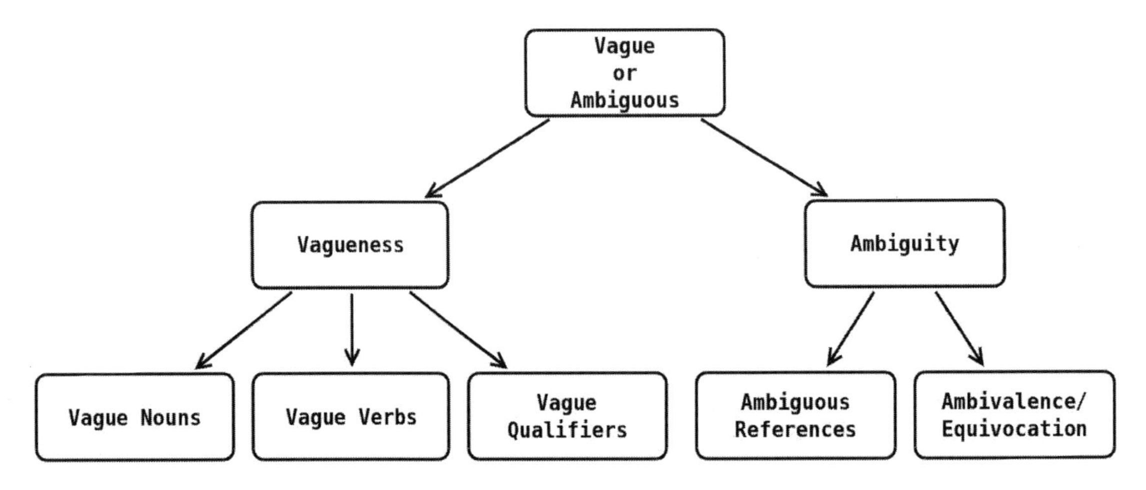

Vagueness

- **Vague nouns** are unspecific and leave it to the reader to "fill in the details" from their experience or imagination.

Nominalisation: "The *study* into the *identification* and *characterisation* of the *infection* of a healthy individual was ..."
In this example, the nouns *study*, *identification*, *characterisation* and *infection* represent more complex processes with multiple steps. When a noun is used to represent a process, then it is known as a *nominalisation.* Nominalisations can be an acceptable and useful shorthand *if all your readers* use the same jargon. Otherwise they don't provide enough detail to actually know what is happening.

Generalised nouns: "Today, the ***government*** announced that ***civil servants*** would have their pensions adjusted in view of the current ***economic situation***."
All of the indicated nouns are vague and leave the specific details to our imaginations. Which department within the *government* issued the announcement? Are *all civil servants* affected or only some? Which specific aspects of the *economic situation* are responsible for this readjustment of pensions?

- ***Vague verbs*** are verbs that identify some activity or process in a generic way while omitting important specifics. Examples of vague verbs include ***characterise, elucidate***, ***investigate***, ***study*** ...
  - If you are going to ***characterise*** or ***investigate*** something, then what does this mean specifically? What specific steps are you going to take?
  - Would an *investigation* involve the same techniques and methods in different fields? Would research medical staff *investigate* something the same way that a chemist or a physicist would? The answer is no. The difficulty is that more and more research is *interdisciplinary,* so we need to assume that our work may be read by people from other fields, who would not do the same things when *investigating* that we would.
  - Another danger with vague verbs is that they give the illusion that something is being done and that we know what it is. Unfortunately we have seen too many cases where vague verbs have concealed careless thinking, especially in project planning, politics and organisational leadership.

- ***Vague qualifiers are adjectives or adverbs*** that do not increase the information content in any useful way.
  - Examples include: ***somewhat***, ***quite***, ***reasonably***, ***most***, ***majority***, ***minority***, ***negligible***, ***some***, ***notably***, ***significantly***, ***substantially***, ***interestingly***, ***fairly***, ...

Vague Qualifiers: "One of ***many*** things that can be said about ***some*** research papers is that they are ***quite*** consistently ***somewhat substantially*** difficult to comprehend within a ***reasonably*** short time by a ***majority*** of international readers from a ***variety*** of countries." (38 words)
(Thirty eight words to say nothing useful!)

In Ted's workshops, he asks participants to specify how much "most" means to them expressed as a percentage. He gets answers ranging from "more than 50%" to "95%". So what will happen when you write the word "most" thinking "more than 50%" and your reader sees "most" and thinks 95%? Will the reader have correctly understood what you meant?

Ask yourself:

"*How much* does this mean? Can I specify or quantify the amount?"

If not, then why not? And if you can't define it, then how do you actually know that it is what you are claiming it is? How would you defend this claim in your PhD defence?

Titles of papers and presentations are particularly prone to clusters of vague nouns, verbs and adjectives.

Title: An ***investigation*** into the ***relationship*** between sonic hedgehog and cochlear ***protein expression*** in mutant and wild mice.
What does this title *mean* specifically? What kind of *investigation*? Genetic, chemical, ... What is the *relationship*? Does it increase, decrease or have no effect? Which proteins are expressed?

Title: ***Identification*** and ***characterisation*** of ***meso-scale bacterial endocytoplasmic structures*** by ***incoherent scattering*** of ***short wavelength energetic photons*** with ***detection*** and ***resolution*** of ***angular dispersion***.
What kind of *identification* and *characterisation*? These are vague and also pointless since the authors then go on to tell us the characterisation method is incoherent scattering of short-wavelength photons with detection and resolution of angular dispersion. And why didn't the authors simply say X-rays instead of "short-wavelength energetic photons"? What kind of *endocytoplasmic structures* and what kind of *meso-scale bacteria*? What kind of *detection* and *resolution*?

We frequently hear complaints about titles of seminars or papers that led people to believe the subject would be one thing and then the actual seminar/paper was something completely different. This is another disadvantage of these vague keyword-laden titles.

Vague and generic is seductively easy to write because you don't need to think about what you mean specifically. However, vague writing is useless to the reader.

Ask yourself:

- "Could this be misinterpreted by a reader?"
- "Could this be expressed more simply, directly and specifically?"

Ambiguity

This is a form of uncertainty concerning the *meaning* of a sentence.

- ***Ambiguous References*** are where the ambiguity concerns what is being referred to.

"This is the *best* option."
Compared to what other alternatives? In what way is it the best? By how much?
"Car crashes due to the use of seat belts are not always fatal."
Did seat belts *cause* the crashes or were they responsible for more people surviving?

"After 30 minutes of gamma irradiation we examined the metal samples."
Were the researchers exposing themselves or the metal samples to the gamma rays?
" ... massive cell death ... "
Was this the death of very large cells or the death of a large number of cells of normal size?
" ... normally fertile ... "
Does this mean that it is *usually* fertile or that it is fertile in a normal way?

- ***Ambivalence / Equivocation***

  This is when the writer says it could be ⟨*this*⟩ or it could be ⟨*that*⟩.

"We are *hesitantly confident* that *perhaps definitely* it could be either ⟨*A*⟩ or ⟨*B*⟩."
Are they *hesitant* or *confident?* Is it *perhaps* or *definitely*? And which is it: ⟨*A*⟩ or ⟨*B*⟩?

Irrelevant Or Unnecessary

This heading covers various ways in which the writer uses additional words that contribute nothing extra towards the meaning. This is also called ***padding*** or ***being long-winded***.

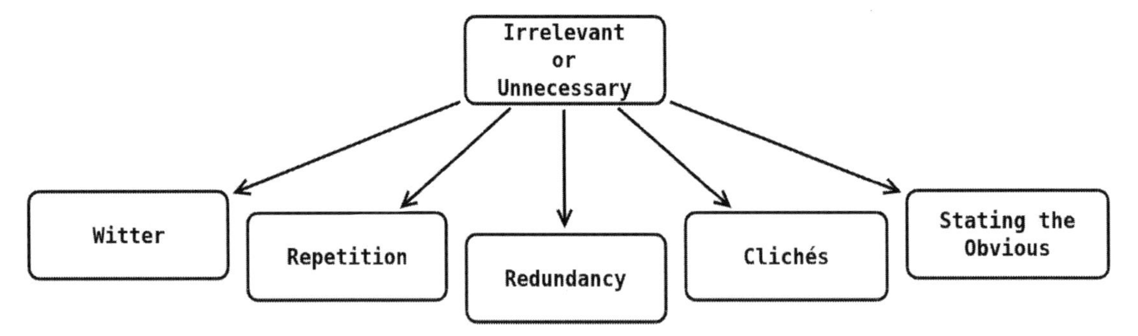

Witter

This is the use of 4 or 5 words when 1 or 2 would suffice.

"... it is evident that ..."	→ *evidently*
"... the rate of speed ... "	→ the *speed*
" ... in the event that ... "	→ *if* (or *when*)
"In conclusion, our studies suggest that ..."	→ "We conclude ... "

" ... by carrying out a comparison ... "	→ " ... by comparing ... "
" ... was found to cause ... "	→ " ... caused ... "
" ... may induce a suppressive effect ... "	→ " ... may suppress ... "
" ... at least one if not more ... "	→ " ... at least one ... "
" ... does not provide support for ... "	→ " ... does not support ... "
" ... make a recommendation ... " ⇒	→ " ... recommend ... "

Repetition

This is the unnecessary restatement of the same idea with words of similar meaning. Often the writer is polite enough to warn the reader that s/he will be repeating themselves by using phrases such as:

- " ... in other words ... "
- " ... that is to say ... "
- " ... which is to say ... "
- " ... *i.e.* ... "
- " ... by which we mean to say ... "

Repetition: "One thing that can be said about some research papers is that they are repeatedly incomprehensible, which is to say that regardless of how many times you have read them, they still don't make sense." (35 words)
Revised Version: "Some research papers don't make any sense, regardless of how many times you have read them." (16 words)

Redundancy

This is when one or more words are unnecessary because the meaning has already been expressed.

" ... actually occurred ... "	→ If it *occurred* then actually is unnecessary.
" ... circular in shape ..."	→ If it's *circular* then of course it is a *shape.*
" ... advance warning ... "	→ A *warning* that isn't in *advance* isn't a warning, it is an "I told you this wouldn't work!"

" ... in close proximity to ... "	→ *Proximity* means *close.* You can't have a distant proximity!
" ... absolute certainty ... "	→ *Certainty* means 100% and there aren't degrees of certainty.
" ... tentatively propose ... "	→ The word *propose* means that it's a suggestion, so *tentative* is redundant.
"It has been demonstrated previously ... "	→ The past-tense means it has already happened, so *previously* is redundant.
"At some time in the past, during the first half of the twentieth century ... "	→ If it was in the first half of the twentieth century then it must have been "some time in the past"!

Clichés

This refers to the use of tired old phrases that everyone has read or heard "a thousand times before". In addition to being boring, clichés are culturally specific and won't make sense to readers in other countries. Please remove clichés.

Stating-the-Obvious

This is when the writer states something that is obvious to anyone, like this definition of stating-the-obvious!

Indirect, Implicit Or Evasive

This is when the writer does not clearly state what they mean, or is possibly being deliberately evasive.

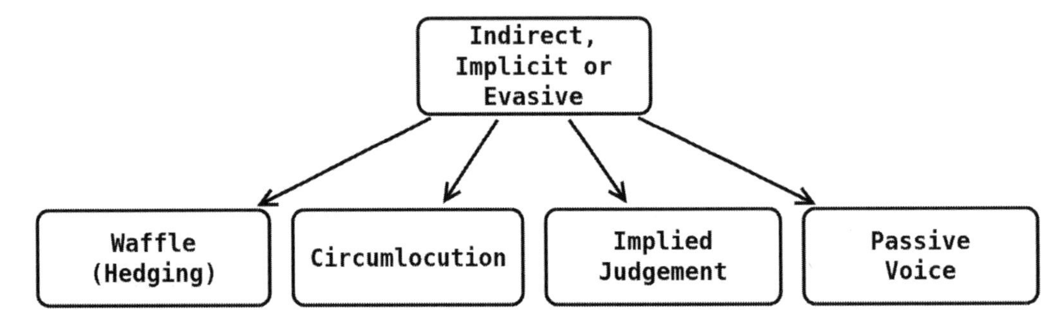

Waffle (Hedging)

This is when the writer avoids committing themselves to any interpretation or recommendation. This is usually revealed by the overuse of conditional words such as ***might***, ***maybe***, ***could be***, ***possibly***, ...

Waffle: "It ***might*** be ***possible*** that ***in some but not necessarily all*** situations a ***certain proportion*** of people ***might*** be ***somewhat reasonably inclined***, to a ***greater or lesser extent***, in ***harbouring the suspicion*** that ..."
We're not going to *try* fixing this sentence! The author is doing his/her utmost to avoid making any kind of commitment.

Circumlocution

This occurs when there is the initial illusion that the argument is developing in a direction, but eventually the reader realises that the writer is going around and around in circles without coming to a conclusion. Either the writer is confused or they are hoping to confuse you.

Implied Judgement

This is when the writer is *hinting* or *implying* something without being explicit and direct. Additionally, the author hasn't presented the reasoning, evidence or criteria for this assessment, so the reader is unable to verify the conclusion for themselves.

- Words like ***should***, ***ought***, ***must***, ***have to***, ***need to***, ***obviously***, ***interestingly*** reveal the presence of a covert interpretation.
- " ... the ***main disadvantage*** ... " → What are the other disadvantages and how do we know this is the most significant?
- "We ***should*** do ... " → *Why* should we do something? What are the reasons and what were the criteria that were used as a basis for the assessment?
- "It is extremely ***interesting*** that ... " → Why or in what way is something interesting?

Passive Phrasing Or Passive Voice

This is a sentence construction where the subject (active agent) is *not* defined and attention is focused upon the actions and results.

It is valid to use the passive voice when the actor/subject is generic or an unimportant detail.

"The ***mail was delivered*** this morning."
This is a legitimate use of the passive voice because the only concern is whether the mail was delivered and not who delivered it.

Researchers often use the passive voice to remove repetition of first person pronouns or to emphasise research actions and results rather than who did a particular experiment.

However using the passive voice has disadvantages.

- Passive sentences are often longer and more awkwardly constructed than their corresponding active sentences.
- The inverted sentence structure (object first, verb following, no subject) generally requires more mental processing to make sense of the sentence than the corresponding active form. For shorter and simpler sentences, this extra mental processing doesn't pose a problem for the reader.
- If the passive voice is used in combination with long sentences, the resulting text can be very difficult for readers for whom English is a foreign language.

"A rather limited number of families of signalling *proteins have been implicated* in these inductive processes and the importance of both cellular context and *signal-strength has been reflected* in the complexity of the *range of responses that have been induced*." (41 words)
This single sentence is manageable, but can you imagine what it would be like to read an entire paper written like this?

Passive sentences are used when someone is attempting to avoid or conceal responsibility for actions or results because they:

- were biased/prejudiced; or
- made a flawed or ill-considered decision; or
- lacked essential skills or experience to correctly perform the activity.

"The *applications were reviewed* by a committee at the end of last month and *none were accepted*."
This is both passive and vague. • Who was on the committee? • Were they competent to assess the applications? • Were they unbiased?

"Today, the *Minister of Transport* announced that *mistakes had been made* in the design and implementation of the new air traffic control system and that *several million pounds had been inadvertently misallocated*."
This is vague and evasive! Unfortunately, everyone is familiar with how politicians and CEOs use the passive voice to conceal their responsibility for bad decisions.

NOTE

If a journal or institution insists upon the use of the passive voice, then you will have to comply if you want to publish there.

When you are using the passive voice, then our recommendation is to keep your sentences as short, simple and direct as possible.

Complicated Or Confusing Sentences

Some sentences can be too complicated or confusing to understand.

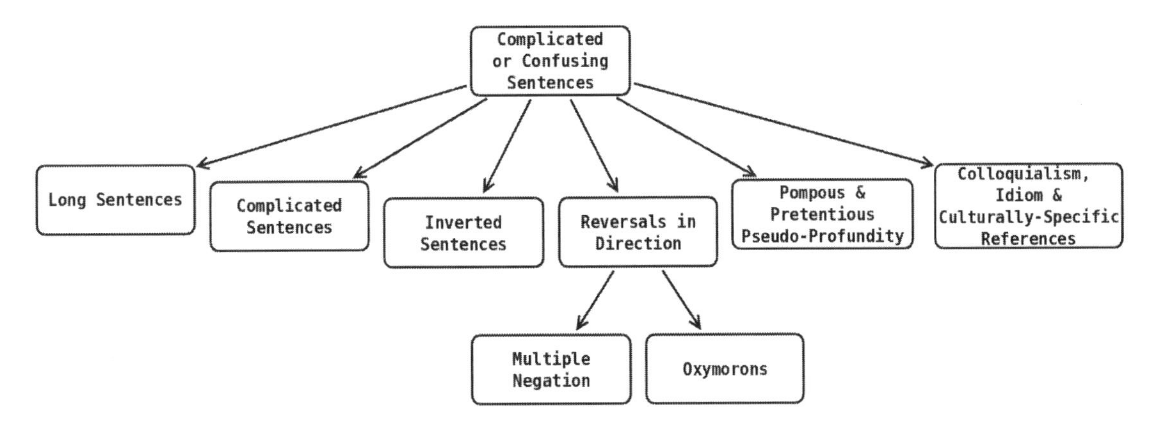

Long Sentences

- Long sentences are an attempt (unsuccessfully) to communicate more than one idea.
- Research on how people process language has shown that when sentences become longer than 20 words, the amount of mental processing required to understand them begins increasing dramatically. The longest sentence Ted has found (so far) in a research paper is 106 words, although sentences of 70 – 80 words are commonly encountered.
- Long sentences also overfill short-term memory and information is lost. It becomes necessary for the reader to re-read the sentence several times in order to retain enough of the information to make sense of it. This re-reading obviously will slow the pace and annoy the reader.
- Finally, imagine what a non-native English speaker must suffer when they try to make sense of these ridiculously long sentences!

Original Sentence: "Despite an extensive list of mutations in the LDLR that affect the LDLR life cycle, very little is actually known about other proteins that play a role in and possibly regulate LDLR synthesis, maturation, trafficking to the cell surface or degradation of receptor molecules originating from the secretory or the endocytic pathway." (52 words)
Rewritten By Workshop Participants: "Many mutations in the LDLR affect its life cycle. However little is known about the other proteins involved in this process." (21 words) (Note: the use of *many* in this sentence is vague but it is not serious in this case because a specific number is not required for the sentence to be meaningful.)

Complicated Sentences

- ***Compound*** sentences contain two or more ideas in two or more main clauses and they are frequently encountered in longer sentences and they are more difficult to comprehend. (Note that the previous sentence had 3 main clauses!)
- ***Compound-complex*** sentences are a nightmare, especially for an international audience, because they contain at least two ideas in two or more main clauses plus descriptive subordinate clauses.

Types of Sentences

	Main Clause(s)		**Subordinate Clause(s)**
Simple	1	+	0
Complex	1	+	1 or more
Compound	2 or more	+	0
Compound Complex	2 or more	+	1 or more

Inverted Sentences

This is when subordinate clauses come before the main clause. Generally, the main clause (or point) in a sentence should go first because this is the position of most emphasis. Supporting information should appear in a subordinate clause which follows.

Inverted Sentence:

"When subordinate clauses, which provide supplementary information, come first in the sentence and the main clause appears afterwards, then until the reader reaches the end of the whole sentence they can't understand the principal meaning."

Rewritten Version:

"It is easier for the reader to get the principal meaning of the sentence when the sentence begins with the main clause and the subordinate clauses follow."

Which of these two examples requires less brainpower to process?

If you read a sentence out-loud and your co-workers can't understand it without having you re-read it aloud several more times, then it's too long and/or too complicated!

If you read a sentence out-loud and you have to take a breath before you have finished the sentence, then it's too long! Imagine reading that 106 word sentence!!

Reversals In Direction

This is when the reader's brain is required to keep track of several closely-spaced changes in direction.

- ***Multiple Negation***
  - Double negation is bad enough, but triple and quadruple negation will confuse your reader and melt their brain. Ted knows of a hypnotist that puts his clients into trance by speaking in sentences containing multiple negations.

Multiple Negation: "It doesn't seem improbable that under not too dissimilar circumstances, we might not be unjustified in concluding that what we thought was true is no longer indeed the case."
Revised Version: "It seems probable that under similar circumstances we might be justified in concluding we were mistaken."

Multiple Negation: "This is not to say that you shouldn't necessarily be disinclined to avoiding not using multiple negation in all circumstances, but rather the disutilisation of indirect multi-negational statements is not to be underestimated in terms of not inhibiting clarity."
(We're not going to even try to unravel this one!)

- ***Oxymorons*** (↑ ↓ or ↓ ↑)

  This is the juxtaposition of apparently contradictory words. A similar effect occurs in research writing when adjacent words have opposite implied *directions* and the reader's brain has to "flip back and forth" to make sense.

  Their occasional use won't hurt anyone, but too many and your reader will become confused and tired.

Uncertain	Definite
"... much (↑) less (↓) ..."	"... the decrease was substantially ..."
"... increasing ↑ inhibition (↓) ..." (It is unclear whether it is the *amount of* inhibition or the *rate of* inhibition that has increased compared to ...)	"... the extent of inhibition was 37% greater than ..." (amount) "... the rate of inhibition was 37% greater than ..." (rate)
"... decreasing (↓) growth (↑) ..." (Again it is unclear if *growth* refers to *amount of* or *rate of*.)	"... the rate of growth decreased compared to ..."

"... proliferation (↑) decrease (↓) ..."	"... the rate of proliferation was 27% lower than ..."
"... over (↑) 10^6 times less than (↓) ..."	"... at least 10^6 times smaller than ..."
"... much (↑) lower (↓) increase (↑) ..."	"... 24% increase was much less than expected ..."

Rephrasing these examples may take a few more words than the cryptic version *but* the gain in clarity, precision *plus* the avoidance of the confusing juxtaposition of words with opposite directions is well worth it.

Pompous And Pretentious Pseudo-Profundity

In its various forms, this is when a writer tries to sound more intelligent and educated by the use of unnecessarily big words or complex sentences. Examples can include ***verbal puffery*** and the excessive and/or unnecessary use of ***acronyms*** and ***technical jargon***.

" ... wakefulness-promoting pharmacologically-active heated aqueous filtrate ... "
Rewrite: "... coffee ... "

"A proper functioning of this unit is critically contingent upon it maintaining dimensional integrity and a proper spatial orientation between its component parts as well as a functional interaction between its relevant sub-systems."
Rewrite: "This won't work if it is dropped or broken."

Colloquialism, Idiom And Culturally-Specific References

This is when the writer uses an expression that only makes sense within their culture or country.

"If this research project is successful then it will count as a ***home run*** in the fight against cancer."
The term "home run" would only make sense to someone familiar with the sport of baseball. In countries and cultures where baseball isn't common, the reader will be wondering what a successful research project has to do with running home.

Inaccurate, Distorted Or Misrepresented

This is when the results and reasoning are inaccurate or expressed in any way that distorts or misrepresents the situation.

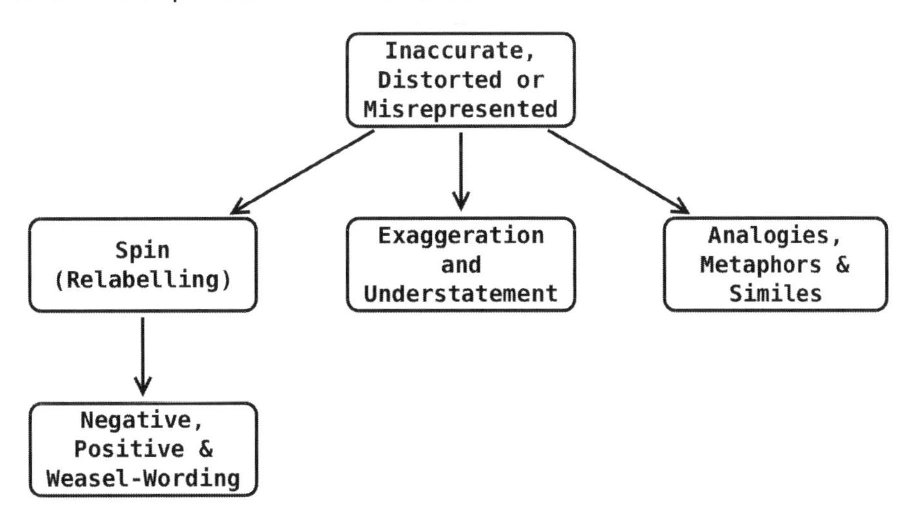

Spin (Relabelling)

This is where events are relabelled or *spun* to make them sound better or worse than they are. Unfortunately, we're all familiar with spin because of politicians and business leaders who seem incapable of speaking plainly and honestly. There are actually several different types of spin depending upon how someone wants to distort the facts.

- ***Negative Spin (Dysphemism)*** to make something sound worse than it really is.

Negative Spin: "Our enrolment *crisis* will be investigated by a select committee of academics who will produce a white-paper of recommendations."
Translation: "Student enrolment is down 2% this year and we're going to waste time having some pointless meetings and expensive lunches that won't fix anything."

- ***Positive Spin (Euphemism)*** to make something sound better than it is.

Positive Spin: "The corporate *reorganisation* will *flatten our administration* and leave our company *leaner* and more *cost-effective*."
Translation: "The company is firing 800 mid-level management staff with a salary-saving of £35 million."

Weasel-wording

This is a phrasing that is used to get around a rule, regulation or law.

"After Christmas Sale – this week only! Up to 80% off!"
On reading this advertisement, most people would imagine large savings on the products in the shop. However, literally the advertisement says that the *maximum possible* discount is 80% and discounts less than this would still be entirely legal.
"Prices start as low as ⟨...⟩ while quantities last ..."
In reality, if the buyer wants the usual features, then these will cost extra. However, as long as at least one basic model is available at the low price of ⟨...⟩, the vendor is being *legally* honest.

Exaggeration And Understatement

These are forms of distortion that involve amplifying or minimising some characteristic through the use of adjectives and adverbs. Exaggeration can occur when researchers are attempting to "sell" their work.
Look for ***extreme*** words like: *completely, extremely, totally, every, each, always, all, never, none, negligibly*.

> **Exaggeration:**
> "This work has addressed the ***extremely*** important question of ⟨...⟩. Our findings have ***completely*** resolved the issue and addressed ***all*** questions which have ***never*** been answered previously.

Analogies, Metaphors And Similes

These are comparisons where the writer is claiming that *(this)* is approximately like *(that)*.

- Inherent in the use of an analogy or metaphor is some degree of misrepresentation.
- Analogies and metaphors can also be culturally-specific, so they may not make sense to people in other countries or in other languages.
- When used carefully and judiciously, analogies, metaphors and similes can aid understanding by simplifying a complex situation.

> **Useful Analogy:**
> "This enzyme operates by a ***lock and key*** mechanism."

- When used carelessly, analogies, metaphors or similes can distort the situation or obscure important aspects. The danger with analogies, metaphors and similes is that they strongly guide our thinking and inhibit consideration of alternatives.

Poorly chosen metaphor:

"Research is a ***competitive game*** and there will be ***winners*** and ***losers***."

Here the analogy is that research is like a game. There are several ways that this analogy misrepresents the true situation and could prove counterproductive:

- Once a normal game is finished, there are no permanent losses. Both sides begin the next game from an equal footing. In research, the "players" never finish one game and begin another, so the "score" of the game is cumulative. The "losing side" never gets another chance to begin from an equal footing.
- Another misleading aspect comes from referring to "winners and losers". Are researchers ***either*** winners ***or*** losers? Or is it actually a question of degree where some researchers are more successful and others less successful?
- The winning or losing mindset will hinder cooperation with other researchers and institutions because for you to "win", others must "lose". This will interfere with the openness and collaboration that is a part of research.
- Games usually involve two competing sides at a time, which doesn't apply for research where everyone is competing simultaneously.

Your audience has limited time, memory and concentration. When a piece of writing has poor style then it becomes progressively more difficult and time-consuming for the reader to uncover and make sense of the embedded message and its structure.

They can *waste* their time and brainpower on making sense of your writing style or they can use it in making sense of your research. Which would you prefer?

We are not saying that it is necessary to find and fix *every single* fault in order to make your writing easier to understand.

We are saying that the more of them you find and fix, the better your research, reasoning and evidence will come across to your international audience.

Additionally, finding and fixing the style faults can shorten a piece of writing by 30% – 70% which will be appreciated by your busy readers!

Writing clearly and concisely will apply equally to progress reports, theses and papers for publication.

How Is Good Style Achieved?

Once you have prepared the structure of your message, how do you write it so that the importance, reasoning and evidence aren't obscured or interfered with by the writing style? Because a research presentation is from one professional to other professionals, there is no need to be fancy or flashy. It's not expected and it is no substitute for a meaningful and important message.

Grammar and spelling contribute to communicating clearly, but they are not enough on their own. Without good structure and good style, even perfect grammar and spelling will not get your message across! The best style is one that doesn't get in the way of the importance, reasoning and evidence.

Unfortunately, it is difficult for many people to write "from scratch" with good style. And focusing on style while writing can make it even harder to write! From our experience, it is better to write without worrying about your style and later revise what has been written to improve the style. The slogan Ted uses is:

"Write first; find and fix the stylistic problems later."

This approach also makes sense for another reason. People tend to have their own personal writing habits, which they repeat consistently. Once you know what your particular habits are, it simplifies what you need to check for.

Meaning comes from the larger pattern that is formed by the pieces of information. It is essential that each sentence has a *purpose and meaning* rather than simply being a collection of words terminated with a full-stop.

Meaning can be difficult to determine when the sentences are poorly written.

It is the *responsibility* of the author(s) to get their research, its meaning and its importance across clearly and correctly to the reader.

Ask yourself:

- "Why am I writing this sentence?" (What purpose does it serve?)
- "What am I trying to say?" (Meaning)
- "How does this connect/link with the rest of the material?" (Context & Relevance)

Sentences express one idea at a time. **A sentence does not convey an entire chain of reasoning!** Don't put more than one idea into a sentence – this will give the reader "mental indigestion".

Your aim is to present and explain the information in manageable chunks and at a steady pace. Avoid overloading the reader's language processing capabilities. A useful analogy is to feed the reader "bite-size chunks" at a rate where they have time to chew and swallow. If the pieces are too big or delivered too fast then you can be sure they won't enjoy the meal.

- The less you explain, the more mental "chewing" the reader has to do, which slows things down even further. Explain meaning and importance rather than tell information.
- Keep sentences simple, specific, direct, active, and positive.
  - *Active* sentences have Subject – Verb – Object structure. For greater clarity, keep the subject and object as close to the verb which connects them as possible.
  - Sentences should preferably be stated in the *positive*. Stating what something isn't still doesn't state what it is.
    - *Negative:* "I don't like chocolate, strawberry or coffee ice cream." (This doesn't indicate what flavour of ice cream the person *does* like.)
    - *Positive:* "I like vanilla ice cream."

Examples of Sentence Rewrites	
Original Sentences in Papers	**Rewrites by Workshop Participants**
Few topics in immunology have inspired such passionate debate or as great a profusion of ever more complex hypotheses as that which tries to explain how a developing thymocyte commits to the CD4 or CD8 lineage. (36 words)	The mechanism by which a developing thymocyte is directed towards either the CD4 or CD8 lineage is an important question. (20 words)
Thus although it is not clear how phosphorylation affects the function of the flexible loop, it is possible that phosphorylation may promote a conformational change that somehow inhibits the negative function of the loop domain. (35 words)	Phosphorylation may change the molecular conformation which then inhibits the negative function of the loop domain. (16 words)
In fact, mitochondrial phospholipid fatty acid profile correlates consistently with proton leakage across different species and in different conditions, in that in conditions in which proton leak changes the mitochondrial phospholipid fatty acyl composition also changes in a specific manner. (40 words)	Mitochondrial phospholipid acyl composition correlates with proton leakage for different species and conditions. (13 words)
Total word count = 111	**Total word count = 49** (44% of the original length and easier to read!)

Everything up to this point is applicable to any kind of writing you may do. What follows are some suggestions for specific situations.

Writing Papers For Publication

- Formatting and layout will usually be specified by the journal. Follow these specified guidelines!
- In many cases the *Guidelines/Instructions for Authors* will also specify aspects of the writing style that are acceptable, such as verb tenses to use and whether first person pronouns are allowed.

Writing Dissertations/Theses

The dissertation/thesis is an exercise in persuasion and reasoned argument! You are trying to convince the examiners that you and your work are worth a degree. Structure and present your thesis as an argument to persuade them. Have a point. Explain, defend and justify all choices and statements.

The three "BIG" questions Ted always asked his students when he proofread something they had given him were:

- "So what?", which concerns the meaning and importance.
- "Who cares?", which concerns relevance, usefulness and novelty.
- "How do you know?", which concerns the reasoning and evidence which supports some claim.

Because a dissertation/thesis is a work of persuasion, think in terms of three questions: **Why**, **What** and **How**. For example:

- When you explain what you did, also explain why it was important or necessary.
- When you explain how you did it, explain why it was done that way, using those methods.

Remember, you are justifying or defending the value of your work, results and interpretations and the choices that you made as you carried it out.

Dissertations/theses are not judged by weight, number of pages or number of references. They are assessed on the basis of *originality* or *novelty,* and *quality* of work, results, analysis, discussion and presentation. Quantity is always a poor substitute for quality. Our recommended formula for success is:

Good Idea(s) + Good Work + Good Structure + Good Style = Success

Be ruthless about what is relevant. It will make your job of writing and revising much easier. Our motto is: "If in doubt, leave it out."

- Waffle and padding will take you extra time to write it, proofread it, print the extra unnecessary pages and bind it.
- Waffle and padding will take the examiners extra time to read and *it will be spotted!* It will bore them and it will make a poor impression of your ability.

The ***Introduction*** serves several vital functions.

1) It sets the ***context***. When and where was this work done? Where does it fit in the body of knowledge? What is it connected or related to? Is it filling a gap in our existing knowledge or is it extending our knowledge into new areas?
2) It defines your ***purpose***. What is it that you were attempting to accomplish? What was the problem you wanted to solve or the question you wanted to answer? This is the *aim* of your thesis. (Remember, the thesis is not a diary of how busy you were, but of what you accomplished.)
3) It defines the ***importance***. Why did the field/subject need this? What was the value or importance of resolving the problem or question? How is your work and knowledge valuable? How can we make use of the knowledge?
4) It justifies the ***approach*** to solving the problem/question. Why was your chosen approach suitable for achieving your aim?
5) It highlights the ***necessary background*** information that the reader will require to make sense of the results, analysis and discussion that follow.

Anything beyond fulfilling these five functions is simply waffle or "data dumping".

When reading the thesis the examiner is going to be looking for "complete thoughts". They will unconsciously be checking for two things:

"What are the facts/evidence?" *plus* **"What does it mean?"**

If they read just a collection of facts and data, then their response will be "Yeah, so what? What does this mean?" Conversely, if you make some interpretation or conclusion without providing the data, then they're going to think "Where is the evidence for this? Prove it!" Get in the habit of providing the evidence ***and*** the meaning of the data.

Assuming that you consistently provide your reader with *evidence + meaning*, then the more subtle questions they will be wondering about concern *relevance, novelty* and *usefulness:*

- "What is the relevance?"
- "Where does this fit?"
- "Why is this valuable or important?"
- "How can we use or apply this practically?"

References

In research papers and your thesis, anything without a reference or citation, you are claiming is your work, your results or your idea. If you are asked to explain or defend that statement and you admit that it's actually "so and so's work" then you will appear to be guilty of either carelessness and incompetence or plagiarism and professional dishonesty.

Our recommendation is that you **only cite papers you have actually read**. If you haven't read the paper, then how do you know that it actually says what you are claiming it does? How do you know those authors did the work correctly and interpreted it correctly? If you are citing a paper simply because another paper cites it, how do you know the citing authors aren't misrepresenting or misunderstanding the paper they are citing?

And while we are on the subject of the literature, when you are reading the literature, you should also be asking:

- "What is the evidence?"
- "What does it really mean?"
- "How do they know?"
- "Is this important?"

The literature is filled with unproven speculations which eventually become accepted as truths by simple force of repetition. Go back to the original paper and check for yourself.

- How did the original authors do the research?
- What was the evidence?
- What was their logic/reasoning?

Formatting And Layout

- Formatting and layout for dissertations/theses (and reports) will usually be specified by the institution. Follow the specified guidelines.
- Font sizes of 10 points or smaller are difficult to read. Font sizes of 11 or 12 point are preferred depending upon the chosen font face. For example *Times Roman* usually needs to be one point larger so that it looks the same size as a sans-serif font.
- Avoid excessive use of different font types (serif, sans-serif, script, ...), font sizes and font styles (bold, italic, underline) which make the text harder to read.
- Left justified text is easier to read because the spacing between words is consistent. Fully justified text has margins that are straight on both sides with the disadvantage is that it is harder to read due to the variable spacing between words. In some cases you will even see "rivers of white" running down a page of text.

NOTE

In printed materials, we never recommend underlining.

- Underlining makes it more difficult to read because it obscures the downstrokes of the letters g j p q y.
- Because of the internet, underlining is now normally used to indicate links that can be clicked. When it's printed on a piece of paper, it can't be clicked, so why have it underlined? If you want to emphasise a word, then **bold** or *italics* are better choices than underlining.

Your Future And The Workplace

- 10 -
Thinking Creatively About Your Future

Your Masters or Doctorate is finished (or soon to be finished)! Before you throw yourself into looking for a job, it's worthwhile to do some creative thinking about your future and your plans, using the questions which follow as a starting point. These questions are important not only because they help you think about your future career but also because they come up in interviews.

1) What would you like to do next?
    - More research?
    - Teaching?
    - Something that is a stepping-stone towards a longer term goal?
    - Applying some or all of what you learned in a different area?
    - Doing something radically different from your research? (A PhD is not a life-sentence!)
2) What are your professional skills?
3) Which supplemental skills have you acquired as a result of your professional and personal activities?
    - Which transferable or "soft-skills" have you learned? For example: Patience, planning, organising, managing individuals and/or teams, negotiation, persuasion, presenting, writing and so on.
4) Which hobbies and sports have you been involved in?
    - Have you played an individual or team sport to a good level?
    - Have you taken part in amateur or professional theatrics?
    - Have you been involved in charity work or fund-raising?
    - Have you travelled extensively?
    - Which memorable experiences have you had?
      Ted knows one young man who bicycled all the way from the UK, across Europe and Asia to Australia. His bicycling skills probably didn't improve dramatically but the scale of the adventure is impressive and could serve as a springboard to something else.
5) What are your personal qualities?
    - Do you like/prefer working alone or as part of a group/team?
    - Do you prefer leading and taking responsibility or are you more comfortable following someone else's lead?
    - Do you have initiative and self-discipline?
    - How well do you tolerate uncertainty and risk?
    - Are you willing to relocate or are there reasons for staying in the city/country where you are now?

6) What makes you different from the other students graduating with a similar degree?
   - Where can you make a unique contribution? This implies a *niche* where you have a competitive advantage.
7) What are the opportunities (locally or globally)?
   - Where could your knowledge, skills and experiences be relevant?
     - This could be in a field or business that already exists.
     - This could be one that you create yourself.
   - From the opportunities available, which ones would be more interesting?
   - Are there any obvious trends that will affect your decisions?
8) Given you answers to the first seven questions, are there any additional knowledge or skills that would contribute towards what you would like to do?

There was one student who came up to Ted at a coffee-break and asked him if he had any advice about looking for a job. Ted asked him what was his PhD research and he responded Databases and Computer Engineering. Ted replied that this sounded a bit vague and could the postgraduate be more specific? The student then answered that it had to do with knowledge management – how an organisation can make optimal use of what it knows and measures. Ted replied "Cool! Where could this be useful?" After several minutes of the postgraduate talking and Ted asking questions requiring specifics and explanations, the student had come up with the following areas where his skills would be useful:

- Data-mining
- Decision-Support
- Troubleshooting
- Risk-management:
  - maintenance of critical systems, such as planes, power stations, hospitals
  - weather
  - insurance
  - finance, loans, investment
- Early-warning systems:
  - design
  - testing
  - deployment

This list is not exhaustive, but it was enough to get the student thinking! And he realised that the area in which he was most interested in applying his PhD skills was the financial sector.

Ted then asked if there were any steps the postgraduate could take that would help him to make a transition towards the financial sector. He thought about it for a minute and then his face lit up and he exclaimed: "I know what I'm going to do next! I'm going to take the one year course to qualify in ... !

After you have considered the above questions, then what would be a reasonable next step? Possibilities might include:

- start looking for a job;
- get some additional training;
- do some volunteer work to gain useful experience;
- start your own business.

How do you search for jobs in the areas that match your skills and interests?

1) Advertisements in trade and research journals.
2) Advertisements in generic subject periodicals – for example, *Science* or *Nature* for people in scientific disciplines.
3) Advertisements in relevant magazines or newspapers.
4) Networking
    - About two thirds of jobs are found through personal contacts. Everyone you know should know you're looking for a job! Use your connections in your search for employment.
        - The average person knows approximately 250 people. So if all of your contacts speak to their contacts, then you have access to 62500 people!
    - Many positions are available but not advertised for a variety of reasons. Meeting and talking to people is your only way of discovering these unadvertised jobs.
    - Meeting and talking to people creates a more favourable and lasting impression than anything you can do online.
5) Professional networking sites, such as *LinkdIn.*
6) Employment websites
7) Professional employment agencies/bureaus
8) If it is possible, visit local companies/institutions that are doing what you're interested in. They may not let you or want you to visit, but if they do, then anything you learn can be useful in your job search. And they may be impressed by your initiative.

Remember, there are more *good* possibilities than you imagine.

- 11 -
Applying For Jobs

This chapter contains advice that is most suited to UK and North American readers. Please remember that there can be important differences between different fields of research and/or countries. Do what is accepted practice for the field, industry or country where you are applying.

Covering Letters Or Emails

Before applying for a position, do as much research as possible about the relevant industry and the particular employer. Use the internet, newspapers, telephone calls, trade journals, and any contacts you know. The answers you find will help in preparing your application. This research will also prove useful if you are called for an interview!

The Covering Letter/Email and CV/Résumé must be prepared for ***each*** position. The combination of employer and position determine what is relevant and useful from the various aspects of your career information. Ask yourself:

> "*How is this information relevant or useful to this position and employer?*"

If you don't have a convincing answer to the above question, then leave that information out! Including irrelevant information will do more harm than omitting one piece of information that *might* be relevant.

For example, if you're applying for a computer programmer's position that doesn't involve visiting clients, then how is it relevant that you have a driving licence?

Purpose Of The Covering Letter/Email

The Covering Letter/Email makes the case why they should be interested in you and your CV. If the Covering Letter/Email is successful, then they will look at your CV/Résumé with more interest. And if your CV/Résumé performs *its* role, then they will invite you for an interview.

Your Covering Letter/Email and CV must be self-explanatory! The employer will not email/telephone you about anything that is unclear! If there is any doubt, then your application goes into the *Reject* pile.

The employer could have a stack of hundreds of applications, so your application will receive at most 30 seconds of their attention during the first pass and probably 60 seconds on the second pass. You must make it relevant, easy and favourable!

- Good layout and presentation
- Bullet points and short phrases/sentences. (They don't want to read paragraphs of text!)
- Short, direct and to the point

Structure Of The Covering Letter/Email

1) Name and contact details at the top.
2) Indicate the position and reference for which you are applying. You can either:
    - Put it in a header below the address and before the body of the letter; or
    - Make the first sentence something like the following:
        - "In response to you advertisement in ... for the position of ... I have enclosed my résumé for your consideration."
        - "I am applying for the ... position advertised in ..."
3) Explain your interest in this position and/or this company. What would be your answers to questions like:
    - Why is this position a logical next step for you?
      e.g. "This position is the logical next step in my career because ... "
    - What interests/excites you about this position?
      e.g. "I am interested in this position (or your company) because ..."
4) Demonstrate/explain how you match the stated job requirements.
    - There are two ways to quickly compare your competencies to the requirements of the position: vertical or horizontal.

Example Layout for Vertical Comparison

The position requires:

- NMR/MRI experience
- Laser spectroscopy experience
- Teamwork and leadership skills

Relevant skills and training:

- B.Sc. in NMR spectroscopy with Professor M.J. Knox
- Ph.D. in Pulsed Laser spectroscopy with Professor I.M. Nobel
- Team captain of local football club for 8 years

Example Layout for Horizontal Comparison	
Requirements Of The Position	**Capabilities**
NMR/MRI experience	B.Sc. NMR spectroscopy with Professor M.J. Knox
Laser spectroscopy experience	Ph.D. Pulsed Laser Spectroscopy with Professor I.M. Nobel
Teamwork and Leadership skills	Team captain of local football club for 8 years

- Do you have any additional skills that are relevant and useful to the position?
- Mention any accomplishments (professional or personal) that demonstrate successful past performances.

5) Make a clear request for the response you want. This could be a telephone call, an informal meeting or, as is often the case, an interview.
   - "I would welcome an interview to discuss this project/position further ..."
   - "I look forward to arranging an interview to discuss my suitability ..."
   - "If my skills and experience are relevant, then I would be pleased to come for an interview."

   Because step 3 and step 4 establish the possibility of a mutually beneficial exchange, then step 5 – your request for an interview – is reasonable.

Good Practice In The Covering Letter/Email

Address it – *by name* whenever possible – to the relevant person!

- If the application is in response to an advertisement, then send it to the person(s) named in the advertisement.
- If you aren't responding to an advertisement and you're taking a chance to see if there are any unadvertised positions available, then send it to the appropriate line-manager. Employers rarely think badly of someone who shows initiative.

If it is a covering letter, then use good quality paper.

- Heavier paper makes a better impression when handled, so use 90 – 100 gsm (A4 or comparable size of 8½ inches x 11 inches in North America).
- Choose white, pale cream, beige or ivory. Avoid coloured or patterned papers and coloured text because these interfere with scanning and photocopying.
- Don't fold or staple the covering letter to your CV. This makes it difficult for someone to make copies for meetings, or the interview.

If it is a covering email, then don't send some specialised file format that requires some specialised program to open it.

- File formats like PDF are generic and will be correctly readable on any Operating System (Windows®, Mac®, Linux, BSD, Unix). PDF files can be protected from being altered by third parties.
  Another advantage of PDFs is that if your computer is infected with malware (viruses, trojans, spyware) then any PDFs you create on your computer are unlikely to be infected.
- The *MS-Word®* format, *.doc, is generally readable. The latest *MS Word®* format, *.docx, requires a corresponding version of *Word®*. Note that *Word®* documents can be altered by third parties unless you password protect them.
  If your computer is infected with malware, then it is possible for your *Word®* documents to be infected as well. If you send an employer an infected document, they will *not* be amused.

Formatting And Layout

- Line spacing: single or 1.5 maximum. Double and triple spacing is harder to read because of the larger spacing and it will make your letter appear longer.
- Use a simple serif or sans-serif font and a point size of 11 – 12. Avoid fancy font faces and excessive use of **bold**, *italics* and <u>underlining</u>!
- Avoid large paragraphs of text! They are unappealing and they won't be read.

Be active, positive, direct and specific.

e.g. "lifetime in research" isn't active and the word *lifetime* makes you sound old.

e.g. "10 years working in biomedical research ... " is better.

CVs / Résumés

Purpose Of The CV/Résumé

The purpose of your CV/Résumé is to demonstrate three points to the potential employer:

1) **Your *interest* in this job** (Career Aims + Professional Profile);
2) **Your *ability* to do this job** (Key Competencies + Training);
3) **Your *accomplishments* both professional and personal.**
   Results are much more important than simply having shown up for work!
   Compare the following and decide which person you would prefer to hire:
   "Worked in the sales department for 2 years." or
   "Increased sales by 10% after 2 years."

During one workshop, a PhD student was interested in applying for a position. One of the requirements was the ability to organise complex projects. He was disappointed and didn't know what to do since his PhD hadn't involved organising a complex project.

After asking him questions about his PhD and his hobbies, it turned out that his hobby was amateur theatre. After further questioning, it turned out that he had organised a complete play from scratch. He'd been involved with choosing and assisting the director, building and painting of the sets, casting, booking the university theatre for the run of the play, and so on.

Finally, Ted asked him if he thought that his experience with organising and delivering a complete play from scratch might be relevant experience for organising complex projects and the position he was interested in. He was amazed that something like that counted as relevant experience!

Principles Of The CV/Résumé

Employers can receive literally hundreds of CVs/Résumés for a position and they will normally invite for interview 3 – 7 people.

Question: How did they reject the other 99% of the applicants so quickly?

Answer: Employers skim and scan, they do not read!

Various surveys have shown that 80% of CVs/Résumés receive *less* than 30 seconds of attention!

CVs/Résumés will pass through several filtering stages.

1) Select *possibles* (approximately 20 - 30 seconds per CV).
2) From the reduced pile of possibles, select *probables* (approximately 1 minute per CV). This stage will focus on comparing requirements of position with competencies and work-experience.
   By the end of the first two filtering stages, you will be lucky if your CV has had 2 minutes of attention in total!
3) From the pile of probables, select interview candidates.

Because they have hundreds of applications to get through, they will not have time to go through each one in detail. They will be quickly scanning the application and looking for *any* reason to reject an application. Often, the initial filtering stages will be done by clerical staff who have no knowledge of the field and are comparing applications quickly against a list of keywords they have been given. Once the hundreds have been filtered to 10 or 20, these remaining applications will be considered by the people more directly involved in the hiring of an applicant.

Structure Of A Good CV/Résumé

NOTE

Length of CVs/Résumés:

- Approximately 10% are 1 page
- Approximately 80% are 2 pages → Two pages has become the 'de facto' standard.
- Approximately 10% are 3 pages

Realistically, if you haven't got enough good stuff in your first two pages to convince them, then additional pages of the same will not increase your chances of getting called for an interview.

The recommended sections in a CV/Résumé are the following:

1) Contact Details

2) Catchphrase – Slogan – Professional Promise *(Optional Section)*

If this is done well, it can hook their attention and provide them with a catchy personal summary. If it is done badly then it comes across as tacky. If you choose to try this, then come up with *at least* 10 catchphrases and then check these with as many work-related acquaintances as possible. If there is one that the majority of people like, then that is probably an acceptable catchphrase.

The catchphrase can also be used on your business cards.

3) Professional Profile – Professional Summary

This is a sales-pitch that answers the interview question – "Tell us a little about yourself." – in approximately 50 words.

- ***Briefly*** summarise your career.
- ***Highlight*** your ***relevant*** skills and accomplishments.
- We recommend never making any claims about your personality in the CV/Résumé because personality traits are difficult to prove on paper.
  - No one ever says anything bad about themselves! So many applicants claim to be "highly motivated, honest, hard-working team-players", that statements like this sound trite and unoriginal.
  - If you claim that you are "highly motivated", then how would you prove this in your CV?
  - And one of the purposes of the interview is for the employer to assess your personality and how you would fit with your potential co-workers.

A trick to writing the Professional Profile/Summary is to write about yourself in either the *first* or *third* person and then delete the personal pronouns and/or adjectives:

1) Think of sentences such as the following:
   - "I have passed my Level 4 ... " (1st person)
   - "My research experience in ... "
   - "S/he is skilled in ... " (3rd person)
2) Remove the first part containing the personal pronouns or adjectives, leaving the remainder of the sentence:
   - "[~~I have~~] Passed Level 4 ... "
   - "[~~My~~] Research experience in ... "
   - "[~~S/he is~~] Skilled in ... "

Alternatively use a construction that combines a factual statement with its meaning:

- "Rising from Lecturer to Reader in 5 years is evidence of my research abilities."
- "Ten years of experience in (...) have prepared me for ..."
- "Increasing sales by 160% in 4 years demonstrates my novel approach to working with customers."

Remember:
You will need to be able to substantiate any claims you make (*e.g.* honesty, motivation, communication skills, *etc.*) in your application.

4) Career Aims

- This is a brief statement about how this position fits with your career direction/aims.
- How is this position a logical next step in your career progression?
- Make sure that your stated career aims are consistent with the position for which you are applying.

5) Key Competencies = Knowledge + Skills *(Optional Section)*

- This section is optional because you will have shown how your skills match the requirements of the position in your covering letter and your work-history follows immediately after this section.
- We would include this only if you have exceptional skills that you want to highlight in a separate section.

6) Work Experience / Career History

- Normally, the focus is upon the most recent 10 years and/or 3-4 positions.
- What were your positions, tasks and responsibilities?
- What did you accomplish that was of value when you were in each position?
- Unless the employer was exceptional or well-known, it can be useful to briefly say what they do, as in the examples later in this chapter.

- Length of time in post is the least important, but it is still considered. For example, if you have had 6 – 8 positions in the past three years, then warning bells will start ringing and they will wonder why you had so many positions in a short period of time.

7) Education, Training and Qualifications

- Education
- Training courses (on-the-job or privately attended)

8) Awards

- Include *any* professional prizes or awards you have won.
- Include any personal awards that are relevant and demonstrate accomplishment.

9) Professional Memberships

- Include membership and status of any *relevant* professional associations or societies.

10) Personal Hobbies and Interests *(Optional Section)*

- Only include a hobby or interest if it is relevant and useful to the position in some way.
  - Running/Swimming ⇒ fit, healthy and disciplined;
  - Club Treasurer ⇒ trustworthy and responsible;
  - Charity/Volunteer work ⇒ unselfish, helpful and *possibly* team-player;
  - Black belt in a martial art
    - ⇒ disciplined, persistent and fit (positive);
    - ⇒ possibility of injury (negative);
  - Travel
    - ⇒ ability to deal with other cultures, ability to plan, willingness to relocate (positive);
    - ⇒ possibility that this person may want their vacation in a block or at an awkward time of the year (negative);
  - Team sports ⇒ team-player
  - Bridge, chess, backgammon, ...
    - ⇒ discipline, logical reasoning and competitive (positive);
    - ⇒ possibly only comfortable solo or in small groups (negative).
- Be sparing in terms of which hobbies or interests you include. Unless it helps with your work, they don't really care. Include too many hobbies/interests and they will wonder when you find time for work.
- Don't mention surfing the internet, video-gaming, drinking or partying as hobbies!

11) Patents, Papers and Presentations

- If it is an *academic* position *and* you have the space (or they specifically ask for it), then you can list your publications here.
  - Often it is sufficient to state how many papers you have published in refereed journals and that a full list can be provided if desired.

    - Highlight any publications that are particularly relevant to the position.
    - With the ease of on-line searching, it is more common for them to do a quick search to see what you have published.
    - Remember that a list of papers is just a list which can be tedious.
- If it is a *non-academic* position:
    - It is sufficient to state how many papers you have published in refereed journals and that a full list can be provided if desired.
    - Be sure to list any patents you have because these will carry more weight than papers.
    - List presentations you have made. If you have made lots of presentations then you can state the number.

12) References

- If the application requires you to provide your references with your CV/Résumé, then include them here.
- If you aren't required to provide references on your CV/Résumé, then omit this section completely. Don't write the phrase "References available upon request." Of course they're available on request! This is stating the obvious.

Never include someone as a reference without first having their agreement that they will act as a reference for you!

In the past, references were only requested and checked after the interview. Now there is a growing trend for organisations to request the references from the beginning, usually to save some administrator some time and work later.

If you provide a list of references with your application then:

- Ensure your referees are qualified and relevant to comment on your work-related capabilities. This would include anyone who has supervised your work either professionally or personally.
- Ensure your referees are easy to contact and will respond promptly.
- Assume your references will have been checked before the interview and that these might serve as the basis for some of the questions you will be asked.

Later in your career, you will need to carefully consider if you really need to include your current employer as a reference.

- What are your reasons for leaving or looking elsewhere?
- Will your current employer 'sabotage' your application so that they can keep you?
- If you end up staying in your current employment, will you be penalised or marginalised for looking elsewhere?

Good Practice In CVs/Résumés

Your CV/Résumé must be:

- Visually pleasing and clean. No stains or smudges on any pages!
- Easy to skim/scan and to find key information;
- Relevant and targeted to the position – essential information only;
- Direct, positive, specific and accurate;
- As brief as possible;
- Suitable for OCR scanning and/or photocopying.
- If hardcopy:
  - Use good quality paper 90 – 100 gsm (A4 or comparable 8½ inches x 11 inches in North America).
  - Use white, pale cream, beige or ivory. Avoid coloured or patterned papers and coloured text because these interfere with scanning and photocopying.
  - Use a board-backed envelope and send your covering letter and CV flat.
  - Send your covering letter and CV Recorded/Registered/Special Delivery. This makes a good impression and guarantees it arrives.
  - Don't put your CV/Résumé in some sort of a cover. It makes it harder for them to deal with. They want to quickly check your CV/Résumé, not unwrap it like a Christmas present! The fancy cover will be thrown away. The cover will also interfere with scanning or photocopying your CV.
  - Don't fold or staple your CV/Résumé. It makes it harder to photocopy or to scan into the computer. Remember, your CV ideally only covers 2 sides, preferably back-to-back.
  - Don't use a two-column format, like newspapers, magazines and journals.
- If it is electronic:
  - Send the covering email with attached CV and request a return-receipt. This means that when it is received you will receive an automatic confirmation.

Formatting And Layout

- Use symmetry and balance in the layout.
- Don't write *Curriculum Vitae* or *CV* or *Résumé* at the top of the page! They know what it is and you will look silly for stating the obvious!
- Use indenting, margins, banding, —— lines ——, borders, frames or highlighting to separate sections and make it easy to navigate.
- Line spacing: 1 to 1.5 but not double-line spaced. 1.25 is a good compromise.
- Use a simple serif or sans-serif font and a point size of 11 – 12. Avoid fancy font faces and excessive **bold**, *italics* and underlining! Bold, italics and especially underling can interfere with optical scanning of your application. Don't use decorative fonts or mixtures of fonts.

- Keep the CV/Résumé short – 1 or 2 pages is ideal. Use three pages only in exceptional circumstances.
  - A long CV/Résumé indicates that you can't select what is relevant and important with respect to the position for which you are applying.
- Use tables and bullet points whenever possible. In general:
  - Work from the top (most important) downwards (least important) *e.g.* present back to the past (reverse chronological).
  - Work from left (most important) to right (least important).
  - For example, several possible formats for your work experience would be:

Format A:		
Chief Executive Assistant	**Megatronix Ltd.** Megatronix does X and has Y staff with an annual turnover of £Z million. • Reported to the Executive Vice-President • Principal Activities and Responsibilities • Major Achievements while there • Important knowledge/skills learned while in this position	2000 – 2004

Format B:	
Chief Executive Assistant / Megatronix Ltd. Megatronix does X and has Y staff with an annual turnover of £Z million. • Reported to the Executive Vice-President • Principal Activities and Responsibilities • Major Achievements while there • Important knowledge/skills learned while in this position	2000 – 2004

Format C:	
Chief Executive Assistant 2000 – 2004	**Megatronix Ltd.** Megatronix does X and has Y staff with an annual turnover of £Z million. • Reported to the Executive Vice-President • Principal Activities and Responsibilities • Major Achievements while there • Important knowledge/skills learned while in this position

Writing Style

- Your CV needs to show your skills and accomplishments quickly and efficiently. It doesn't need to be 'great literature'.
- Minimise, *as much as possible*, the use of personal pronouns (I, me, my, mine, we, ...) and the use of articles (a, an, the). It is futile to attempt to eliminate *all* personal pronouns and articles, but do your best to reduce their usage.
- Be factual, definite and specific. Avoid vague and general statements.
- Use definite, positive, active verbs.
    - Avoid vague or passive verbs. *e.g. elucidated* or "... results were obtained ..."
    - In your covering letter and CV, you want to present the impression that you are active. The passive voice makes it sound like things happened and that you were a spectator.
- Use short sentence-fragments or phrases beginning with concrete and active verbs.

  e.g. "Measured the viscosities of 23 room temperature ionic liquids between 10 to 70 °C. This was the first time that this data was reported in the literature."
  This statement shows an activity (measuring) and 23 results (viscosity data) and indicates the value of the result (first time in literature).
- Show dates as either years (2004–2009) or month + year (Oct 2004 – Sep 2009).

Information/Content

- Tell the truth and only the truth. If the employer finds that you lied about anything, it can give them grounds for unconditional dismissal at a later date.
- Include only what is relevant and useful information. Too much information just bores them and it interferes with them finding the good bits.
- Don't include a photograph (unless the advertisement or application form specifically asks for one). Some positions (*e.g.* acting) will require a photograph and this is not considered discriminatory. A photograph:
    - Does you no favours unless it is professionally taken.
    - Gives them an opportunity to discriminate on the basis of your age, gender, ethnicity or simply your facial expression.
    - Can give the impression you are an egomaniac if you are the only applicant that included a photo.
- Don't include personal details that are irrelevant to performing the job, such as:
    - Age or Date of Birth
    - Gender
    - Nationality (unless you aren't allowed to work legally in the country until the prospective employer has obtained a work permit.)

    - Marital and family status
    - Religion, race, culture or ethnicity, political beliefs
- Don't disclose current or previous salary details.
    - It can be considered to be in poor taste and it implies that you are focused on money.
    - More seriously, from your point of view, it may give them a chance to offer you less money than they had planned or to reject your application because you look too expensive.
- Don't disclose your reasons for leaving any previous employers in your covering letter or CV/Résumé. It may come up in the interview as a question, for which you will have prepared a good answer – won't you?

Appendix 5 has examples of bad and good covering letters and CVs.

Keep Track of Your Applications!

Make sure to keep a check-list of the applications you have sent. There is nothing worse than being contacted by an employer you don't remember having sent an application!
We suggest keeping a table or spreadsheet that has columns for:

- position + reference number;
- company + address;
- contact person + telephone/email;
- date sent;
- response;
- follow-up.

Keep a copy of your Covering Letter/Email + CV/Résumé by the telephone and another copy with you at all times. Telephone interviews are becoming more common as a method for an initial screening of candidates, before inviting them for interviews in person. It makes a poor impression if you don't remember what you put in your application!

- 12 -
Interviews

Purpose Of The Interview

The interview is:

- your attempt to determine whether you really would like to work there;
- the employer's attempt to assess how you will perform and fit in.

Formal interviews with a panel are typically 20 – 60 minutes. Some positions may require a series of interviews and/or tests over a period of days or weeks. For other positions, such as academic ones, a visit of an entire day might be involved. This would include an interview, giving a seminar and having discussions with various members of staff.

Consider your *entire* visit as the interview.

Presume that *everyone* you talk to will be reporting back to the interview panel about what you said and did, as well as their impressions. The same is true even if you share a meal with prospective colleagues, which is common in an all-day interview/visit. The conversation may turn to lighter non-research related topics but it is safe to assume that they are still trying to get a sense of who you are and whether you will fit in with the group.

It is not over until you have left the building and sent them a thank-you note or email.

What Are *You* Looking For?

- See if you like the position, the company and the people you will be working with. Remember, they will always treat you nicer at the interview than they will when you work for them!
  - If you fit the company, but not the position then see if they have other positions available.
  - If you fit the position, but not the company then look for similar positions with other employers. Don't take this job unless you're desperate.
  - If you fit the position and the company and they think you are the best candidate, then they will offer you the job. Accept it if you are happy with the working conditions and terms of employment.
- Check whether they are being open or if they seem to be hiding anything. What do their questions or statements imply or suggest about them as employers? For example if they ask:
  "Do you mind working long hours? We have a company culture of putting in long days." then this could imply:

  → They emphasize hours-worked over productiveness and efficiency.

→ They are *seriously* understaffed.
→ They mismanage projects and duties.
→ There is a lot of stress and unrealistically short deadlines.

What Are *They* Looking For?

They've seen how you look on paper and now they want to see what you are like in person. They will be looking for answers to the following questions.

1) Can you do the job?
   - Do your competencies (Knowledge and Skills) and personal characteristics match the requirements of the position?
2) Why do you want this position?
   - What is your interest in this occupation, position and/or the employer?
3) What have you accomplished in the past?
   - Motivation is important but past accomplishments are the most reliable indicators of future performance.
4) Will you fit in and get along with people?
   - Personality *e.g.* optimist/pessimist
   - Interpersonal Skills (Teams, Communication, Leadership, ...)
5) Will you stay?
   - This is an important question because staff turnover is a major operating loss for any organisation.
6) Will you be cost-effective?
   - How much will you cost?
   - Will your value to the employer be greater than your cost?
   - Will you be an efficient choice? For example, available sooner, less training required, more skilled, cheaper, more cooperative, ...

Approximately 70% of operational expenses are associated with salaries and various staff-support functions. Since salaries comprise such a substantial fraction of operating expenses, the employer will want value-for-money.

Salary

When you go to the interview, you must be clear on the absolute lowest salary you can afford to accept. If their final offer is less than this, then you will need to refuse. If you accept a lower salary than your minimum you will not be happy working there and you won't have enough money to pay your bills.

If they bring up salary during the interview, then this is a good sign. At this point, you can begin to be more assertive in the interview. They may ask about salary for any number of reasons. For example:

- they are genuinely interested in you as a candidate;
- they want to hire you at the lowest salary they can. Getting you to name your price first is a standard negotiating tactic, since inexperienced negotiators often make their opening bid too low.

Defer answering questions about salary until as late as possible, preferably after they have offered you the job (and you have decided you would like it). For example:

- "I will need to know more about the position and responsibilities before I would be in a position to decide what I would consider an acceptable salary."
- "I would base my decision to accept or reject an offer on the basis of the overall negotiated package. Salary would be one part of this and would be negotiable depending upon the other terms."
- Alternatively you can answer with a *salary range* that either you would find acceptable or is typical for that position, in that industry, in that geographical area.

Salaries Are Negotiable!

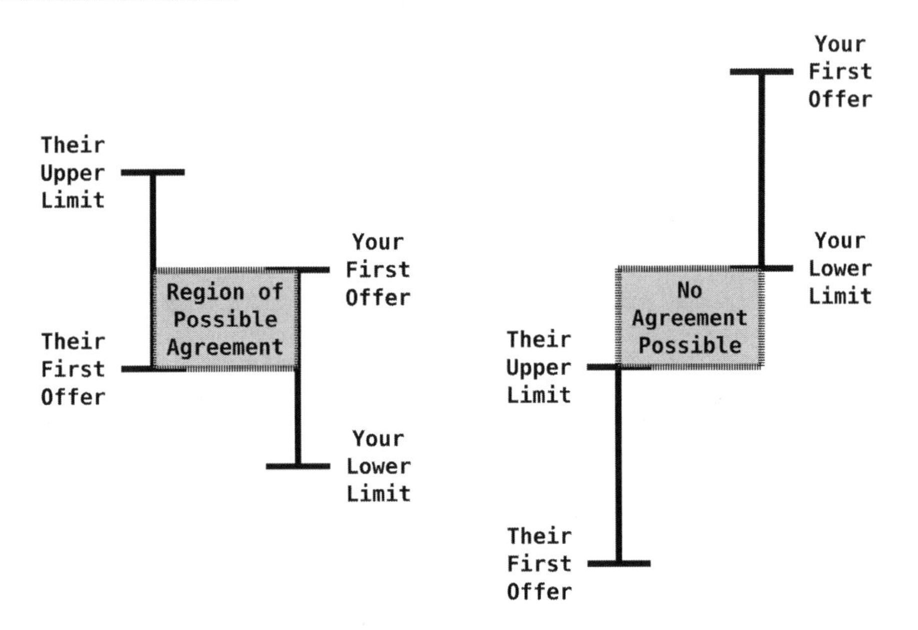

Their first offer will generally be at the bottom end of their range. Avoid suggesting a salary first and if you must, then suggest something at the top end of the range you want – because they will usually argue you *downwards* towards their minimum. If they offer you a salary that you find unacceptable, then this is either a test to see how you respond or they are serious. You have several ways you could respond to this, for example:

- "Is that your final offer?" (Ask gently, not aggressively.)
- "As it stands, that isn't acceptable. Are there any additional non-salary benefits?"

- "I see." and then remain silent – as if thinking – for as long as it takes for them to speak again. By indicating hesitation, you are forcing them to raise their offer without giving them your own figure. This option is the toughest to execute but generally produces the best results. It also works well with sales-people.

Although salaries are negotiable, there will be an upper limit to what they are willing and/or able to offer as a salary. Beyond that, they will decide to offer the position to their second or third place candidates.

At the end of the interview, you need to decide if the job, salary, working conditions and other benefits are good enough. Make sure you don't have any doubts or questions before you accept the offer. Once you have been hired, if you leave within a year then it looks bad on your CV and the employer you leave is unlikely to give you a good reference.

Remember that other things have value besides salary!
For example:

- Are there health or dental plans?
- Are the working hours flexible? Can you work from home some days?
- Will they contribute towards some or all of your commuting costs?
- Are there on-site facilities for childcare or fitness?
- Are the rates for bonuses or commissions negotiable?

The above non-salary items would save you money and/or make your life more convenient. Non-salary items often come out of other budgets, so it can be easier to negotiate gains on these non-salary elements than on salary itself.

Surveys indicate that when employees quit, salary is the reason for approximately 10% of the cases. This means that 90% of the time, people leave for reasons ***not*** related to salary.

Your current salary is *personal* and there is no obligation to tell them. They won't be telling you *their* salaries will they! Furthermore, what you are currently paid is irrelevant to both job-performance and what you should be paid for this new position, if they hire you.

If they have a "Current Salary" box on the application and you leave it blank, they have no grounds for rejecting you.

If they have a "Desired/Expected Salary" box then you need to think carefully what you will put in it.

- If you state too high a salary, then you will be rejected as unreasonable.
- If you state too low a salary then you risk being paid less than the employer would have been willing to pay. By underpricing yourself, you will also look desperate.

You could put *Negotiable* or a salary range in this box. If this upsets them, then you probably wouldn't be happy working there anyway!

Telephone Interviews

Although face-to-face interviews are the norm, telephone interviews are becoming more frequent:

- for initial screening of candidates before inviting people for face-to-face interviews;
- when there is some urgency; or
- when the distances involved make it difficult to book flights and schedule an interview within the required time-frame.

To cope with telephone interviews:

- Keep copies of your covering letters and CV by the telephone at home and with you at all times. You will need to refer to it during the interview.
- Make sure your home telephone has an answer-machine or voice-mail.
- Keep your mobile fully charged at all times. Also, realise that a telephone interview on your mobile could prove to be expensive, especially if you live in Europe. You may want to suggest a mutually convenient time when you can use a land-line.

Preparation For The Interview

It is useful to have answers to as many of the following questions as possible.

The Industry/Market

- How has the industry been performing?
- What are the trends in their market?
- What are the new factors or developments which may play a role?
- What is the market volume (*i.e.* total sales per annum)?
- What geographical variations are there in the industry?

The Employer

- What is their market-share?
- What is their product or service?
- Who are their clients/customers?
- Who are their competitors and how do they rank?
- Does this employer have a reputation for paying a fair salary?
- Does this employer have a reputation for good relations with its employees?

The Position

- What are the *responsibilities* of the position?
- What are the *deliverables* which you are expected to produce?
- How do these deliverables contribute to the company's success and survival?
- How might they check and assess your performance (activity) and effectiveness (results)?
- How much does this position pay in this industry and this geographical area?

Having answers to these questions will demonstrate that you are well-informed and up-to-date. These answers also have implications for the salary you can expect and how much the employer will be willing to spend to have this job done.

Anticipate Questions And Prepare Answers

Anticipate possible questions that you will be asked on the basis of your covering letter and CV. Preparing answers before the interview, means that you will give better and quicker answers to their questions and make a better impression.

For The Interview

- Dress conservatively and formally. Dark colours are preferred but not essential.
- **Turn off your mobile!** If it rings during the interview, then you have probably just lost the job because you didn't think of this beforehand and/or you value talking on your mobile phone more highly than finding employment.

During The Interview

- In terms of the impression you make on people:
  - **60% is visual** ⇒ appearance and body language (stance, gestures, facial expressions, eye contact)
  - **30% is auditory** ⇒ volume, pitch, inflection, pace, pauses, emphasis
  - **10% is verbal** ⇒ what you say
- Make eye contact and smile as often as justifiable.
- You want to come across as patient, polite and professional.
- Show them you can solve their problems, make them rich, successful and famous.

Never:

- Chew gum, smoke, play with personal items, fidget, bring food or drinks with you, answer your mobile phone or arrive late.
- Argue with them, unless you've decided you don't want the job.
- Interrupt them while they are speaking. If you must interject something before they go too far, then interrupt by using a gesture such as raising your hand slightly.
- Dominate the conversation.
- Blame, make excuses, complain, criticise. This makes you sound ineffectual.

Questions They Are Allowed To Ask You

- They may ask about anything which is relevant to performing the job.
- They may 'discriminate' on the basis of job-related performance issues. They *may* ask things like the following:
  - "Can you lift a 40 kg box to waist height?" They may not discriminate on the basis of *gender*, but they may discriminate on the basis of *strength* if the job requires lifting heavy objects.
  - "Are you old enough to serve liquor?" if you are applying to work in a pub.
  - "Are you legally entitled to work in this country?"
  - "Are there any issues that might interfere with the amount of international travel that is involved in this position?"

Questions They Aren't Allowed To Ask You

- If it is *personal* and/or *irrelevant* to performing the job, then they *should* not ask. *e.g.* race, religion, political beliefs, sexual preferences, family status, health, ...
- They might ask you a disallowed question:
  - to see how you handle a potentially awkward situation; or
  - because they are inexperienced and weren't aware of the issue.

Subject Areas For Questions

- Situations/Circumstances/Conditions
  - Yours, the employer's, the employer's industry, ...
- Competencies (knowledge and skills)
  - Thinking and reasoning abilities
  - Planning, organizing and managing
  - Problem solving and creativity
  - Interpersonal skills (Communication, Teamwork, Leadership)
  - Numeracy and literacy
  - Computing skills
- Training, Education and Qualifications

They won't generally ask questions to test your factual professional knowledge since this should have been established by your qualifications and experience and it is a waste of valuable interview time.

If they do ask factual questions, then it might indicate that:

- they have some doubt about your knowledge, skills or experience;
- they are checking your problem-solving skills; or
- they are inexperienced interviewers and don't really know what they should be asking.

- Work Experience
- Professional Memberships
- Opportunities and Obstacles
  - How have you recognized these?
  - How have you responded to them?
- Achievements, Accomplishments and Awards
- Failures and Mistakes
  - What were they? What did you learn?
- Personal Characteristics
  - Initiative and motivation
  - Persistence, perseverance and discipline
  - Awareness and sensitivity
  - Flexibility and adaptability
  - Resilience and fluidity
  - Personal preferences, attitudes, values, ...
- Personal Interests – often used to "break the ice" when the interview begins.

Types Of Questions

- **Open** = Interpretive or explanatory
  e.g. "How would you assess market trends for the next 5 years?"
- **Closed** = Yes/No or Factual
  e.g. "How many years did you work at ...?"
- **Probing** = digging deeper for detail and specifics
  e.g. "Tell us more about the project failure at ...?"
- **Leading/Presupposed** = hinting, implying or suggesting something about you or the expected answer. This can sometimes be a trick question.
  e.g. "Wouldn't you say that your performance was mediocre at ...?"
  e.g. "Isn't it fair to say that ...?"
- **Conditional**, **Hypothetical** or **What if** ...?
  e.g. "What would you do if ...?"
  e.g. "How would you estimate the number of Indian restaurants in the UK?" Make your answer as concrete and tangible as possible. Think out loud so they can hear your reasoning.
- **Feeling/Experiential/Personality/Motivational**
  e.g. "How did you feel about ...?"
- **Values/Ethical/Moral**
  e.g. "What do you think about truth in advertising?" or "What do you think about animal rights?"
- **Cartesian** (checking both sides of an issue or point)
  e.g. Strengths and Weaknesses, Opportunities and Threats, Successes and Failures, Likes and Dislikes

Behavioural Interviewing is becoming more common. This uses questions about how you have performed in particular situations in the past. Your past performance is considered to be the most reliable indicator of your future performance. The principle is that: "If you have done it in the past, then you are likely to do it in the future."

They will be noticing:

- Incomplete answers;
- Vague answers or missing information;
- Hypothetical answers;
- Ambiguous or evasive answers;
- Responses where you used words like *all*, *every*, *none*, *never*, *always*;
- Responses that were emotionally charged (tone of voice or choice of words);
- Rambling or long-winded answers.

Answering Questions

- If you need to, pause to think before answering.
- Keep your answers direct, positive, active and specific. Aim for answers that are not longer than 1 to 2 minutes.
  - Avoid dominating the conversation. Initially, you are there to answer *their* questions.
  - Avoid overloading them with details for which they haven't asked.
- When they ask a question, ask yourself what is the concern or issue that is motivating their question. What are they really concerned about?
- For any weaknesses, mistakes, failures, ... explain:
  - the situation was ... ;
  - the corrective actions you took;
  - what you learned or have improved;
  - why it shouldn't happen again.

Brief stories or anecdotes (60 – 90 seconds) about how you have dealt with similar situations in the past are excellent ways to answer questions, as long as you keep it to the point. The stories should follow the approximate guidelines below:

10% on what was the initial **Situation** and **Problem**?

60% on what **Choices** and **Actions** did you take and why?

20% on what were the **Outcomes** and **Consequences**?

10% on what was **Learned**?

The story needs to be strong, clear and *brief*!

- When answering questions about teamwork, make sure to mix "I" and "we" pronouns so it sounds like you were an active member of the team and you still give credit to the contributions of the other members.
- When they ask "How ... ?", they are looking for a 'recipe' or step-by-step procedure which you either have followed in the past or would follow in the future.
- Options for answering:
  - Answer the question.
  - Ask further specification and clarification if the question is vague or ambiguous.
  - Check their assumptions. *e.g.* "When you ask ... are you assuming ... ?"
  - Ask them to rephrase the question.
  - Ask them to repeat the question.
  - Take time to think about it and then answer.
  - For multi-part questions, remember and answer the first part. Then ask them to repeat the 2nd, 3rd, 4th parts. Your job is to answer the questions. Their job is to ask the questions and this means that they are responsible for keeping track of their questions – not you.

NOTE

There is a principle of balanced or reciprocal disclosure of information.
For example, if they are unwilling to reveal anything about the other candidates they are interviewing, then you don't need to reveal anything about the status of your other job applications.

Examples Of Some Questions With Answers

"Tell us about yourself."

Good:

"I'm interested in this position because it will build upon the skills and experience I have and let me work on proteins which is something new for me. Your position requires experience with NMR/MRI and laser spectroscopic methods. My BSc project involved NMR of carbohydrates and my PhD project involved laser spectroscopic measurements of DNA denaturation. Although I have not worked directly with proteins, working with carbohydrates and DNA means that I'm familiar with proteins. The position also specifies the ability to identify and rectify electronic artefacts caused by high magnetic fields. Dealing with instrumental problems was a part of my BSc and PhD research. Because of this, I also voluntarily attended two postgraduate courses, one in Electronics and the other in Instrumentation. Your advertisement mentioned computing skills in a general way. My computing skills include the usual software, such as *Word*, *Excel*, as well as specialist software used in NMR, laser spectroscopy and data visualisation. I also have some experience programming in BASIC and FORTRAN. In terms of teamwork, I worked in large research groups during my BSc and PhD projects, so I have experience of coordinating my activities with other team members. In the final year of my PhD I was in involved in helping the new postgraduate student who would be continuing the work after I left."
(220 words ≈ 2 minutes at a speaking rate of 100 words-per-minute)

Mediocre:

"I was born in France. My father was English and my mother was French. We moved to the UK when I was ten, so I am bilingual. I did my A levels at East Finchley School, my BSc at King's College and my PhD at UCL. I'm honest and hard-working and I'm really excited by this position and I think I can make a valuable contribution."
(66 words ≈ 40 seconds)

Poor:

"What do you want to know? Personal or professional stuff?"

"Tell us about how you handle obstacles or problems – either in your research or in your interactions with colleagues."

Good:

"Well last week, two of the new postgraduate students were set up to repeat an important experiment. But after they began, the signal progressively disappeared over a thirty minute period. They asked me if I could help. Although I had a pretty good idea what the problem was, since it had happened to me. I wanted the students to learn how to deal with situations like this in the future without me, so I asked them questions to get them to think about the possibilities of what might have happened. We started by checking the power connections, the leads and the indicators on the equipment. These were all OK. Next I asked the students to show me the reagents bottles they used and then their lab book where they calculated the concentrations for the reagents. I asked them about what would happen with their DNA samples when various changes were made to the ionic strength and the p*H* of the solution. That's when they realised that the DNA must have condensed and precipitated out of solution. When they lowered the p*H* and resonicated the solution, the signal reappeared."
(188 words ≈ 2 minutes)

Mediocre:

"I encountered frequent experimental problems during my BSc and PhD projects. I always approached them in a systematic way. I'd figure out what the possible causes could be and then I'd check each one. In terms of interpersonal problems, I got along with most of the group except for this one postdoc from ... We just did *not* get along. Finally I suggested we have a chat with the Prof. and we managed to come to a workable compromise. We still didn't get along personally, but at least we got along at work."
(94 words ≈ 1 minute)

Poor:

"I didn't really have any problems with either of my projects. They were pretty routine and everything worked smoothly. I got along with most of the group and we'd always go out for a few beers every night after we'd finished."

"Why do you think you're the best candidate for the position?"

Good:

"There is no way for me to know if I'm the best candidate since I don't know the other candidates or their backgrounds. I have demonstrated that I'm interested in this position and capable of performing it. It is up to you to decide if I best match your requirements."

Mediocre – Poor:

"I have demonstrated that I'm interested in this position and capable of performing it. Add to that the fact that I'm highly motivated and hard-working and you have the best person in front of you."

Note: This answer includes vague statements such as "highly motivated" and borders on arrogance.

"This position requires a security clearance. Is there anything that would prevent you passing a security screening?"

Good:

"No, there is nothing to my knowledge that would prevent me from passing a security screening."
Note: If there is something that will show up in a security screening, then you will need to answer "Yes" although you are not obligated to give them specifics. For some positions, they won't expect you to be a saint, but they will expect you to be completely *honest.* If there is something in your past, then perhaps you probably shouldn't be applying for this job.

"What do you think is an appropriate salary for someone with your experience?"

Good:

"For this sort of position, in this industry and this area of the country, the salary would range from ⟨...⟩ to ⟨...⟩. What I would be willing to accept would depend upon how the rest of this interview goes and what the total remuneration package is like."
Note: This answer shows that you have done the background research and know what a reasonable salary range is for this position.

Mediocre:

"I wouldn't accept anything less than £30,000 per year."
Where did the £30,000 figure come from? Is this even reasonable as a starting salary?

Poor:

"I don't know. What are you offering?"

"Do you have any other offers?"

Good:

"I have made several applications for other positions. It will be a question of which one produces the best offer."
Note: This shows that you are actively pursuing opportunities. This is an example of *reciprocal disclosure*: if they do not tell you about their other candidates, then you are under no obligation to tell them about your other applications.

Poor:

"I have one offer already, but I'm waiting to see how this interview goes before I tell them one way or the other."
Note: This is a negative-hire answer. It indicates that you don't deal fairly.

"I don't know why you think you are suitable for this position."

Note: This *question* is not a question, but a confrontational assertion of your unsuitability. It is also inherently illogical since they invited you for an interview, which means that a majority of them decided that you were suitable. So this is either a test question or these employers are illogical and/or bullies.

Good:

"The position as advertised required ... I have demonstrated my ability and experience in those areas. Are there aspects of this job that weren't advertised?"

Good:

"What are your specific doubts?"
Note: This is asking them to specifically identify the issues they are criticising. It forces them to commit themselves to particular points, which you can then address.

Risky:

"If I'm unsuitable for the position, then why did you invite me? It seems like a waste of everyone's time."
Note: This answer is definitely "cheeky". Only use it if you're willing to risk losing the job.

"What would you do if your partner telephoned that your child was taken ill?"

Note: This question is probing for personal details irrelevant to performing the job – so it is not normally allowed. Even if you have already mentioned earlier in the interview that you have a partner and/or children, this is not relevant to how you would perform if you were hired.

Good:

"Hypothetically speaking, if I received a call that my child was ill, then my decision would depend upon how serious it was. If it was the flu, then it could wait until I returned home. Out of curiosity, does your company have a policy on this sort of occurrence?"

Good:

"Is this question indicating that your company rates business more highly than the health of the children of its employees?"
Note: This is *Interview Question Jujutsu*, where you have flipped the question and they are now on the defensive. This could be a risky approach depending upon how they take it.

"Do you thrive under pressure?" or **"How do you handle stress?"**

Good:

"Is this a stressful position? Is it under-resourced in terms of personnel, equipment or budget? Are the deadlines unrealistically short?"

Poor:

"I can't handle pressure at all. I just fall apart like a wet tissue."

"How would your partner respond if we offered you the post and this required relocation to ...?"

Note: This question is also probing for personal details irrelevant to performing the job – so it is not normally allowed.

Good:

"S/He certainly wouldn't be thrilled about relocating, but it will depend upon how attractive the overall package is. I would need to discuss any offer with them before I could accept."
Note: This confirms that you have a partner/spouse and uses this fact to put pressure on them to offer a more attractive package, since there is an absent third party who must be satisfied.

Good:

"Relocating to ... would not be a problem. Would you be providing any help with the relocation, such as temporary accommodation or covering the expenses of moving?"
Note: This response doesn't say anything about a possible partner, while confirming a willingness to relocate. You then use their question to probe for what support the employer would provide to assist with the relocation which they would want you to make if hired.

Good:

"How is the opinion of my possible partner relevant to my on-the-job performance?"
Note: This answer is potentially confrontational. If you've decided you don't want this job, then enjoy the fireworks!

Some Possible Questions To Ask The Interviewers

What questions must you have answers to, before you can decide whether or not to accept the position? Make sure to ask these questions before you leave the interview! Realise that when you ask *certain* questions you will be revealing personal information. But if you need the answer, then it is a fair trade-off. For example, if you ask:

- "Does the company have a day-care facility on-site?" This implies that either you have children or are planning to have children. This offers them personal information about which they are not allowed to ask, but since *you* raised it first then they can pursue this with follow-up questions.

- "What is the company's policy on sickness leave?" They will wonder why this is so important that you have asked a question about it.

The questions which follow will provide you with useful information with which to judge the position and employer. These questions also don't imply anything unfavourable about you as a candidate.

- "Do you have any reservations about my suitability? If so, what are they and what would you need to know to remove these reservations?"
- "How many candidates are you interviewing for this position?"
- "Is this a new position or is it refilling a vacancy?"
    - If it is refilling a vacancy, then ask why did the previous person leave and how long has it been available? The employer may not want to answer this question because it might reveal unfavourable aspects to working there. Either way, the answer or their evasion will be useful to know.
    - "How long has the position been vacant?"
- "What is the average turnover in the company?" Again they may not want to answer this question, but it can tell you a lot about how satisfying it is to work for this employer.
- "What is the turnover for this position?" or "What is the average length of stay in this position."
- "How did you arrive at that salary figure (or range)?"
- "Did you attempt to fill this position internally?"
- "What are the main deliverables/objectives of the position?"
- "How does this position fit within the corporate strategy?"
- "What are the major concerns of this position?"
- "What areas would you like to see improved?"
- "To whom would I report?"
- "Who reports to me?" (The more people who report to you, the larger you should expect the salary to be, since you have more responsibility.)
- "What annual budget would I be responsible for?"
- "When are the heavy and light periods you mentioned and what percentage of the annual workload do they comprise?"
- "How will you assess performance?"
- "Are there performance-related incentives?"

If they are hiring you from outside instead of promoting or transferring an internal candidate, then be prepared for the internal candidate either to cause problems for you or to quit soon after you arrive. You certainly shouldn't expect the internal candidate to give you willing cooperation, since they were 'passed over' for you.

At the end of the interview confirm what happens next, when and by whom.

- When will they notify you one way or the other?
- Is there anything that they have agreed to do or to send you? When is the deadline?
- Is there anything that you have agreed to send them? When is the deadline?

After The Interview

- Make notes:
  - The questions you were asked and the answers you gave (that you can remember).
  - If necessary, prepare better answers for future interviews.
  - What is the next step, who makes it and when?
- Add the notes from the interview to your file with the Covering Letter and CV that you sent. Keep a file for each position for which you apply.
- A note or email thanking them for their time and consideration never hurts.
  - Politeness is always appreciated and you may apply to these people again at a later date. Or they might move to a company to which you will someday apply.
- Send anything you agreed that you would, before the deadline.
- If you aren't interested in the position, say so and wish them well in their search.
- If you weren't offered the position then:
  - Ask to be considered for future positions (assuming that you are interested in working for this organisation).
  - It is worth asking the interviewers and/or HR people for feedback on your covering letter, CV and interview performance. They may not tell you but if they do it will be extremely useful for future applications.

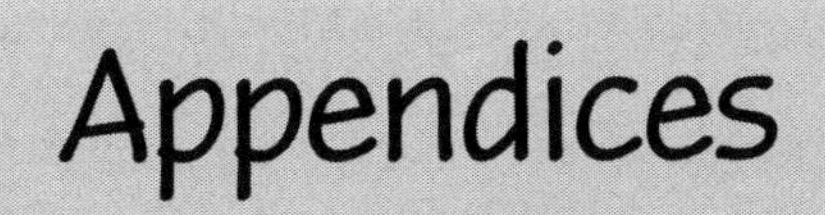

Appendices

- Appendix 1 -
Guidelines For Causal/Concept-Mapping

Because we have blurred the boundary between causal- and concept-mapping in this book, we will refer to both techniques by a more generic label: *C/C-mapping*.

A Bit Of Theory

Causal/Concept-mapping is a method for representing information and interactions as a networked structure, without the distraction of sentences or paragraphs. There are several books published on both techniques, as well as papers and material on the internet.

The advantages of C/C-mapping are:

- It reduces the reliance on words and represents the material more visually.
- It is more generic/flexible than a hierarchical format because there is no central idea that is imposed upon the material from the beginning.
- It emphasises and respects the network/systemic structure of information.
- In a map of a logical argument, it can:
  - represent the pattern or structure of the information;
  - represent the flow or sequence of inferences in a logical argument.
- The representation of flow means it can also represent dynamic or time-dependent events in a developing situation.
- It can represent more complex interactions, such as systems with feedback loops.
- It can reveal contradictions, inconsistencies, and gaps in the material or the logic of the argument. This leads to more constructive questioning.

We don't use mind-maps (spider diagrams) or text-outlines because:

- they presume one central concept;
- they presume and impose a hierarchical structure;
- they don't represent the flow or sequence of ideas which is required for mapping out logical reasoning;
- they can't represent the development over time.

Drawing C/C-Maps

Nodes

- Nodes are typically represented as closed figures, such as ellipses, rectangles, circles or squares.
- Nodes can contain:
  - an *agent* or *entity* – anything that can take action of some kind.
  - an *action* or *task* that needs to be performed. This makes the map more like a PERT diagram.
  - an assertion or claim, when they are used to represent the logic of an argument.
  - a question
  - a concept or idea
  - a measurable or qualitative aspect of something, such as *(Birth Rate)* or *(Quality of Life)*.
  - a *condition* or an *event*
- Nodes have ***neutral*** labels.
  - Examples of neutral labels would be:
    - "Age of Population"
    - "Exercise" or if relevant, a specific type such as "Cardiovascular Exercise";
    - "People on Sickness Benefit"
  - Examples of labels that aren't neutral because they indicate a *direction* or a *change* would be:
    - "*Increasing* Age of Population"
    - "*Less* Exercise"

    Don't use adjectives/adverbs such as *more, less, faster, slower, younger, older* ...
- When redrawing a map, it can improve the clarity of the map if you group related nodes closer together and minimise the number of crossing arrows.
- When mapping a logical argument, you can add a note for the source of each piece of evidence, for example Table 1, Figure 2, Reference 7, ...

Arrows

- The arrows connect the nodes.
  - If one node has no *direct* effect on another then there should be no arrow connecting them!
- Arrowheads indicate the direction and flow of the relationship or interaction.
  - When an interaction is mutual (two-way), this is best represented by two separate single-headed arrows.

- The two ends of an arrow could have the following possible meanings/interpretations:

Precedes ... comes before ...	⟶	Follows after/from ...	Time
Leads to ...	⟶	Follows after/from ...	Causation
Causes ... contributes to ...	⟶	Results from ... or Is an effect of ...	Causation
Stimulates ... initiates ...	⟶	Is the response to ...	Causation
Sends Is the source of ...	⟶	Receives Is the sink for ...	Flow or Transfer
Is a precondition to ... Is a prerequisite to ...	⟶	Is a consequence of ...	Logic
⟨...⟩ is transformed ...	⟶	Into ⟨...⟩	Process

- Feel free to develop additional ways of indicating anything important (*e.g.* aspects, characteristics or relationships) by using colour, line style or the shape of nodes.
  - For example, we use:
    - single-headed thick dashed lines (||||||||||||||||||||||▶) to indicate that ⟨*node A*⟩ *implies* ⟨*node B*⟩; and
    - double-headed thick dashed lines (◀||||||||||||||||||||||▶) to indicate a *comparison* between two nodes.
- If you share your C/C-maps with others, then make sure you provide them with a legend for the symbols you use, especially if your symbolism might be non-standard.

Arrowheads

- The arrowheads can be labelled with words or symbols to define the nature of the interaction. For example:
  - If a change in one node changes another node in the same direction, then this relationship is indicated by a plus (+) sign or "s" for *same* direction:
    - if ⟨*node 1*⟩ *increases* then ⟨*node 2*⟩ *increases;* or
    - if ⟨*node 1*⟩ *decreases* then ⟨*node 2*⟩ *decreases.*

  - If a change in one node changes another node in the opposite direction (inverse/reciprocal) manner, then this relationship is indicated by a minus (–) sign or "o" for *opposite* direction:
    - if ⟨*node 1*⟩ *increases* then ⟨*node 2*⟩ *decreases;* or
    - if ⟨*node 1*⟩ *decreases* then ⟨*node 2*⟩ *increases.*
  - *Uncertain/questionable* connections could be indicated by a large "?" indicating that they need to be verified.
  - *Contradicts* or *inconsistent-with* could be indicated by "≠" or a large "X".

Let's take an example which was in Chapter 3. This example shows:

- nodes which have *neutral* labels;
- arrows indicating the interactions; and
- signs on the arrowheads indicating the *direction* of the effects.

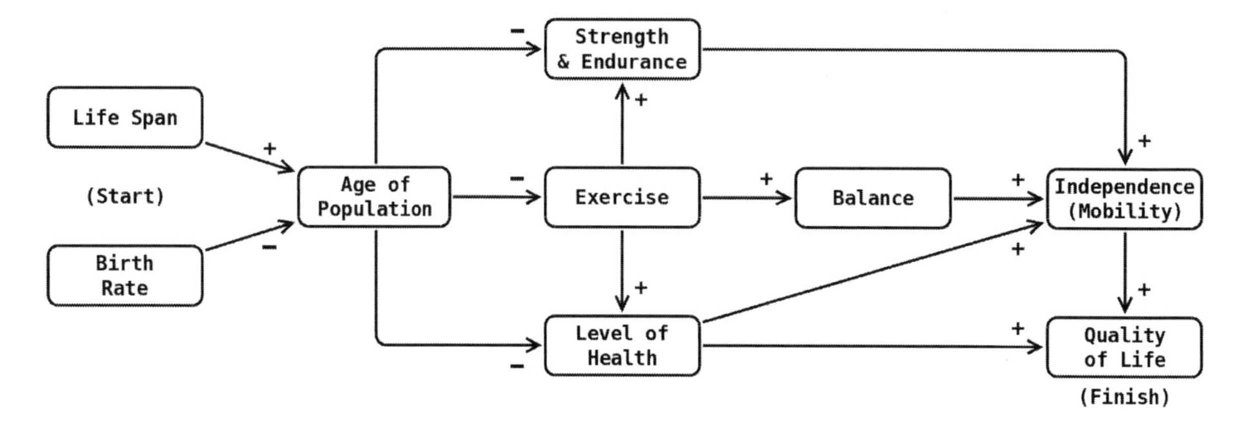

Including The Element Of Time: Working Upstream And Downstream

In some situations, you will want to explicitly represent the element of time in your C/C-maps.

Working Upstream

The question which typically indicates working backwards in time is something like:

What must come before this?

- This is working backwards in time and Ted calls this working *upstream*, like going up a river towards its source. People from engineering backgrounds also refer to this as *reverse design*.
- Working *upstream* defines the necessary and/or sufficient preconditions, prerequisites or causes for a given condition/state.

As an example, let's imagine the reverse design process when engineers first had the idea of making a portable CD player in the late 1970s. If they were going to design and build a portable CD player that was successful commercially, then what things would have to be true in order for people to want to buy it? These would be ⟨*Competitive price*⟩, ⟨*Light weight*⟩, ⟨*Small size*⟩, ⟨*Useful battery life*⟩ and

⟨*Plays CDs*⟩. Then what else would have to be true in order for these to be the result? Notice that as we work upstream, we can see that using speakers is going to be inconsistent with the desired low weight, small size and long battery-life. Headphones are consistent with light weight, small size and low power consumption, which is why they were chosen in reality. Similarly, low weight and competitive price would be favoured by the use of as many plastic parts as possible.

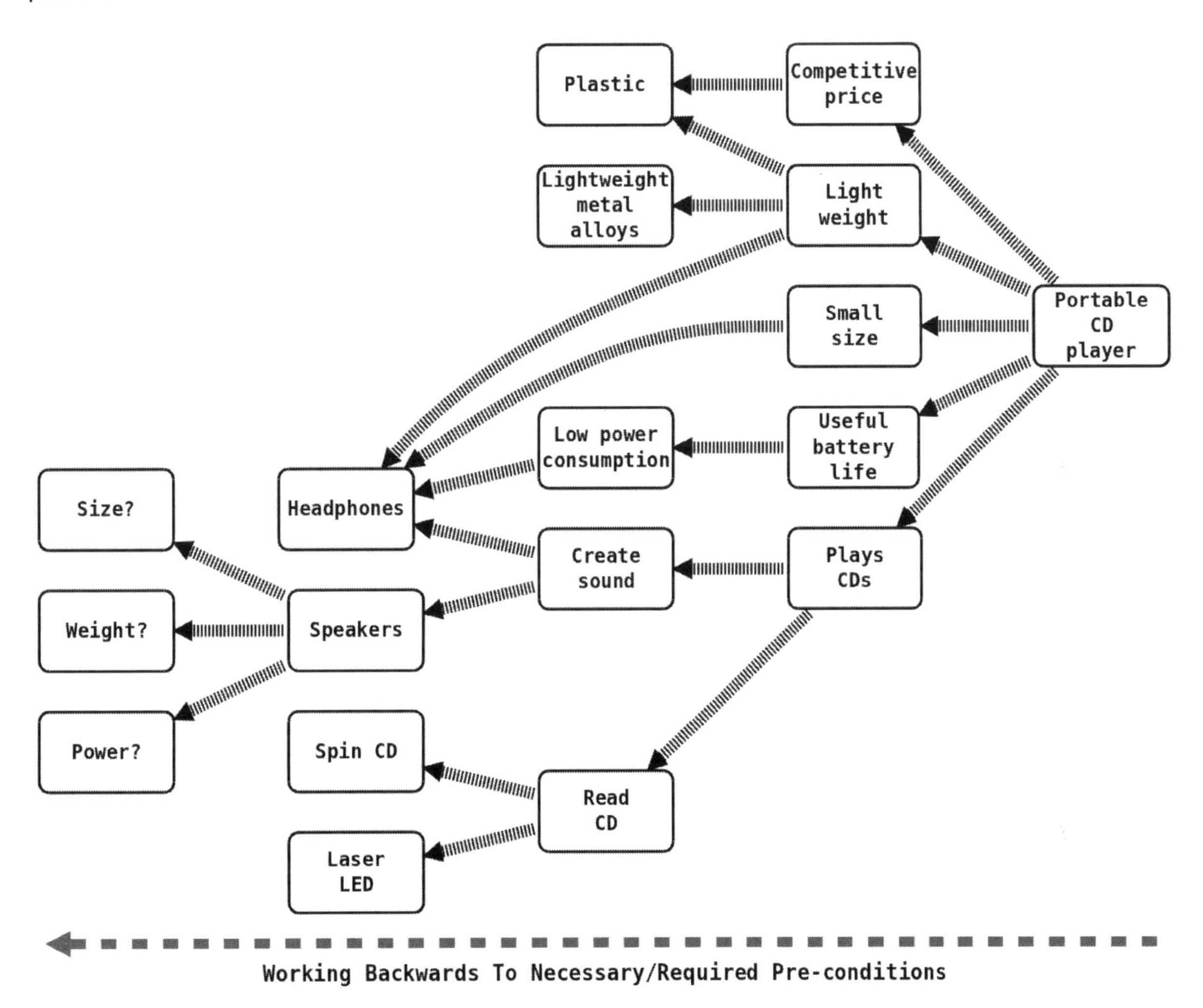

Working Downstream

The question which typically indicates working forwards in time is something like:

What would be the consequences if ⟨...⟩ happens?

- This is working forwards in time towards what could come after. Ted calls this working *downstream.*
- Working *downstream* defines possible consequences or effects of a given action.

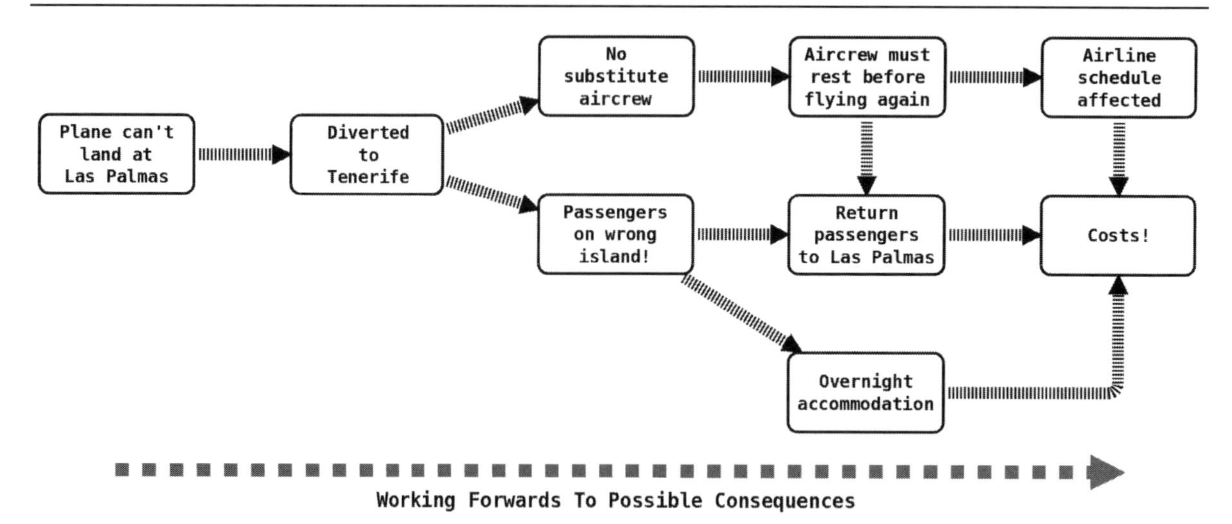

When you draw the first draft of the map, don't worry about how "pretty" it looks. Focus on getting the nodes and arrows correct. Then you can redraw it to make it neater. Many of the diagrams in this book took 2–4 redraws.

While redrawing it, you will also have the chance to think about the material further.

We recommend drawing the first version by hand. Then for later drafts there are several freeware or open-source programs that can be used, such as *Dia, Vue* and *CMap.* Ted used *Dia* to draw the C/C-maps for this book.

Any program that can draw a flowchart can be used without difficulty. Most drawing packages will also serve perfectly adequately for drawing C/C-maps.

If you are drawing a C/C-map to help you understand a paper or report and you find it *difficult* (or impossible) to construct the C/C-map, then there are several possibilities:

- it has no logical structure;
- it has poor/weak structure;
- the structure is obscured by a poor writing style.

If the resulting concept-map is *messy*, then the paper is either:

- poorly structured and is little more than a collection of facts, citations and suppositions; or
- overly complicated.

Things To Look For In Any C/C-Map

During the drawing of your C/C-map, you will have already been looking for:

- missing nodes or arrows;
- sections that are uncertain;
- inconsistencies.

It is worthwhile to continue looking for the above even when your C/C-map is finished. In addition, it is also useful to look for:

- feedback loops;
- delays/time-lags;
- entry (start) and exit (finish) points.

Feedback Loops

- When you are working with complex maps, one thing to look for is *feedback loops*. A feedback loop is where a closed loop or path can be traced around a circuit of nodes.

Feedback Loop	Not A Feedback Loop
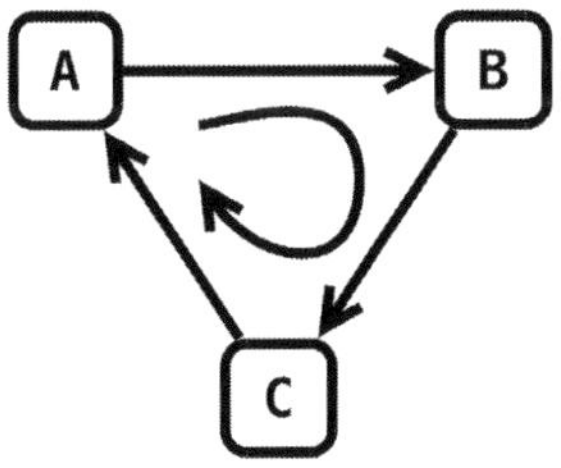 A, B, C ⟨*A*⟩ → ⟨*B*⟩ → ⟨*C*⟩ → ⟨*A*⟩ forms a closed loop.	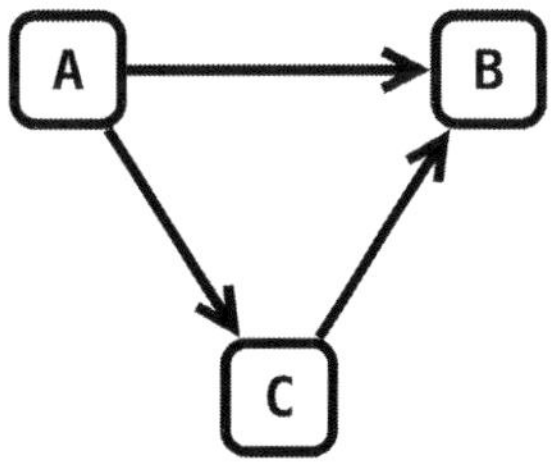 A, B, C This is two pathways from ⟨*A*⟩ to ⟨*B*⟩: ⟨*A*⟩ → ⟨*B*⟩ and ⟨*A*⟩ → ⟨*C*⟩ → ⟨*B*⟩
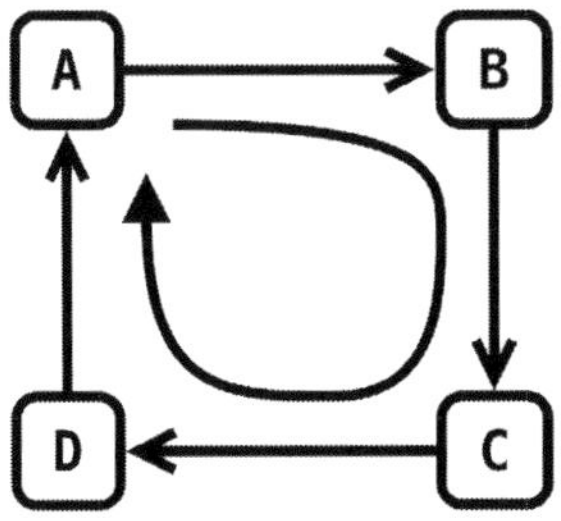 A, B, D, C ⟨*A*⟩→ ⟨*B*⟩ → ⟨*C*⟩ → ⟨*D*⟩ → ⟨*A*⟩ forms a closed loop.	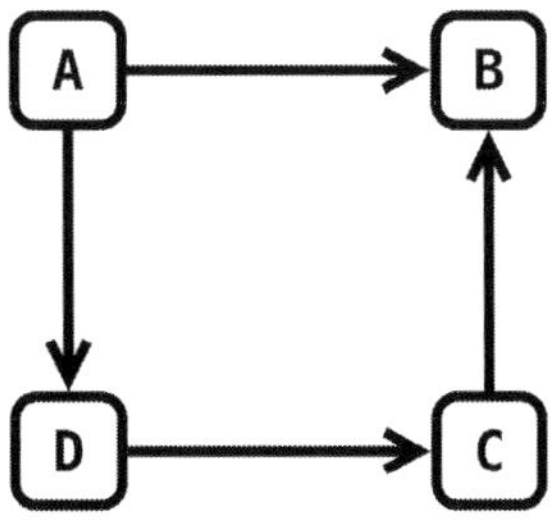 A, B, D, C Two paths from ⟨*A*⟩ to ⟨*B*⟩.

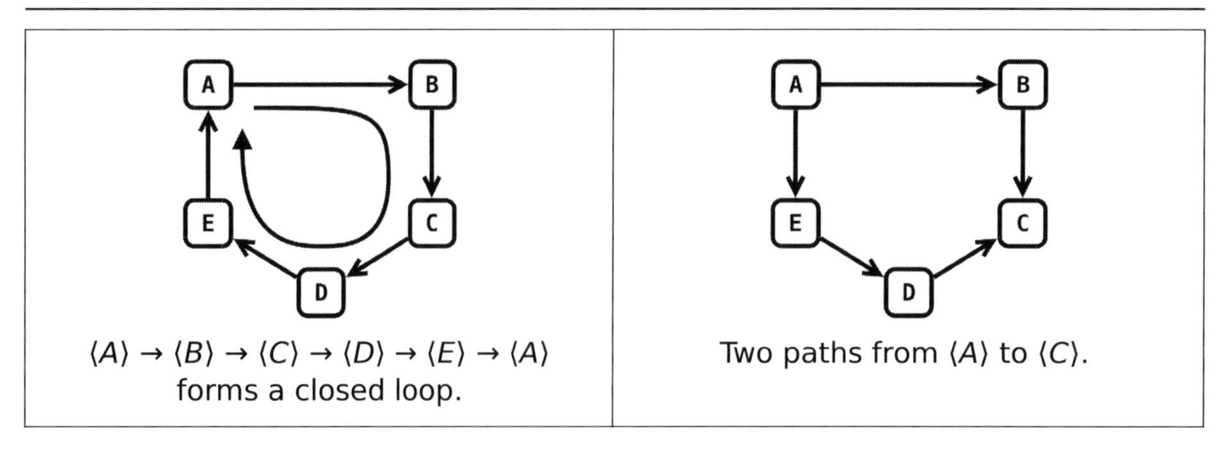

⟨A⟩ → ⟨B⟩ → ⟨C⟩ → ⟨D⟩ → ⟨E⟩ → ⟨A⟩ forms a closed loop.	Two paths from ⟨A⟩ to ⟨C⟩.

- Larger maps can have more than one feedback loop and the loops may even be interconnected/interacting.
- When you are working with a causal map (signs on the arrowheads) *and* there are feedback loops, then it is useful to consider the effect(s) of the feedback loop(s).
- Feedback loops can be either *negative* or *positive*.
  The two following examples illustrate the general rule for determining whether a feedback loop is *positive* or *negative.* In these examples we have labelled the arrowheads with (a), (b), (c) and (d) which represent the sign on the respective arrowhead.

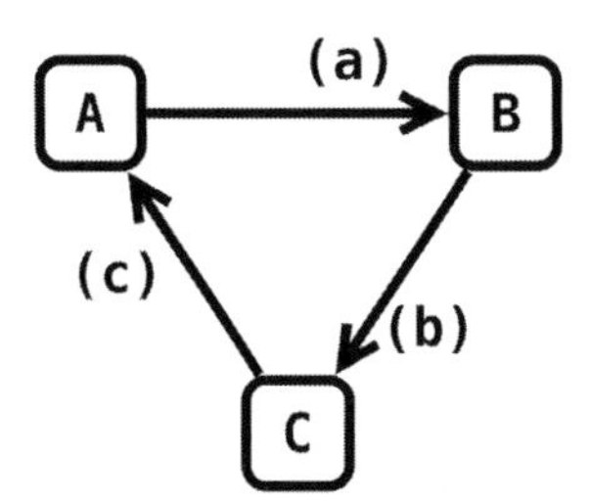

If (a) is ...	**If (b) is ...**	**If (c) is ...**	**then**	**Feedback is ...**
+	+	+	⇒	**+**
+	+	−	⇒	**−**
+	−	+	⇒	**−**
+	−	−	⇒	**+**
−	+	+	⇒	**−**
−	+	−	⇒	**+**
−	−	+	⇒	**+**
−	−	−	⇒	**−**

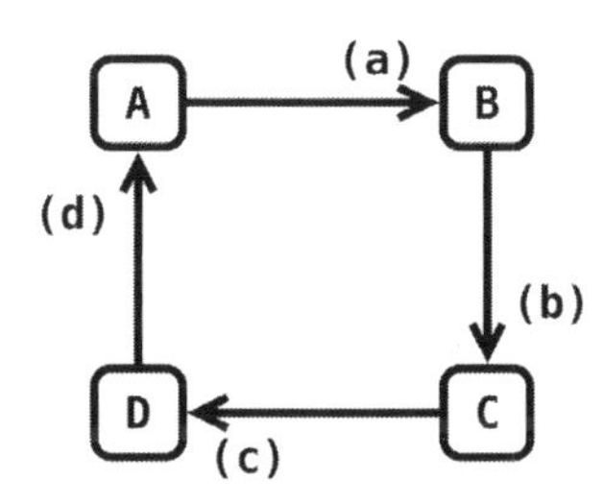

If (a) is ...	If (b) is ...	If (c) is ...	If (d) is ...	then	Feedback is ...
+	+	+	+	⇒	+
–	–	–	–	⇒	+
+	–	+	+	⇒	–
+	–	+	–	⇒	+
+	+	–	+	⇒	–
–	+	–	–	⇒	–

If the product of the signs around the loop is – then it is a *negative* feedback loop. An alternative way of defining this is if the number of – signs around the loop is *odd* then the feedback loop is *negative.*

If the product of the signs around the loop is +, then it is a *positive* feedback loop. An alternative way of defining this is if the number of – signs around the loop is *even* then the feedback loop is *positive.*

Negative feedback can also be called *balancing* or *restraining* feedback because the negative feedback loop automatically *restrains* or *resists* any change to the nodes within the loop. It will be *stable* in the sense that if something tries to change one node then the loop as a whole will automatically readjust in a way to minimise that change. The diagram below shows a negative feedback loop. Let's imagine that something from outside the loop increases node ⟨*A*⟩.

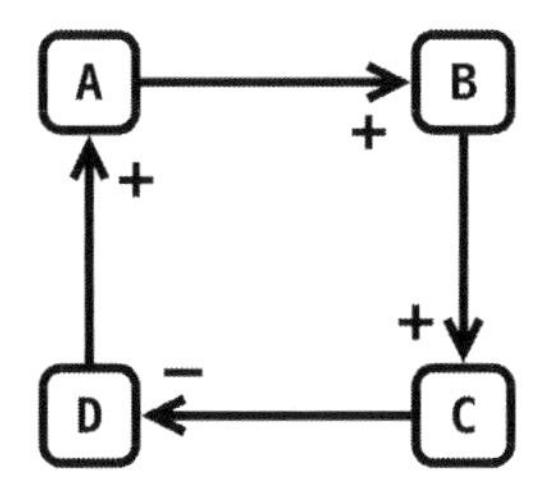

If we follow the effects of this increase in node ⟨A⟩ around the loop then we see that:

- if ⟨*A*⟩ increases then ⟨*B*⟩ will increase also;
- if ⟨*B*⟩ increases then ⟨*C*⟩ will increase;
- if ⟨*C*⟩ increases then ⟨*D*⟩ will decrease; and
- if ⟨*D*⟩ decreases then ⟨*A*⟩ will decrease as well.

The feedback loop has responded in the *opposite* direction to the initial change at ⟨*A*⟩. Let's look at an example. In nature, populations normally stabilise at a number that is suited to the space and food available. How does that happen? Through the action of various negative feedback loops, one of which is shown below.

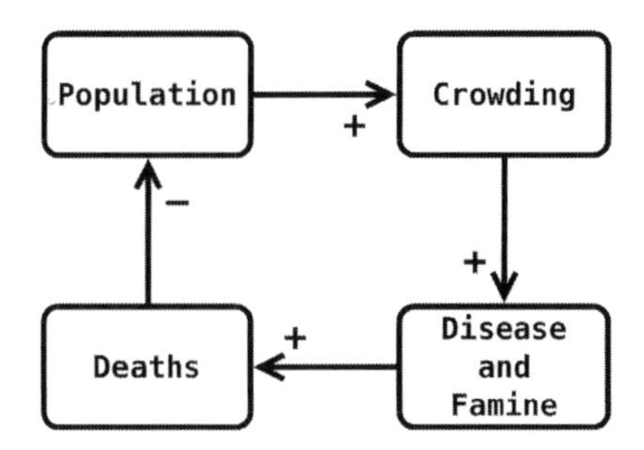

If ⟨*Population*⟩ increases, then so will ⟨*Crowding*⟩ and as a result of increased ⟨*Crowding*⟩ there will be an increase in ⟨*Disease and Famine*⟩. Increased ⟨*Disease and Famine*⟩ will increase ⟨*Deaths*⟩ which will decrease the ⟨*Population*⟩.

Positive feedback can also be called *unbalancing* or *reinforcing* feedback because the positive feedback loop will automatically reinforce or accentuate any change to the nodes within the loop. It will be *unstable* or *destabilising* in the sense that if something tries to change one node then the loop as a whole will automatically react in a way that amplifies the change. The diagram below shows a positive feedback loop. Let's imagine that something from outside the loop increases node ⟨*A*⟩.

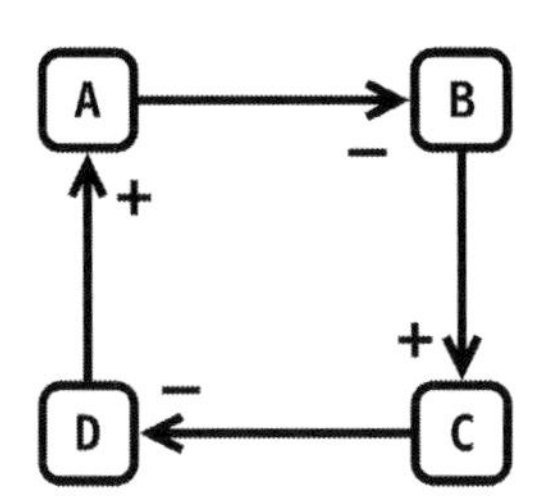

If we follow the effects of this increase in node ⟨A⟩ around the loop then we see that:

- if ⟨*A*⟩ increases then ⟨*B*⟩ will decrease;
- if ⟨*B*⟩ decreases then ⟨*C*⟩ will decrease as well;
- if ⟨*C*⟩ decreases then ⟨*D*⟩ will increase; and
- if ⟨*D*⟩ increases then ⟨*A*⟩ will increase further.

The feedback loop has responded in the *same* direction to the initial change at ⟨*A*⟩ and has reinforced or amplified the change.

Positive and negative feedback loops are neither good nor bad. Whether they are helpful or harmful depends upon the circumstances and the desired outcome.

- In situations where you want things to remain stable and constant, then negative feedback loops will be useful and positive feedback loops will cause problems because they will destabilise matters.

- In situations where you want a change to happen, then positive feedback loops will be useful and negative feedback loops will automatically restrain/resist any changes.

Let's revisit an example from *Chapter 6*, where a politician had made a vague statement that the increasing number of ⟨*People on Sickness Benefit*⟩ was adversely affecting the ⟨*National Economy*⟩. This C/C-map has one positive (+) feedback loop which has been highlighted in grey:
⟨*Disposable Income*⟩ → ⟨*Consumer Demand*⟩ → ⟨*Business*⟩ → ⟨*Workforce*⟩ → ⟨*Disposable Income*⟩

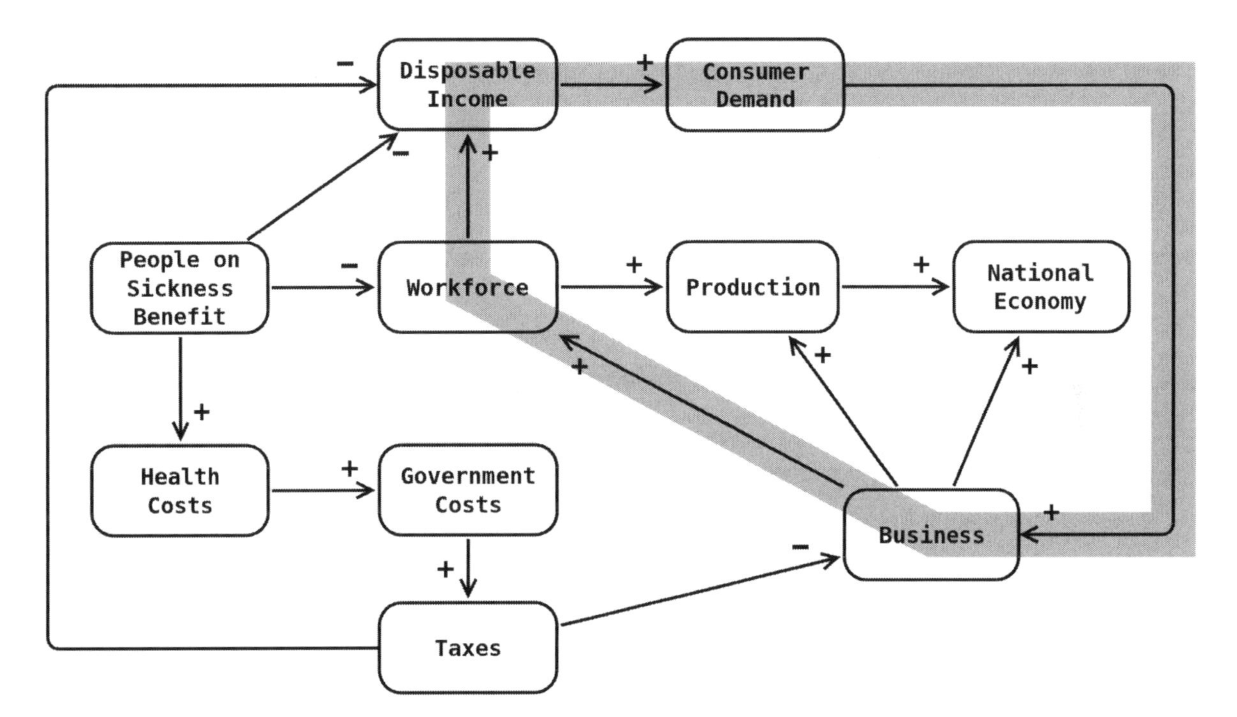

The positive feedback loop means that it is a *reinforcing* loop. There are two possible *directions* of reinforcement:

- the nodes around the loop can increase or improve;
- the nodes around the loop can decrease or deteriorate.

How do you know which way it will go? The node ⟨*People on Sickness Benefit*⟩ affects both ⟨*Workforce*⟩ and ⟨*Disposable Income*⟩. The node ⟨*Taxes*⟩ will affect both ⟨*Business*⟩ and ⟨*Disposable Income*⟩. The nodes ⟨*People on Sickness Benefit*⟩ and ⟨*Taxes*⟩ will act like two separate switches that influence the direction of the positive feedback loop.

- If either ⟨*People on Sickness Benefit*⟩ and/or ⟨*Taxes*⟩ increase, then the feedback loop will be driven into a decreasing spiral, making the economic situation worse.
- If either ⟨*People on Sickness Benefit*⟩ and/or ⟨*Taxes*⟩ decrease, then the feedback loop will be driven into a increasing spiral, making the economic situation better.

- If ⟨*People on Sickness Benefit*⟩ and ⟨*Taxes*⟩ change in opposite directions to each other, then the effect on the feedback loop will be more difficult to predict since the two quantities will be having opposing influences upon the feedback loop.
- If ⟨*People on Sickness Benefit*⟩ and ⟨*Taxes*⟩ remain constant, then the feedback loop will continue in whichever direction it was already going.

Delays/Time-Lags

Another issue of importance in C/C-maps is time-lags or delays and these can occur either along a chain of events or within feedback loops. What this means is that the result is always delayed with respect to the action or event that triggered it.

In the chain of nodes above, ⟨*A*⟩ initiates a sequence of events that eventually results in ⟨*F*⟩. Regardless of how fast each arrow is, the response at node ⟨*F*⟩ will be *delayed* relative to any changes at ⟨*A*⟩.

The same will apply to feedback loops where the feedback will be delayed to some degree because it must travel around the loop. Feedback will not be instantaneous.

Let's assume that all arrows are equally fast and revisit the examples from earlier.

Feedback Loop	Time-Lag For Feedback
A, B, C	If node ⟨*A*⟩ does something to node ⟨*B*⟩, then ⟨*A*⟩ won't feel the effects of its actions until ⟨*B*⟩ has acted on ⟨*C*⟩ and then ⟨*C*⟩ has acted on ⟨*A*⟩.
A, B, C, D	If node ⟨*A*⟩ does something to node ⟨*B*⟩, then ⟨*A*⟩ won't feel the effects of its actions until ⟨*B*⟩ has acted on ⟨*C*⟩ and then ⟨*C*⟩ has acted on ⟨*D*⟩ and then ⟨*D*⟩ has acted on ⟨*A*⟩. The feedback delay will be greater for this loop compared to the previous loop.

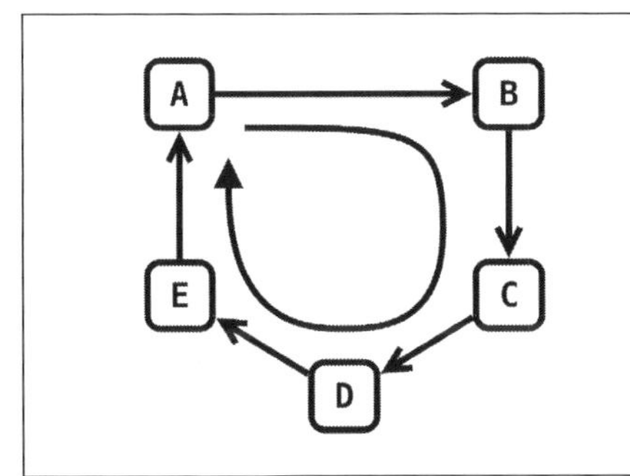	For this case, the feedback delay will be even greater.

Regardless of the speed of the processes represented by particular arrows, the feedback will be delayed to some degree. In general, the more nodes that are present in a feedback loop, the slower the feedback loop will be.

If we revisit the map on ⟨*People On Sickness Benefit*⟩ above, we can see that even if ⟨*Business*⟩ hires people and the ⟨*Workforce*⟩ increases, there will be a delay before the extra ⟨*Disposable Income*⟩ of employed people affects ⟨*Consumer Demand*⟩.

Entry And Exit Points

Once your C/C-map is completed you may find that it has entry and/or exit points.

- Nodes that have only ***leaving*** arrows are called ***entry*** (start) points for the map.
- Nodes that have only ***entering*** arrows are called ***exit*** (finish) points for the map.

In the example on page 160 there are two entry points ⟨*Birth Rate*⟩ and ⟨*Life Span*⟩ and one exit point ⟨*Quality of Life*⟩. When using C/C-maps to represent the flow of ideas, entry-points and exit-points make logical starting and finishing points for your discussion.

Useful Questions To Ask Yourself About Any C/C-Map

- Does the C/C-map make sense? If not, then why not?
  - What are the driving forces behind actions/processes?
  - Do entities interact directly or indirectly?
  - How do the parts fit together?
  - Are there missing nodes or links?
  - Are there isolated or irrelevant nodes? (This suggests irrelevant material.)
  - Are there invalid or questionable links?
  - What are the inconsistencies or contradictions?
- What is missing, uncertain, unreliable, ambiguous or questionable?
- What else would be required to resolve the map? Can this be determined?
- What has been assumed as self-evident without evidence? What can't be verified immediately?

- What is presupposed by the map and its elements?
  - If one thing is true, then what else *must* also be logically true or logically false?
  - If the map is an accurate representation, then are there any consequences or implications that follow from it?
- How does this map fit with other things you know?

It is worth remembering that any node in a completed C/C-map might interact with external environmental factors that haven't been represented within the map. There is always a possibility that something which hasn't been represented could be important.

– Appendix 2 –
PERT Movie Answer

The First Draft

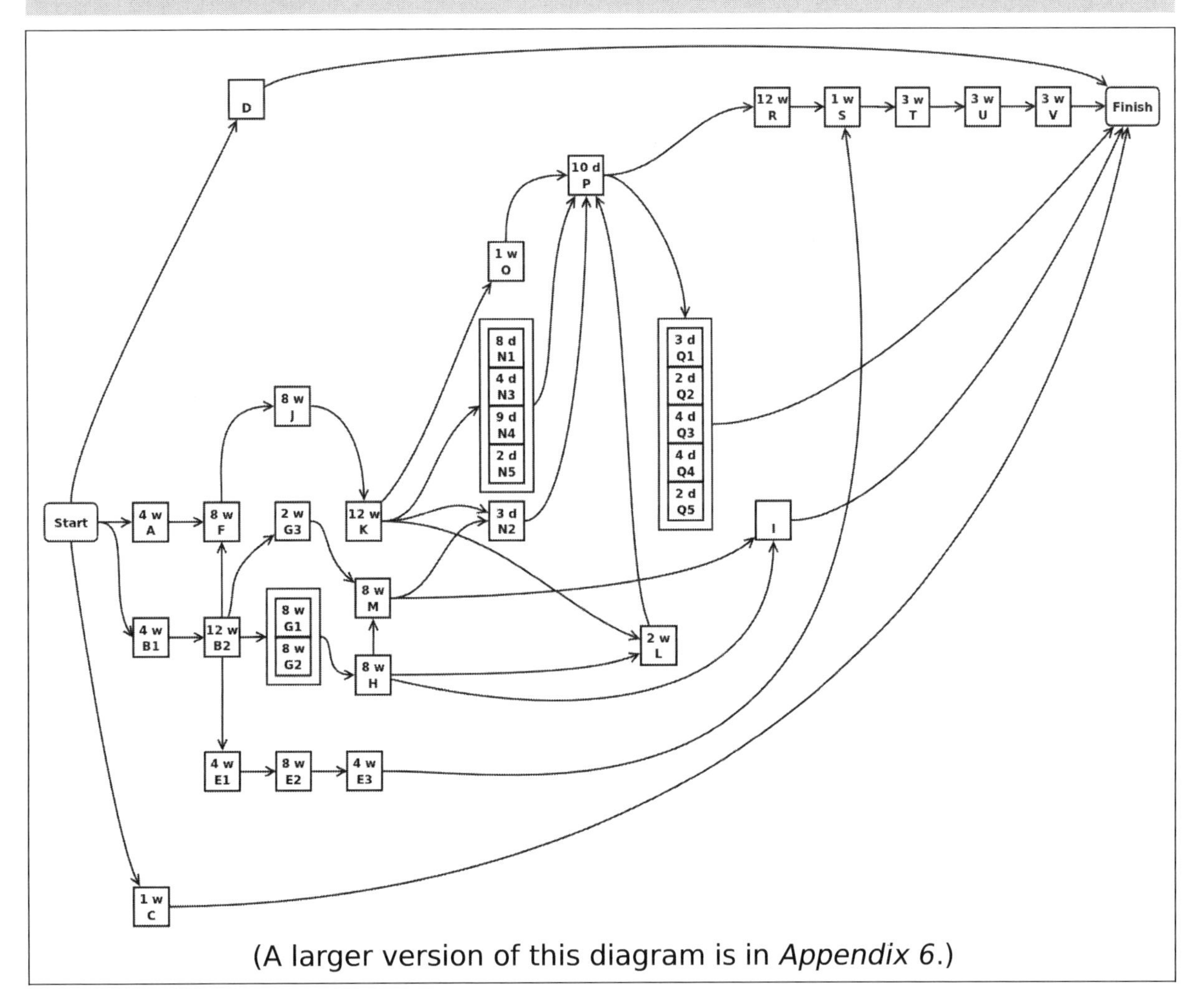

(A larger version of this diagram is in *Appendix 6*.)

Here is a first draft of the PERT–PON diagram for the movie project. Your initial layout may be different which is perfectly acceptable. If your first version is messier than this, then you might want to redraw it so that it is easier to understand. The most important thing is that the connections and sequence are correct.

To simplify the diagram, G1 and G2 which are similar in nature and done in parallel, have been grouped into a single larger box. The same has been done for the groups [N1+N3+N4+N5] and [Q1+Q2+Q3+Q4+Q5]. The task which takes the longest time was the time that was chosen for the grouped box as a whole.

(**Note:** The list of tasks has been repeated at the end of this appendix in case you want to refer to it.)

Identifying The Critical Path

Once you have the first draft of the PERT diagram, the next stage is to find the critical path.

To find the critical path, you use a process of elimination to reveal the longest duration pathway through the PERT diagram. The steps to follow are:

Step 1: Identify The Principal Pathways Through The PERT Diagram.

What are all the major pathways from the Start to the Finish? At this stage, we simply need a "big picture" overview without getting lost in details. In this diagram there are four principal pathways.

Step 2: Identify The Sub-Sections Within The Diagram

With complex PERT diagrams, one way to simplify your life is to break it down into smaller sub-sections (a set of sub-pathways that share a common starting node and finishing node). You begin with the smallest sub-sections and then progressively work up to larger sub-sections. Working from smaller sections to larger sections will save you time later.

To help identify the possible sub-sections, it is useful to pay attention to three types of nodes.

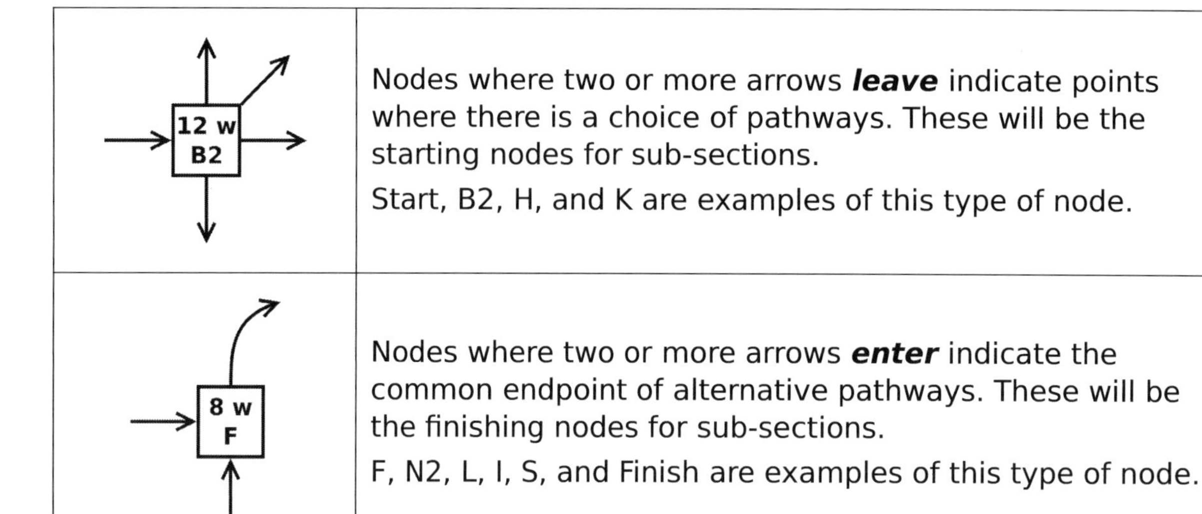	Nodes where two or more arrows ***leave*** indicate points where there is a choice of pathways. These will be the starting nodes for sub-sections. Start, B2, H, and K are examples of this type of node.
	Nodes where two or more arrows ***enter*** indicate the common endpoint of alternative pathways. These will be the finishing nodes for sub-sections. F, N2, L, I, S, and Finish are examples of this type of node.
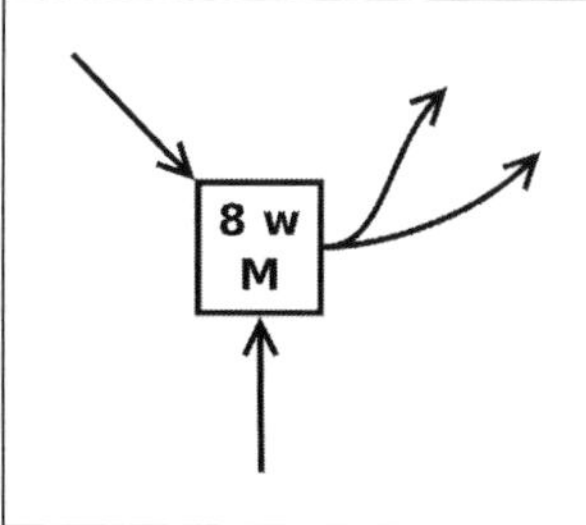	Nodes where two or more ***leave*** and two or more arrows ***enter*** will be combination nodes that serve as either starting nodes or finishing nodes of sub-sections. M and P are examples of this type of node.

Step 3: Within A Sub-Section, Compare And Eliminate

Start with the smallest and simplest sub-sections and progressively work up to larger sub-sections.

Pick a sub-section and compare the durations of the alternative pathways from the starting node to the finishing node. Eliminate all the alternatives with shorter durations leaving only the pathway with the longest duration.

Repeat this process of comparison and elimination with other sub-sections until you have a single pathway through the diagram which remains. This is the critical path.

When comparing alternative sub-pathways, it is the times *between* the common starting node and the finishing node that are important. You exclude the times of the starting and finishing nodes because they are common to all the alternative pathways through the sub-section you are considering.

Let's work through this diagram using the steps.

Step 1

Looking at this diagram we can see that there are 4 major routes from Start → Finish:

- **Start → C → Finish**
  Task C is arranging the insurance and that takes one week, so that isn't the critical path. We can eliminate this pathway.
- **Start → D → Finish**
  Task D is Accounting and it is an ongoing activity. It will take as much or as little time as the movie takes. So the pathway through D is not the critical path. We can eliminate this pathway too.
- **Start → A → rest of messy stuff in the middle → Finish**
- **Start → B1 → rest of messy stuff in the middle → Finish**

Step 2

The possible sub-sections are:

Start → F

K → P

M → Finish

H → P

H → Finish

P → Finish

B2 → M

B2 → P

B2 → S

B2 → Finish

If we have missed any, then well done for noticing and Ted's excuse is that he didn't have enough coffee (wakefulness-promoting pharmacologically-active fluid) the morning he was working on this!

Step 3

Now we need to start working with the smaller sub-sections of the "messy stuff in the middle" which we identified in Step 2.

Start → F

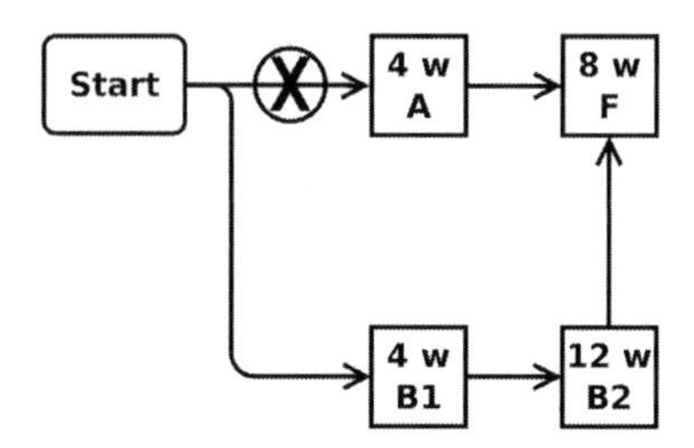

There are two alternative pathways beginning at Start and ending on the node F.

Start → B1 → B2 → F (16 weeks)

Start → A → F (4 weeks)

The sub-pathway through A is shorter duration so we can eliminate (circled X) it from further consideration, because it won't form part of the critical path.

K → P

This sub-section has four alternative pathways:

K → O → P (1 week)

K → [N1+N3+N4+N5] → P (9 days)

K → N2 → P (3 days)

K → L → P (2 weeks)

When we compare the durations of the 4 branches, we can see the first three can be eliminated leaving K → L → P for inclusion and checking in other sub-sections.

M → Finish

This sub-section contains two alternatives.

M → I → Finish (ongoing)

M → N2 → P → R → S → T → U → V → Finish (23 weeks + 6 days)

There is no need to calculate the duration of the branch through I because it is Advertising/Marketing which is ongoing. It will take as much or as little time as the movie takes so it won't form part of the critical path. This leaves M → N2 → P → R → S → T → U → V → Finish for checking in other sub-sections.

H → P

This sub-section has two alternative branches:

H → L → P (2 weeks)

H → M → N2 → P (8 weeks + 3 days)

When we compare these two branches, we can eliminate H → L → P from further consideration and keep H → M → N2 → P for inclusion in larger sub-sections.

H → Finish

This sub-section has two alternative branches as well.

H → I → Finish (ongoing)

H → M → N2 → P → R → S → T → U → V → Finish (31 weeks + 6 days)

We can eliminate the branch H → I → Finish for the same reason we eliminated M → I → Finish from the sub-section involving M.

P → Finish

This sub-section has two alternative branches.

P → [Q1+Q2+Q3+Q4+Q5] → Finish (4 days)

P → R → S → T → U → V → Finish (22 weeks)

We can eliminate the branch P → [Q1+Q2+Q3+Q4+Q5] → Finish because it is shorter duration.

B2 → M

For this sub-section we have two alternative pathways to compare.

B2 → G3 → M (2 weeks)

B2 → [G1+G2] → H → M (16 weeks)

It's easy to see that the pathway through G3 is eliminated.

B2 → P

As a result of our earlier "pruning" of other sub-sections, we have three remaining alternatives to consider:

B2 → F → J → K → L → P (8 w + 8 w +12 w + 2 w)

B2 → [G1+G2] → H → M → N2 → P (8 w + 8 w + 8 w + 3 d)

B2 → [G1+G2] → H → L → P (8 w + 8 w + 2 w)

Comparing the durations of the three branches, we can eliminate both of the pathways through [G1+G2] leaving only B2 → F → J → K → L → P for inclusion and checking later.

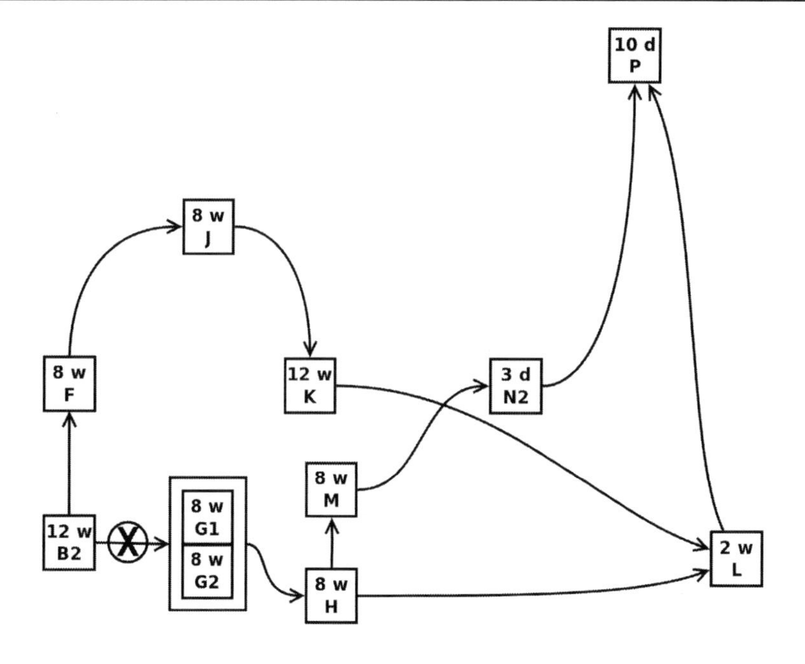

B2 → S

Again, because of our work with other smaller sub-sections, we have only two alternatives to compare:

B2 → F → J → K → L → P → R → S (8w + 8w + 12w + 2w + 10d + 12w)

B2 → E1 → E2 → E3 → S (4w + 8w + 4w)

So we can eliminate the sub-pathway through E1 leaving the branch B2 → F → J → K → L → P → R → S.

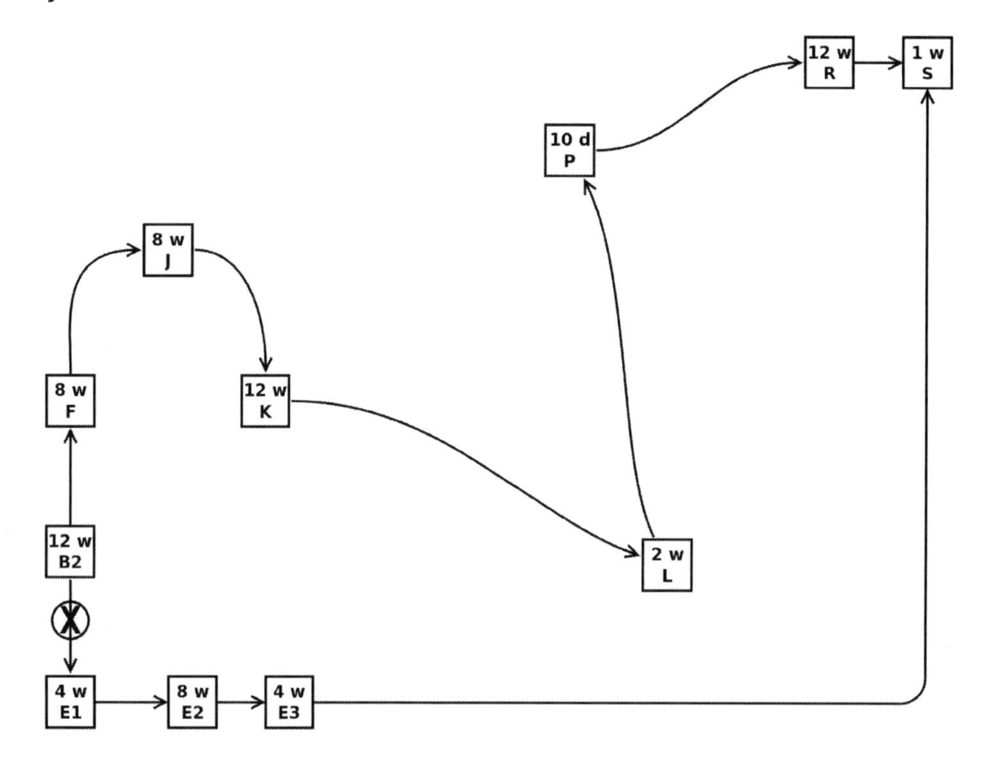

At this point, when we look at the diagram with all the eliminated branches, we realise that there is only one path remaining which must be the critical path.

Start → B1 → B2 → F → J → K → L → P → R → S → T → U → V → Finish

(4w + 12w + 8w + 8w + 12w + 2w + 10d + 12w + 1w + 3w + 3w + 3w)

The duration of the critical path is 69 weeks + 3 days. This is the *best-case scenario* or the minimum possible time, for completing the film, assuming every task is completed on time.

You can mark it on your diagram, for example by using a coloured highlighter. We have highlighted the critical path using thick grey arrows.

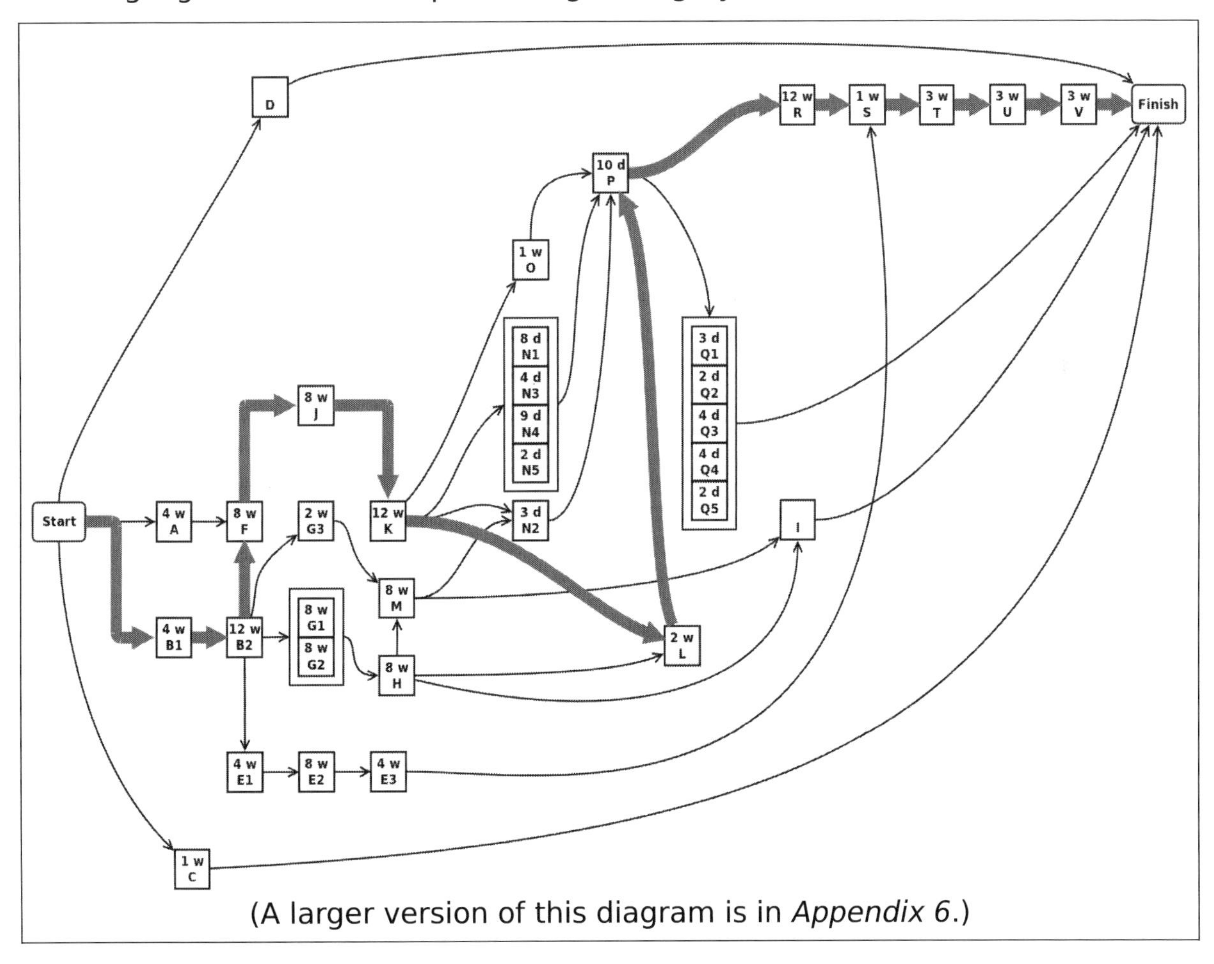

(A larger version of this diagram is in *Appendix 6*.)

Once the critical path has been highlighted, then we can redraw the diagram to make it as clear as possible. Here is the final draft of the PERT diagram.

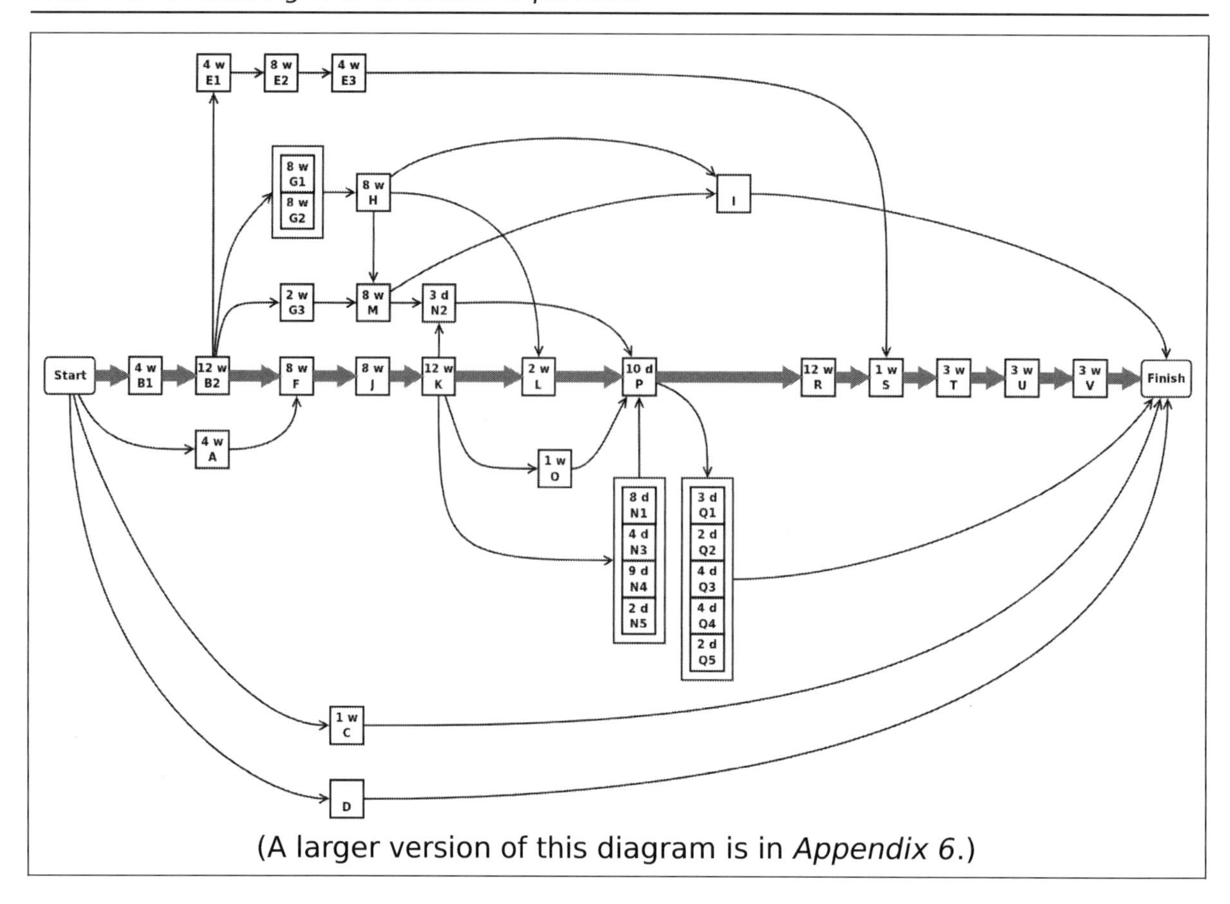

(A larger version of this diagram is in *Appendix 6*.)

This exercise illustrates the important idea that all projects have preparation and "clean-up" which will take time! For this example, the exciting part (filming) only takes 10 days but requires 46 weeks of *pre-production* (preparation). After the filming is complete there are another 21 weeks of *post-production* work.

Planning and preparation of your research will take a significant amount of time. And once the research is completed, then analysis and communication will take more time. For example, many students underestimate the time it takes to write a dissertation/thesis.

Identifier	Activity	Duration	Prerequisite
Start	Producer has financial backing for the film.		
A	Find Director	4 weeks	Start
B1	Find Screenwriter	4 weeks	Start
B2	Produce Screenplay	12 weeks	B1
C	Legal: Insurance	1 week	Start
D	Accounting	ongoing	Start
E1	Find Composer	4 weeks	B2
E2	Produce Musical Score	8 weeks	E1
E3	Find Orchestra/band	4 weeks	E2
F	Storyboard the screenplay	8 weeks	A, B2
G1	Cast principal actors/actresses	8 weeks	B2
G2	Cast supporting actors/actresses	8 weeks	B2
G3	Cast extras	2 weeks	B2
H	Legal: Negotiate contracts	8 weeks	G1, G2
I	Advertising/Marketing	ongoing	H, M
J	Find & negotiate city exterior location	8 weeks	F
K	Legal: Permits & Permissions	12 weeks	J
L	Arrange accommodation for cast & crew.	2 weeks	H, K
M	Costumes: Design & Preparation	8 weeks	H, G3
N1	Props: Preparation & Transportation	8 days	K
N2	Costumes: Transportation	3 days	K, M
N3	Lighting: Preparation & Transportation	4 days	K
N4	Cameras: Preparation & Transportation	9 days	K
N5	Sound: Preparation & Transportation	2 days	K
O	Catering: Arrange catering	1 week	K
P	Filming	10 days	N1 – N5, O, L
Q1	Props: Re-packing & Transportation	3 days	P
Q2	Costumes: Re-packing & Transportation	2 days	P
Q3	Lighting: Re-packing & Transportation	4 days	P
Q4	Cameras: Re-packing & Transportation	4 days	P
Q5	Sound: Re-packing & Transportation	2 days	P
R	Studio: Editing film	12 weeks	P
S	Studio: Recording soundtrack	1 week	E3, R
T	Studio: Editing soundtrack	3 weeks	S
U	Studio: Titles & Credits	3 weeks	T
V	Distribution	3 weeks	U
Finish	Film Première		

– Appendix 3 –
Handling Hostile Questions

Below are some horrible questions and *possible* responses that students have come up with during Ted's workshops. You may not use some of the answers in real-life, but the exercise of exploring what is possible is useful and fun.

Q: "Have You Ever Thought Of Taking Up A Different Career?"

→ "No."
(Literally, the question is asking for a yes or no answer. So answer no and then shut up. If they want to take it further, they have to say more.)

→ "No. Have you?"

→ "Only when I meet someone like you."

→ "If you know of something that is more fun and pays better, then I'm listening."

→ "With dinosaurs like you around, I think this field needs people like me."

→ "Have *you* ever thought of learning some manners?"

→ "I have toyed with the idea of becoming a hit-man."

→ "How is a discussion of alternative career paths relevant to my presentation?"

→ "I'll need to think about this."

→ "Are you trying to say that my work is no good?"
(This is forcing them to bluntly state what they really mean.)

Q: "Is Your Supervisor Aware Of How You've Been Wasting Your Time?"

→ "Yes."
(Again, this question is literally asking for a yes/no answer. Give them a yes/no answer and then be quiet. If they want to take it further, they have to say some more – which provides you with further ammunition and options.)

→ "Yes. S/He's the one who suggested this direction."

→ "S/He is sitting over there if you'd like to ask them yourself?"

→ "I've been doing exactly what was outlined in the project plan which was funded by ⟨...⟩. They seemed to think it was worth pursuing."

→ "At least it was fun."

→ "Do you have a scientific question or are you just cranky?"

→ "Well my work can always serve as a bad example."

→ "I didn't know beforehand that it would be unsuccessful."
(Notice how you have relabelled a *waste of time* as an *unsuccessful attempt*.)

→ "And how is this opinion of yours relevant or useful?" (This relabels their assertion of wasting time as the opinion it really is.)

→ "Can you be more specific?"

- "S/He doesn't know I'm lazy and I'd appreciate it if you didn't disabuse them of this notion."
- "I'm still waiting for ... to be delivered/prepared/provided."
- "Why do you care? How is it your responsibility?"

Q: "Do You Realise That Your Argument Is Completely Specious?"

- "No." and then be completely silent.
  (Their question is literally asking for a yes/no answer which you have provided. If they want to take it further, they will have to come out from under their rock and provide more specifics.)
- "I don't think so."
- "What does *specious* mean?"
- "Oops. Sorry about that."
- "I'm going to lie awake at nights worrying about it now that you've told me. Next question?"
- "That's an interesting opinion. What is your reasoning and evidence?"
  (Note that your answer has relabelled their statement as what it is, an opinion, which is lacking in any specifics. And you ask them to provide support for it.)
- "Can you be more specific?"
- "What reasons do you have for that opinion?"
- "I'll check into what you say."
- "Which part is wrong?" or "Can you elaborate?"
- "I'm afraid that we will have to agree to disagree until further work resolves this issue."
- "It seemed reasonable at the time."
- "How do you know it's wrong/impossible?"
- "Previous literature indicates ... "
- "Our next experiment is to confirm ... "
- "Where is the contradictory evidence?"
- "It is a complicated argument and not everyone understands it the first time. Let me explain it to you more slowly."
- "You looked more gullible than I guess you are."
- "We can't really *prove* anything in science. All we can do is present a consistent case for the inference."
- "We discussed this with others and they seemed to think it was reasonable."
- "This is the best model we have available at present."

Q: "You're Mistaken In Your Analysis. A Complete Beginner Would Have Known Better Than That."

→ "Which *complete beginner* would that be? I may want to consult them next time."

→ "And where do you *believe* there is a mistake?"
(Notice how you have relabelled it as a belief on their part, rather than absolute truth.)

→ "And how would someone have known better? This is a new area that we are researching and we weren't aware that it had already been all worked out and published. Perhaps you could give me the references?"

→ "If you have a different hypothesis which explains all the data, then I'm willing to hear it."
(This is forcing them to commit themselves to tangible facts.)

→ "I must have missed that lecture at university."

→ "We are looking for useful comments and suggestions. Your opinion isn't. Next question please."

→ "You seem irritable. Did you take your medication this morning?"

→ "I see that your eyes and ears are here. Where did you leave your brain?"

Q: "I Don't Agree. You Haven't Proven Your Case At All, Have You?"

→ "Then we'll have to agree to disagree."

→ "Do you have anything more constructive and specific?"

→ "That's nice to know." or the American version is "Thanks for sharing that with us."

→ "OK, you don't agree with the case I've presented. Does anyone have any *questions*?"

→ "What specifically don't you agree with?"
(Force them to be more specific and commit themselves.)

→ "This is a new area of research and different research groups have different ideas about what is happening. It will take some time before workers in the field reach any kind of consensus."

→ "Well, our overall conclusion was ... and we arrived at this conclusion because ..."
(Basically, you repeat your argument and evidence in a brief form.)

→ "Well, I have presented my reasoning and evidence, but you seem to disagree. We won't resolve it here and I think we will have to agree to disagree."

→ "What *have* we shown then?"

→ "What would make it conclusive for you then?"
(This is getting them to suggest additional evidence that would strengthen your case. You could then do the additional work to get the evidence if you decided it was worthwhile.)

→ "I've discussed this with others who ... "

- "I don't know what else to tell you."
- "I have some additional/supplemental data which I did not have time for in my presentation. If we look at ... "
- "Feeling a bit frustrated are we? "
- "This is too lengthy a discussion for the question period. I'd be happy to discuss it with you in detail later."

Q: "Your Whole Approach Is Flawed, Isn't It?"

- "No."
  (Literal answer to their yes/no question.)
- "I'll have to think about that."
- "Really? The whole, entire approach is flawed? There isn't a single solitary bit that is right?"
  (In negotiation, this is known as 'salami slicing' - you get them to back down from 'whole' to part, and then continue to whittle them down. Usually, you will find it is one trivial point with which they disagree and have blown out of all proportion.)
- "It's being fixed."
- "Are you stating this as a preamble to making yourself look clever in front of this audience?"
- "Apparently as flawed as your social skills."
- "Do you agree with what we did here? ... And here? ... "
  (This approach involves working through your presentation point-by-point and checking for agreement or disagreement at each stage. Normally, they will have to agree or accept at least some of what you have done, and in so doing, they have discredited their initial statement that the 'whole approach' was flawed.)
- "Which *part* do you believe is flawed and why?"
- "The journal referees/grant committee disagree with you."
- "That's a big question. To spare the audience *another* lecture, see me after."
- "We attempted to take every reasonable precaution, but I'd be interested in your specific comments since you seem to think we missed something."
- "You were asked for your comments when the project started and you didn't respond. Now is too late to start complaining."
- "There is a compromise between the precision of a model and its usability."
- "Not all factors are equally important."
- "Any evidence apart from hot air?"
- "Because of time-constraints I have shown only a selection of the data available."
- "What makes you say that?"
  (This counter-question asks for them to commit themselves with more specifics.)
- "What else *should* have been done?" or "How much *should* I have achieved?"

→ "What do you think I have missed?" or "What more is needed?"

Q: "Don't You Know That The Work By Blogs *Et Al.* Disproves What You Claim To Have Shown Here."

→ "Thank you for bringing their work to my attention. I wasn't aware their work led them to a different conclusion."

→ "The situation is more complex and there may be additional factors responsible for the differences between our work and theirs."

→ "I haven't come across it. Thank you for bringing it to my attention."

→ "I can't comment until I've seen the paper. Do you have a copy with you?" (It is essential that you never answer a question like this until you have checked the paper for yourself. The work might not be relevant. The questioner might have misunderstood the paper. Or the questioner might be intentionally or unintentionally misrepresenting what the paper says.)

→ "I have seen the work by Blogs *et al.* and what they say is ..." (In this answer you present your understanding of the work by Blogs *et al.* Then it is up to the questioner to provide further specifics if they wish to pursue the point.)

→ "I have seen the work by Blogs *et al.* and their research was conducted under different set of conditions or using a different set of assumptions." (The aim here is to point out the differences between your work and that of Blogs *et al.* The differences in conditions or methods then explain the difference in results or interpretations.)

→ "That is the only paper which disagrees with our work. The rest of the literature agrees with what I/we have presented here."

→ "Could you summarise your understanding of what it says?"

→ "That work was never confirmed/replicated."

Q: "Do You Have Any Real/Substantive Data To Support This?"

→ "In answer to your question, let me summarise my argument, in case I didn't make myself completely clear ... " (Here you briefly summarise your reasoning and evidence. If you want to be a bit more confrontational, then you can say '... let me summarise the argument in case you misunderstood ...'. This option makes it their 'fault' they have it wrong.)

→ "The work is ongoing and all the additional data we have collected so far is consistent with what I have presented here."

→ "Were you awake?"

→ "How much data do you need to be shown?"

→ "What would you consider to be 'substantive data'?"

→ "Can you be more specific?"

→ "I'm listening."

→ "You need to tell me more before I could comment."

→ "There is additional/supplemental data which shows ... "

→ "Does anyone else think so?"
→ "What would convince you?"
→ "Do you want me to explain it again using small words this time?"
→ "I can't discuss it further because of issues of confidentiality."

Q: "Why Did You Do It This Way When It Is Well Known That This Method Is Ineffective/Obsolete/Has Been Replaced By (...)"

→ "Well I knew your life was empty and meaningless so I thought I'd give you something to get excited about."
→ "To repeat myself, the reasons I/we did it this way were ..."
(This is restating your reasons for taking the approach you did.)
→ "Well known by whom exactly?"
(This is attacking their assertion that it is a 'well known fact' and forcing them to substantiate it with specifics.)
→ "How do you know this method is ineffective/obsolete/has been replaced? What evidence do you have for your opinion?"
→ "The method you suggest has the following disadvantages ..."
→ "Both approaches have advantages and disadvantages. These are ... The reasons I/we chose this approach were ..."
→ "We looked at ... and it worked/didn't work." or "We looked at ... but left it out of the presentation because of time-constraints."

Q: "Why Didn't You Think Of (...) ?"

→ "I don't know. Because we didn't."
→ "We did and we decided that it wouldn't work because ..."
→ "This is really an illogical question. If someone hasn't thought of something, then they can't have a reason for not having thought of it because they weren't aware of not having thought of it in the first place! Isn't that so?"
→ "Since I didn't think of it, I can't really tell you how I went about not thinking about it because if I did know how I didn't think of it then by definition I would had to have thought about the thing I wasn't thinking about and the way in which I wasn't thinking about it."
(This answer may put them to sleep.)

Q: "What About The Paper By (...)?"

→ "What about it?"
(This forces the questioner to provide more specifics.)
→ "How is that paper relevant to what I have been presenting?"
→ "Since I haven't seen that paper, I can't comment upon how it might or might not be relevant to what I've presented here."
→ "Can you tell me a bit about it?"
→ "Can you give me the reference?"
→ "It didn't appear in our search."
→ "I'll have a look at it."

→ "We selected these papers to highlight important ideas. It wasn't possible to exhaustively review the literature within the time limits of this presentation."

→ "That was published while ours was in-press."

→ "Ours is different because ... "

→ "We confirm/support their work."

→ "Our focus/approach/assumptions/methods/conditions differed from ... "

→ "Many groups have contributed to this field and time did not permit me to mention every group by name during my presentation. However, this group do appear in my list of relevant references."

Reminder:

The trick to handling difficult questions is to do your homework in advance. Anticipate difficult questions and practise preparing possible responses. The preparation means that you don't need to "think on your feet".

- When you hear (or imagine) a horrible question, write it down.
- Then think of as many ways as possible in which you could respond to it. As long as it doesn't violate the *Laws of Physics* or require a divine miracle, it's allowed as a *possible* response! Even rude, sarcastic answers that you would only dream of saying are allowed!
  - You *will* need to empty your head of the sarcastic answers before you can start thinking of the more professional and polite responses.
  - An advantage of permitting sarcastic responses in this exercise is that they often contain the seed of a good idea that can be developed into a more polite and professional response.
- With more experience, you will create a data-bank of possible polite answers in your mind and all you need to do will be to choose which one you want to use in a given situation.

– Appendix 4 –
Troublesome Words

Hyphen

Use it to join or connect items that should be considered as a single entity.

" ... large **cell-counter** ... " means the cell-counting device is large.
" ... **large-cell** counter ... " means the device counts large-cells.

Conjunctions

Use ***which*** when the subordinate clause provides *supplementary* but non-essential *description.*

"Dangling pronouns, *which include it, one, these or they*, are confusing."
If we remove the subordinate clause: "which include it, one, these or they" then the main clause we are left with is: "Dangling pronouns are confusing." This main clause still makes sense, even if it is vague. So ***which*** is the correct conjunction to use because the subordinate clause provides *supplemental description* concerning dangling pronouns.

Use ***that*** when the subordinate clause provides an *essential definition* of the main clause.

"Pronouns *that are ambiguously related to more than one noun* are said to dangle."
If we remove the subordinate clause: "that are ambiguously related to more than one noun" then the main clause we are left with is: "Pronouns are said to dangle." This makes no sense, because "*dangle*" is *undefined.* So ***that*** is the correct conjunction to use because the subordinate clause *defines* what a dangling pronoun is.

And, Moreover, Furthermore indicate a continuation in the same direction.

Either/or indicates a binary *choice* between either *⟨this⟩* or *⟨that⟩*.

Neither/nor indicates a binary *exclusion* of *⟨this⟩* and *⟨that⟩*.

Although, **But** indicate a change or reversal in direction.

However, **Nevertheless** indicate exceptions.

Consequently, **Hence**, **Therefore** and **Thus** indicate a conclusion or inference.

While/Whereas = see list of troublesome words which follows.

List Of Troublesome Words

Troublesome Words	Meanings
absorb adsorb	goes inside remains on surface
accept except	to agree, receive to make a special case
accurate precise	close to the actual value (statistical definition) small variance (statistical definition)
acute chronic	serious, grave ongoing
adjacent adjoining	nearby, next to in contact
affect effect	to influence to make or cause (verb) or a result (noun)
altogether all together	wholly, completely all of them together
allude refer	indirect, vague direct, specific reference
alternately alternatively	one after the other one or the other
ambiguous equivocal	not certain, unspecific intentionally vague
a an before "h"	"a" if the "h" is pronounced "an" if the "h" is silent
annex annexe	the verb the noun
anyone any one	anybody any single one

anyway any way	regardless in any manner
biannual biennial	twice per year every 2 years
cf.	written abbreviation for "compare". It is incorrect to use it to mean to consult or refer to. (R.L. Trask, *Mind the Gaffe*)
cohesive coherent	sticking together naturally connected or related, an organised whole
compare to compare with	is similar to outline similarities and differences
compatible comparable	fits, is consistent with can be compared to or is similar
complement compliment	fitting, alternative praise
complex complicated	refers to structure refers to understanding
comprehensible comprehensive	understandable thorough, complete
concave convex	sunken inwards)(bulging outwards ()
connote denote	implies, suggests, or hints at explicit indication
continual(ly) continuous(ly)	repeated(ly) steady, unbroken, uninterrupted
credible creditable	believable deserving credit
defective deficient	faulty insufficient, unsatisfactory
definite definitive	clear, precise the defining example
definitely definitively	without doubt, clearly, certainly authoritatively, conclusively, decisively
dependent dependant	depending upon (adj.) a family member that depends upon another (noun)

differ from differ with	difference between disagreement
e.g. *i.e.*	for example that is, in other words
effective efficient	produces a result economical; minimum cost, time, effort
effectively in effect	satisfactorily in practice
essentially substantially	in essence, indispensably in substance, considerably
et al. *etc.*	and others and so on
everyday every day	commonplace (adj.) each day (adv.)
everyone every one	everybody each one
exo endo	outside or external inside or internal
explicit implicit	fully specified implied, suggested, hinted at ...
fatal lethal	has caused death is capable of causing death
fewer less	used for *discrete,* countable quantities used for cont*i*nuous quantities (*e.g.* energy, mass, time)
forever for ever	continually for always
former latter	first of TWO items last of TWO items
formula formulae	singular plural
hence whence	from this time, therefore from this place
hyper- hypo-	over under

imply infer	hint, suggest indirectly to deduce, reason
inherent intrinsic	present naturally as a part of something being part of the nature or character of something
inter- intra-	between *e.g.* Intercollegiate means between colleges. within *e.g.* Intramural means within our walls/organisation.
irregardless irrespective	Don't use this word, it is non-standard/incorrect English. without considering/taking account of ...
it's its	it is possessive
licence license	the noun the verb
lose loose	cease to have, missing, or the opposite of win not tight
material materiel	substance or apparatus *military* equipment or supplies
may might	I *may* have been ... If ... then I *might* ...
maybe may be	perhaps possible existence
mean median mode	average middle valued point most frequent point
medium media	singular form plural form
method methodology	single procedure whole set of procedures, a discipline
monotonous monotonic	boring steadily, smoothly
onto on to	on top of on towards
orient orientate	Although both forms are now accepted in English, researchers have been unable to discover a useful function served by the additional syllable.

perquisite prerequisite	privilege of role or position precondition that must be satisfied in order to qualify
phenomenon phenomena	singular plural
possible plausible probable	can happen is reasonable is likely
practicable practical pragmatic	capable of being done sensible, useful, effective concerned only with outcomes
practice practise	the noun the verb
precede proceed	comes before goes ahead or progresses
principal principle	main (adj.) rule, law, heuristic (noun)
program programme	for computers agenda, timetable, schedule
purposefully purposely	with determination intentionally, deliberately
rational rationale	logical, sensible (adj.) reason (noun)
rebut refute refuse	argue against ... prove false, incorrect or dispute correctness of ... determined unwillingness to accept, consider, cooperate
[*sic*]	used to indicate that an error in a quotation was in the original
significant substantial	important, meaningful large amount, quantity
site cite	a location to quote
sometime some time	at an indefinite time a period of time
split infinitives	This is a grammatical myth. See the section by R.L. Trask in *Mind the Gaffe*.

stationary stationery	not moving pens and paper
systemic systematic	pertaining to a whole system thorough, orderly
theory hypothesis conjecture	hypothesis/model which has been extensively tested proposed explanation to be tested guess, speculation
there their they're	that place belonging to them they are
to too	towards also, excessive
viable feasible	capable of independent life workable, practicable
while whereas	conjunction involving *time*, not comparison conjunction involving *comparison* with a different case/situation
whose who's	possessive (adj.) "who is" or "who has"

– Appendix 5 –
Examples Of Covering Letters And CVs

Here is an example of a fictitious advertisement for a fictitious position at a fictitious university. The example covering letters and CVs are in reference to this advertisement.

University of Hampshire
Department of Biomedical Research
Three Year Postdoctoral Appointment
Salary range: £20,000 – £23,000 + 25 days paid-holidays p.a.

The Department of Biomedical Research is a Grade 5+ department which is at the forefront of biomedical research in the UK. The University of Hampshire is a leading UK university located on the south coast with easy access to a wide range of parks, cities and sporting facilities.

The MRC has funded a three year project (£550,000) to explore the possible adverse effects of protein denaturation in the high magnetic fields within MRI machines. The project will use laser spectroscopic methods to probe the protein structure while it is within the magnetic field of an MRI instrument.

We are seeking a postdoctoral research worker with experience of NMR/MRI and laser spectroscopy to take a leading role within this project. Experience with identifying and rectifying electronic artefacts, particularly those caused by high magnetic fields would be an asset. The successful candidate will have good to excellent computer skills and be able to work as part of a large interdisciplinary research group. The successful candidate must be capable of working with minimal supervision and may be required to supervise several postgraduate students on a day-to-day basis.

Informal enquiries may be directed to Professor J. Dilbert.
Tel: (123) 4567 8910 / Fax: (123) 4567 8911 / E-mail: j.dilbert@hamps.ac.uk

Please send your CV to either Professor Dilbert or
Mr. N.O. Chance, HR Department, University of Hampshire, SH12 3AB.
Quote Reference Code: **JD/CHE67/04**
Closing date for applications is 5 April 2004.
Interviews will be held on 19 April 2004.

Note: The advertisement mentions proteins but these are not listed explicitly as a requirement of the position. Nevertheless, it would be worth indicating any experience that was related to biologically relevant molecules.

(Example of a poor covering letter)

Dominic Herbert
227 Grey Street
Finchley
LONODON
N11 3QP

Chemistry Department
University of Hampshire
Hampshire
SH12 3AB
18 March 2004

To whom it may concern,

I'm writing in response to your recent advertisement in the *New Scientist* for the postdoctoral research position in the department. I'd like to apply for this positon & you'll find enclosed my CV for your consideration.

As indicated in my CV, I did my BSc degree in Chemistry at King's College London where I took courses in all three branches of chemistry: inorganic, organic and physical. Following that, I did a PhD at University College London. I'm a conscientious & hard-working person & I get along well with my co-workers.

I believe I have the skills for the position & I'd be interested in the possibility of coming for an interview to discuss thsi position face to face. I'm available at any time & I hope to hear from you soon.

Yours sincerely,

Dominic Herbert
Telephone: 020-7654-3210
e-mail: dh57@yahoo.com

Faults With The Preceding Covering Letter:

- Spelling mistakes!!! These indicate carelessness and inattention.
- Telephone and email in a different location from name and address. Underlining the email is pointless.
- Which position advertised in which issue? There is no mention of the advertisement or reference number.
- What is the name of the person the letter is sent to?
- Why was it addressed to the Chemistry Department when the advertisement clearly states Department of Biomedical Research or HR? This error indicates carelessness.
- No explanation of why he is interested in this position.
- Talks about where he studied, but was vague concerning the specifics of:
  - what he studied;
  - with whom; and
  - how this is relevant to the position.
- Uses abbreviations and contractions *e.g.* "&", "I'm", "I'd".
- *Excessive* use of first person pronouns and possessives (16 occurrences)!
- States the obvious or includes redundant information.
- There are vague claims without evidence. *e.g.* "I'm a conscientious and hard-working person ... " Everyone says that they are honest, hard-working, *etc.* The question is whether you can prove it or not.
- "I'm available at any time ..." sounds like he has nothing to do.
- Sounds indecisive with "weak" phrases like:
  - "I'd like to apply ..."
  - "I believe I have ..."
  - "I'd be interested in ..."
  - "... I hope ..."

(Example of a good covering letter)

Dominic Herbert
227 Grey Street, Finchley
LONDON N11 3QP
Tel: 020-7654-3210
Email: d.herbert@gmail.com

Professor John Dilbert
Department of Biomedical Research
University of Hampshire
Hampshire SH12 3AB

18 March 2004

Reference Code: JD/CHE67/04
Advertised: *New Scientist* 13 March 2004 – Vol. 181 No. 2438

Dear Professor Dilbert,

I am applying for your advertised postdoctoral position. My interest in this position comes from its combination of NMR and Pulsed Laser Spectroscopy both of which feature in my research experience. The project will also extend my experience with biologically relevant molecules (carbohydrates and DNA) to include proteins.

The position requires:

- NMR/MRI experience;
- laser spectroscopic experience;
- ability to identify and rectify electronic artefacts caused by high magnetic fields;
- computing skills;
- teamwork and leadership skills.

My relevant skills and training:

- BSc: NMR (Prof. M.J. Knox);
- PhD: Pulsed Laser Spectroscopy (Prof. I.M. Nobel);
- Experience with carbohydrates and DNA;
- Two postgraduate courses in instrumental artefacts;
- Computer literate;
- Co-authored 6 papers in refereed journals;
- Postgraduate representative on the Staff-Student Liaison Committee.

I look forward to an interview to discuss this position in more detail. Thank you for your time and consideration.

Yours sincerely,

Dominic Herbert

(**Note:** the address at the top can equally be either centred or right-justified.)

(Example of a poor CV)

Curriculum Vitae

Dominic Herbert
227 Grey Street
Finchley
LONDON
N11 3QP
U.K.
Telephone: 44-(0)20-7654-3210
E-mail: dh57@yahoo.com

Date of Birth: 29 February 1980
Marital Status: Single
Nationality: EU

Personal Profile:

I have five years research experience in studying biologically important molecules (carbohydrates and DNA) using NMR and Pulsed Laser Spectroscopy. I have co-authored 6 papers in refereed journals. During my PhD I attended 3 national and one international conference, presenting a total of 5 posters and two oral presentations. My computer literacy is excellent and I have good communication and interpersonal skills. My time management and problem solving skills have both been developed by my PhD Research.

Carreer Aims:

I am looking for a position which will make use of my experimental skills (NMR and Pulsed Laser Spectrosopy) and extend my experience with biologically important compounds.

Key Knowledge and Skills:

I have 4 years experience of Pulsed Laser Spectroscopy on DNA and a final year project on NMR of carbohydrates. I am computer literate using a wide variety of softwares. I have excellent communication and interpersonal skills. I am hardworking, honest and I respond well to continual supervisions. I have a high degree of creativity and initiative.

Requirements of the Position:

The advertised positon requires experience in NMR and Pulsed Laser Spectroscopy and in the chemistry of biologically important proteins. Another aspect of the project requires the identification and correction of instrumental artefacts in the laser system caused by the high magnetic fields near the MRI instrument.

Work Experience:

May 1998–Aug. 2000 Part-time stock controller at Shah's Pharmacy
Sep. 2000–Aug. 2004 Undergraduate Teaching Laboratory Demonstrator
Sep. 2000–Aug. 2004 Exam Invigilating Assistant
Sep. 2000–Aug. 2004 UCAS Departmental Tour Guide

Education / Training / Qualifications:

Oct 2000–Aug 2004 PhD Chemistry University College London
Oct 1998–June 2000 BSc Chemistry King's College London
Sep 1995–July 1998 'A' Levels Chemistry (C) / Physics (D) / Maths (E) East Finchley School

Post-Graduate Short Courses:

EPSRC Graduate School Programme (2002)
Scientific Presentations (2001)
Scientific Writing (2002)
Problem Solving (2003)
Time Management (2003)
Fire Safety (2000)
Electrical Safety (2000)
COSHH and Laboratory Safety (2000)

Awards:

RSC Young Chemist Award (London 2004)
Pulsed Laser Spec' Poster Prize (Dublin 2002)
University Medal of Science (King's College London 2000)

Professional Memberships:

Graduate Member of the Royal Society of Chemistry
Member of the International Society of NMR Spectroscopists

Personal Hobbies and Interests:

Clubbing, base jumping, mountain climbing, bungee jumping and full-contact martial arts
Surfing the internet and video-gaming
Committee member and fund-raiser for a registered UK charity.

References:

Available upon Request.

Faults:

- It has been labelled *Curriculum Vitae*! What else would it be? This is stating the obvious.
- There are numerous spelling mistakes!!!
- There is unnecessary *Personal Information* (birth date, marital status and vague nationality).
- Why is the email address underlined? We can't click on it.
- It is visually unattractive.
- The formatting is variable and inconsistent:
  - Uneven spacing and layout over the two pages
  - Variable indenting and line spacing
  - Some paragraphs are left justified and others are fully justified, producing "rivers of white".
  - There is a mixture of different fonts and font sizes within the document.
  - None of these issues have been noticed or corrected, implying this applicant is inattentive and careless.
- Blocks of text that are unappealing.
- No specific accomplishments
- 'References upon request.' Of course Dominic will provide references if asked, so this is unnecessarily stating the obvious.
- The hobbies are either dangerous or questionable. When does Dominic actually work? Will he miss work because of hospitalisation?

(Example of a good CV)

Dominic Herbert
227 Grey Street
Finchley
LONDON N11 3QP
Tel: 020-7654-3210
Email: d.herbert@gmail.com

Professional Profile

Research spectroscopist (NMR and Pulsed Laser Spectroscopy) with five years research experience involving carbohydrates and DNA. Proven ability to generate results and communicate (6 refereed papers in the literature, 5 posters and 2 presentations at 4 conferences). Computer skills include word processing, spreadsheets, database, scientific graphing and analysis software. Has worked within two large, diverse research groups.

Career Aims

To extend my experience with biologically important compounds while using my experimental skills (NMR and Pulsed Laser Spectroscopy).

Key Competencies

- Pulsed Laser Spectroscopy
- NMR/MRI
- Biologically important compounds (carbohydrates and DNA)
- Computer Literacy (PC/Windows, Word, Excel, Access, PowerPoint, Origin, Gaussian, Peak-Fit)

Work Experience

Role/Position	**Employer**	**Years**
Part-time stock controller	Shah's Pharmacy (annual sales of £2,000,000) • Reported directly to the owner. • Responsible for ordering non-pharmaceutical products. • Introduced a new ordering method which reduced errors by 10%.	1998–2000
Undergraduate Laboratory Demonstrator	Kinetics, Thermodynamics, Spectroscopy course laboratories. • Reported to the course co-ordinators and academic staff. • Responsible for instructing students and ensuring safe working practices.	2000–2004

Exam Invigilating Assistant	Invigilated exams for a variety of courses. • Reported to the Registrar and Assistant Registrar. • Responsible for preparation of the examination room, collection, distribution and re-collection of the examination papers.	2000–2004
UCAS Departmental Tour Guide	Showed UCAS applicants around the university. • Reported to the Undergraduate Course Tutor.	2000–2004
Student Representative	Staff-Student Liaison Committee (UCL)	2003–2004

Education / Training / Qualifications

Degree	Subject	Institution	Years
PhD	Biophysical Chemistry (*Pulsed Laser Spectroscopy of DNA*)	University College London	2000–2004
BSc	Chemistry	King's College London	1998–2000
'A' Levels	Chemistry, Physics, Maths	East Finchley School	1995–1998

Postgraduate Short Courses:

CV and Interview Skills (2003)
Problem Solving (2003)
Time Management (2003)
EPSRC Graduate School Programme (2002)
Scientific Writing (2002)
Scientific Presentations (2001)
Fire Safety (2000)
Electrical Safety (2000)
COSHH and Laboratory Safety (2000)

Awards

RSC Young Chemist Award (London 2004)
Pulsed Laser Spec' Poster Prize (Dublin 2002)
University Medal of Science (King's College London 2000)

Professional Memberships

Graduate Member of the *Royal Society of Chemistry*
Member of the *International Society of NMR Spectroscopists*

Personal Interests

Committee member and fund-raiser for a registered UK charity.

Questions That Might Be Asked In An Interview Based Upon This CV/Résumé:

- "You talked about your ability to generate results and communicate with others. A lot of stuff that gets published is fairly trivial. How important or useful were your results to the research community and how do you know your assessment is accurate?" *[This question is checking for realistic self-appraisal.]*
- "How well were your posters and presentations received at the conferences? Any interested responses? Any disagreements?"
- "How large were the two research groups you worked in?"
- "How or in what way did working in these two groups develop your team-working? What evidence can you give me?"
- "Teamwork is about a specific group accomplishing a specific project within a deadline. Working in a large research group is about getting along with others and *not* teamwork. What are your views?"
  [This question is a challenging question because it forces him to take a position of agreement or disagreement and then defend it without giving offence.]
- "In your Career Aims, you didn't explain *why* you wanted to extend your experience with biologically important compounds. What is your interest in continuing this work?"
- "You said that you introduced a new ordering method at the Pharmacy which reduced the errors by 10%. Please explain how you came to notice the problem and then went about improving the situation."
- "During your time as an Undergraduate Laboratory Demonstrator, were there any accidents? If so, what happened and how did you deal with it?"
- "Why were you showing *UCAS* students around? Why did you agree to do this?"
- "Why did you serve on the *Staff-Student Liaison Committee*? What did you accomplish? What did you learn?"
- "Which UK charity are you a committee member of? Why did you choose that charity? What have you accomplished while you have been there?"

Remember that you must be ready and able to explain and support with evidence any statements in your CV/Résumé!

Have prepared examples or stories ready for every question you can anticipate.

- Appendix 6 -
Large Versions Of Selected Diagrams

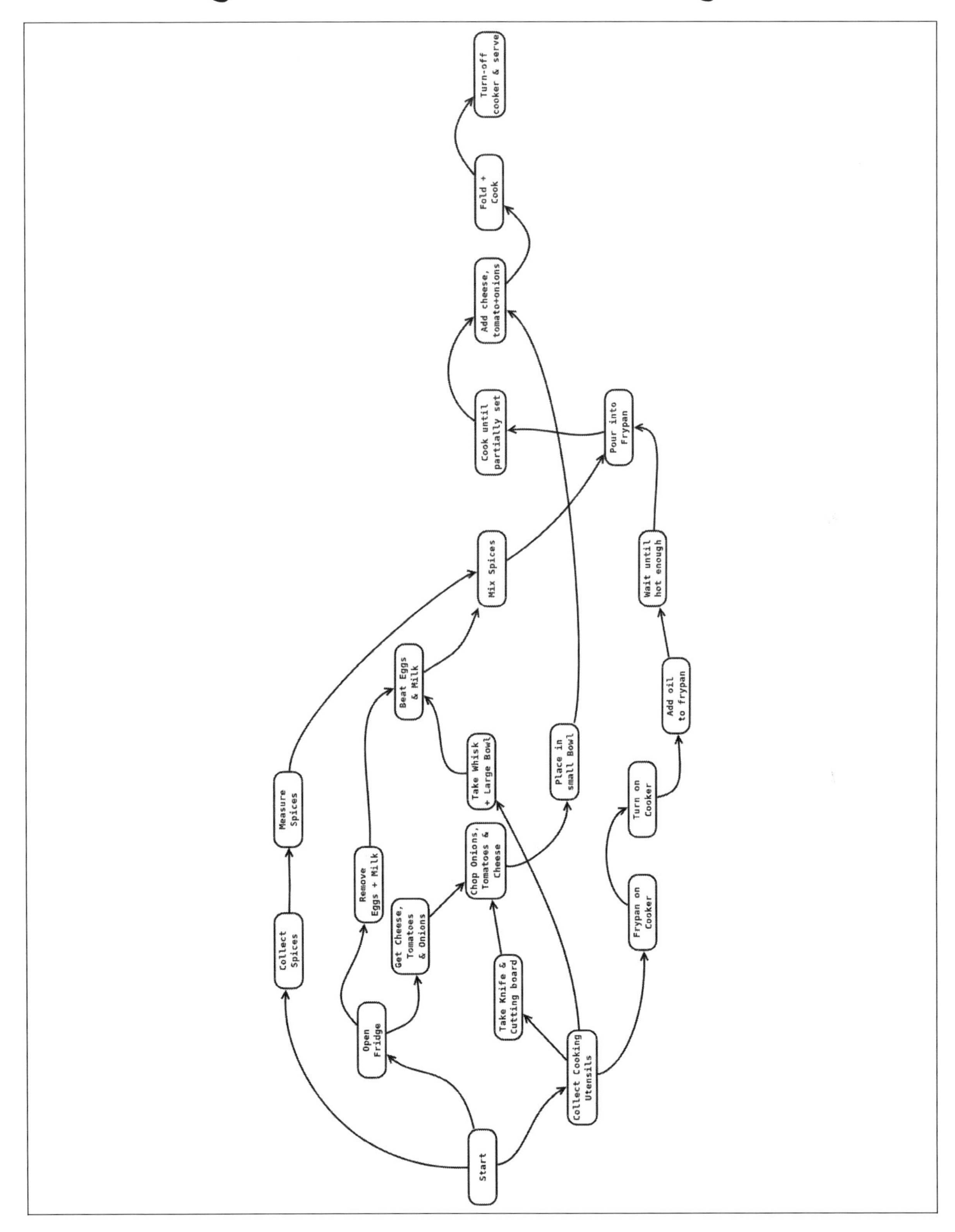

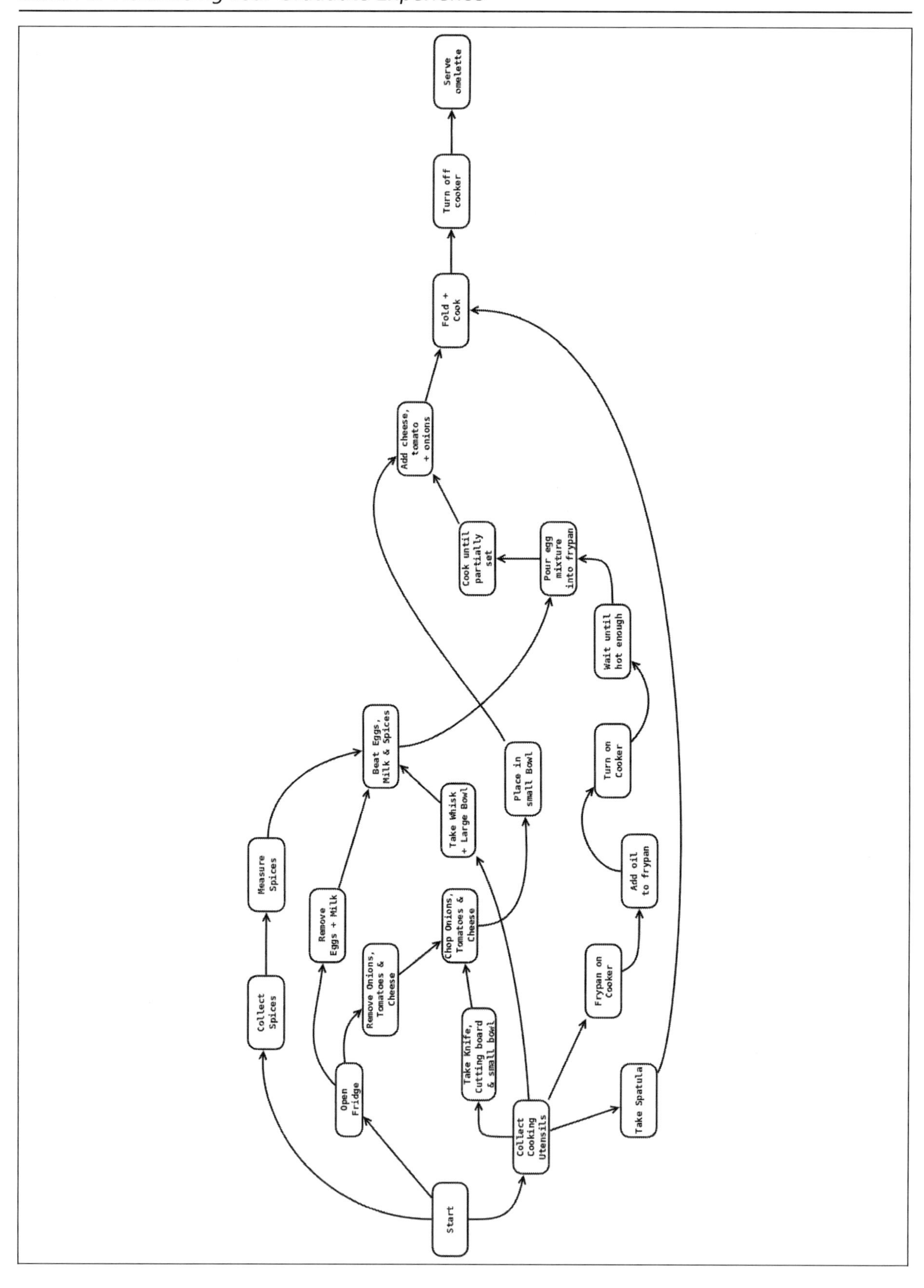
Start
Collect Spices
Measure Spices
Open Fridge
Remove Eggs + Milk
Remove Onions, Tomatoes & Cheese
Beat Eggs, Milk & Spices
Collect Cooking Utensils
Take Knife, Cutting board & small bowl
Chop Onions, Tomatoes & Cheese
Take Whisk + Large Bowl
Place in small Bowl
Frypan on Cooker
Add oil to frypan
Turn on Cooker
Wait until hot enough
Pour egg mixture into frypan
Cook until partially set
Add cheese, tomato + onions
Take Spatula
Fold + Cook
Turn off cooker
Serve omelette

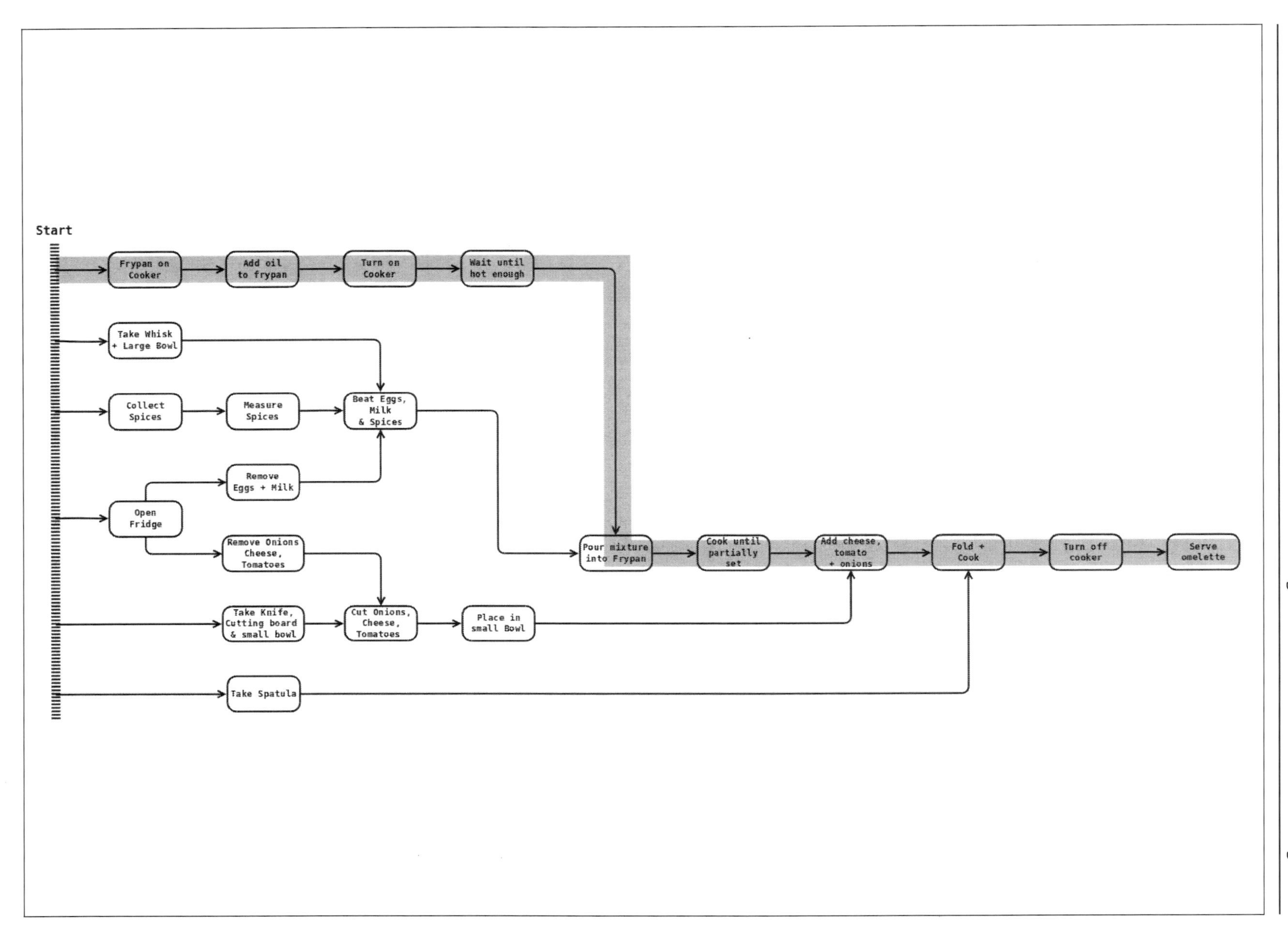
Start
Frypan on Cooker
Add oil to frypan
Turn on Cooker
Wait until hot enough
Take Whisk + Large Bowl
Collect Spices
Measure Spices
Beat Eggs, Milk & Spices
Remove Eggs + Milk
Open Fridge
Remove Onions Cheese, Tomatoes
Take Knife, Cutting board & small bowl
Cut Onions, Cheese, Tomatoes
Place in small Bowl
Take Spatula
Pour mixture into Frypan
Cook until partially set
Add cheese, tomato + onions
Fold + Cook
Turn off cooker
Serve omelette

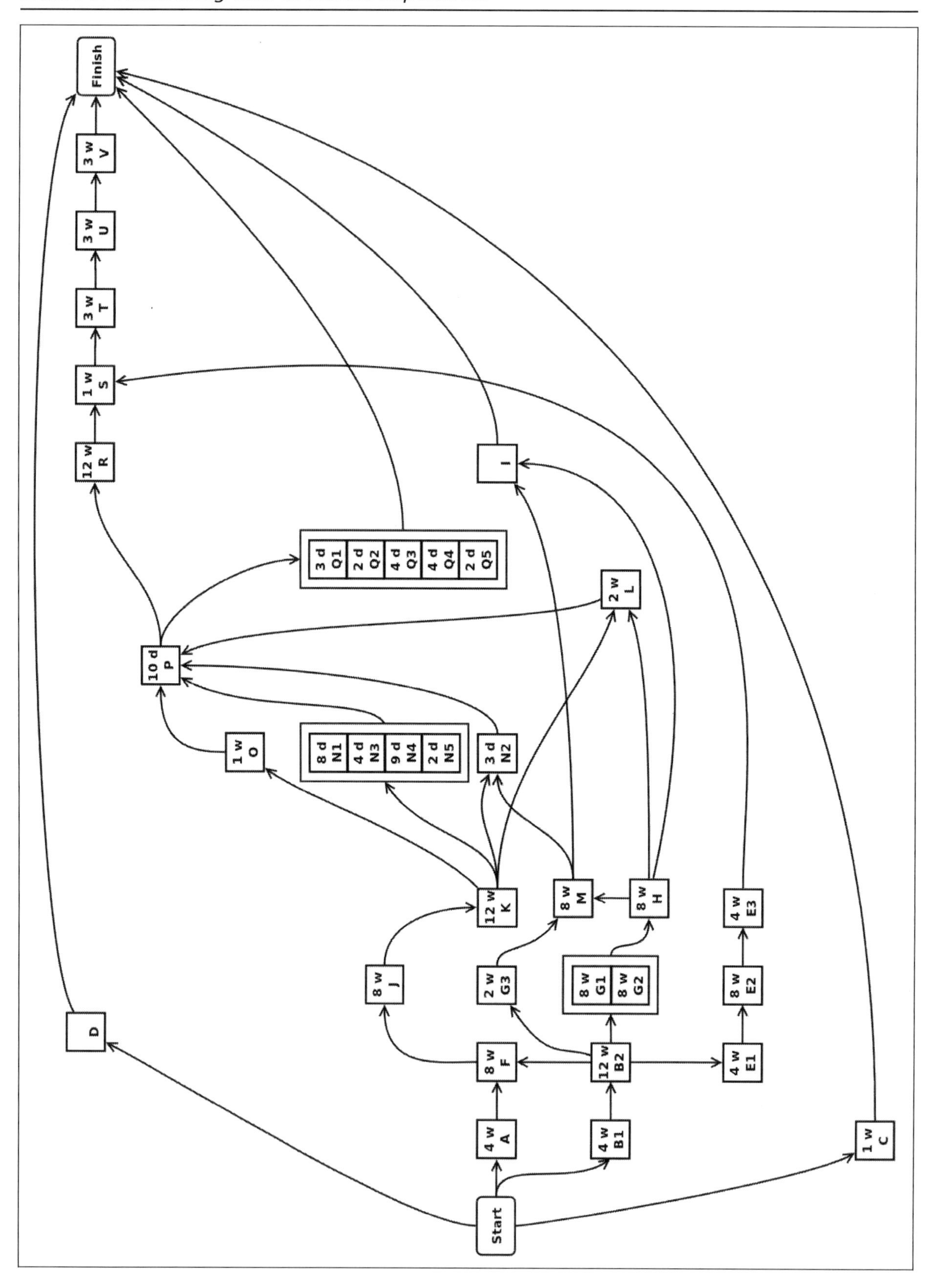
Finish
3 w V
3 w U
3 w T
1 w S
12 w R
I
3 d Q1
2 d Q2
4 d Q3
4 d Q4
2 d Q5
2 w L
10 d P
1 w O
8 d N1
4 d N3
9 d N4
2 d N5
3 d N2
12 w K
8 w M
8 w H
4 w E3
8 w J
2 w G3
8 w G1
8 w G2
8 w E2
D
8 w F
12 w B2
4 w E1
4 w A
4 w B1
1 w C
Start

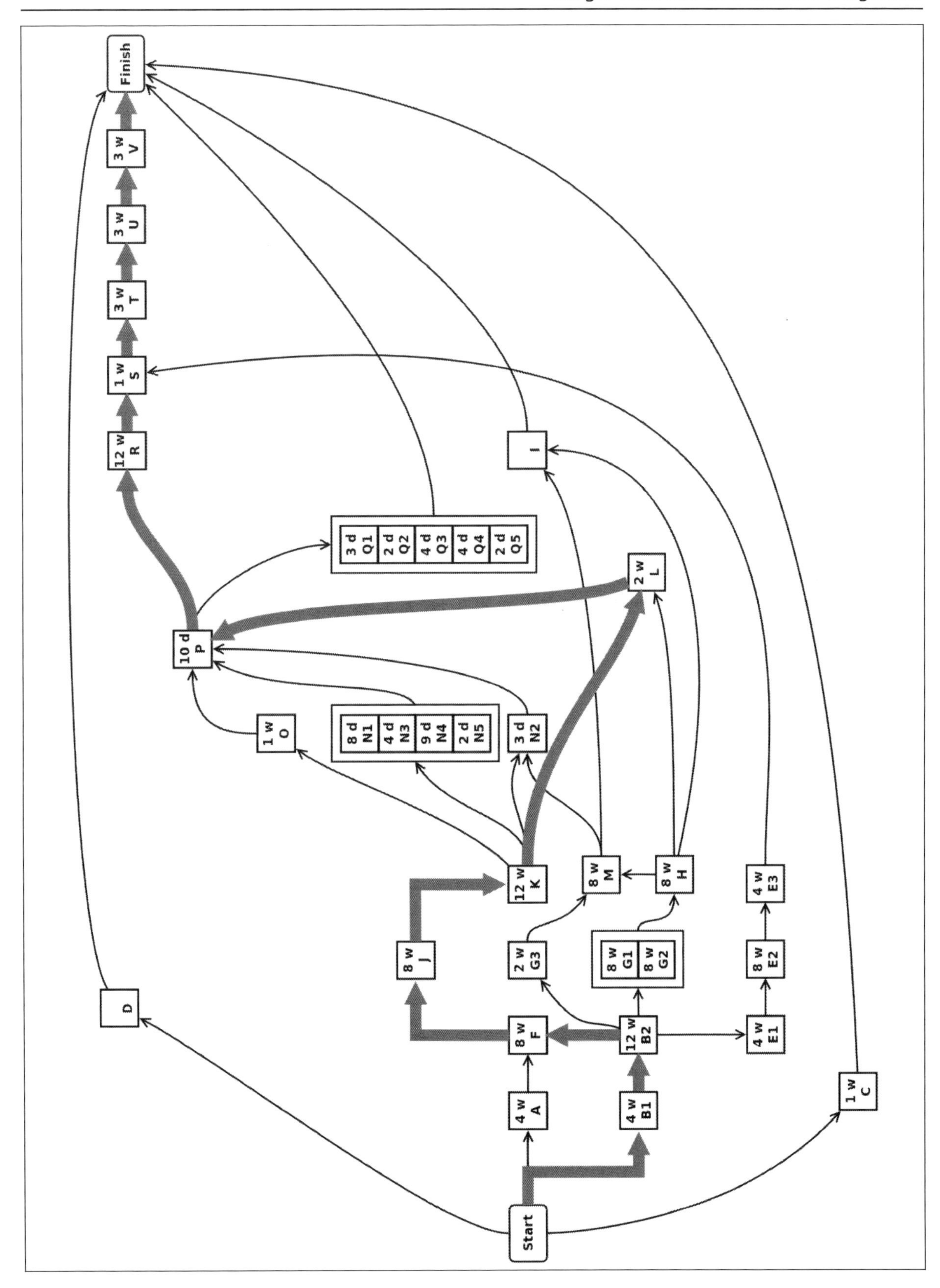
Start
4 w
A
4 w
B1
12 w
B2
8 w
F
8 w
J
12 w
K
2 w
G3
8 w
G1
8 w
G2
4 w
E1
8 w
E2
4 w
E3
8 w
M
8 w
H
1 w
C
D
1 w
O
8 d
N1
4 d
N3
9 d
N4
2 d
N5
3 d
N2
10 d
P
2 w
L
3 d
Q1
2 d
Q2
4 d
Q3
4 d
Q4
2 d
Q5
I
12 w
R
1 w
S
3 w
T
3 w
U
3 w
V
Finish

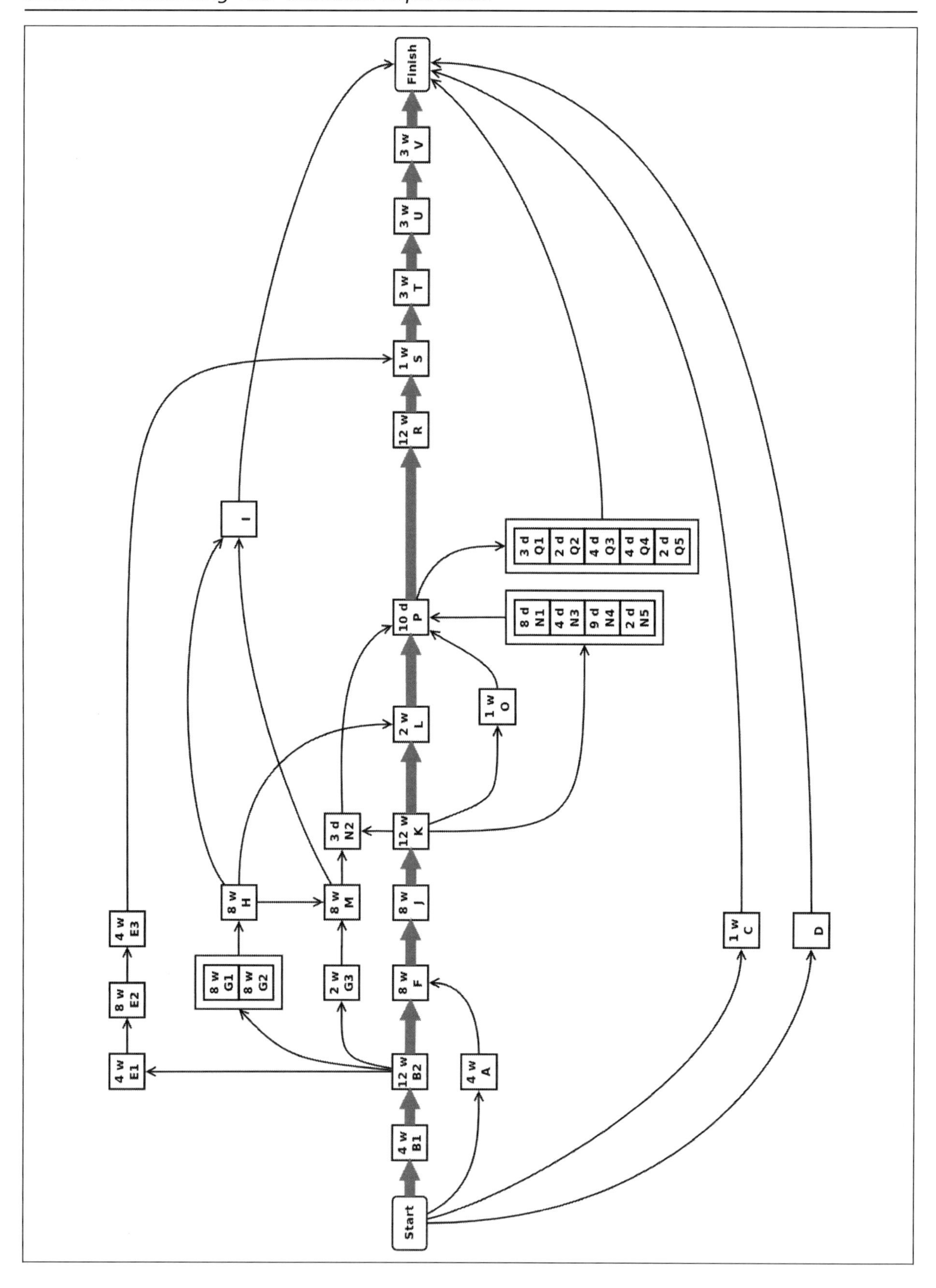
Start
4 w B1
12 w B2
4 w A
8 w F
8 w J
12 w K
2 w L
10 d P
12 w R
1 w S
3 w T
3 w U
3 w V
Finish
4 w E1
8 w E2
4 w E3
8 w G1
8 w G2
2 w G3
8 w H
8 w M
3 d N2
I
1 w O
8 d N1
4 d N3
9 d N4
2 d N5
3 d Q1
2 d Q2
4 d Q3
4 d Q4
2 d Q5
1 w C
D

Printed in Great Britain
by Amazon